BISON
BOOKS

CHARLES MARSHALL

LEE'S AIDE-DE-CAMP

BEING THE PAPERS OF COLONEL CHARLES MARSHALL
SOMETIME AIDE-DE-CAMP, MILITARY SECRETARY,
AND ASSISTANT ADJUTANT GENERAL ON THE STAFF OF

ROBERT E. LEE
1862–1865

Edited by
FREDERICK MAURICE

Introduction to the Bison Books Edition by
GARY W. GALLAGHER

UNIVERSITY OF NEBRASKA PRESS
LINCOLN AND LONDON

Introduction to the Bison Books Edition © 2000 by the University of
Nebraska Press
All rights reserved
Manufactured in the United States of America

∞

First Bison Books printing: 2000
Most recent printing indicated by the last digit below:
10   9   8   7   6   5   4   3   2   1

Library of Congress Cataloging-in-Publication Data
Marshall, Charles, 1830–1902.
[Aide-de-camp of Lee]
Lee's aide-de-camp / Charles Marshall; edited by Frederick Maurice;
introduction by Gary W. Gallagher.
p.   cm.
Originally published: An aide-de-camp of Lee. Boston: Little, Brown, c1927.
Includes index.
ISBN 0-8032-8262-1 (pbk.: alk. paper)
1. Confederate States of America. Army of Northern Virginia.   2. Lee,
Robert E. (Robert Edward), 1807–1870.   3. United States—History—Civil
War, 1861–1865—Campaigns.   4. Marshall, Charles, 1830–1902.   5. Lee,
Robert E. (Robert Edward), 1807–1870—Friends and associates.
6. United States—History—Civil War, 1861–1865—Personal narratives,
Confederate.   I. Title.
E470.2.M35   2000
973.7'55'092—dc21
99-086939

CONTENTS

ILLUSTRATIONS vi

INTRODUCTION TO THE BISON BOOKS EDITION . . . ix

PREFACE xxi

INTRODUCTION xxv

I PREPARATION FOR WAR IN THE CONFEDERACY . 3

II GENERAL LEE ATTEMPTS REFORMS . . . 28

III GENERAL LEE'S MILITARY POLICY 63

IV THE SEVEN DAYS (*a*) BEAVER DAM AND GAINES'S
MILL 77

V THE SEVEN DAYS (*b*) WHITE OAK SWAMP TO MAL-
VERN HILL 104

VI THE CAMPAIGN AGAINST POPE 119

VII THE MARYLAND CAMPAIGN 143

VIII CHANCELLORSVILLE 163

IX THE GETTYSBURG CAMPAIGN (*a*) THE OBJECT OF THE
CAMPAIGN 177

X THE GETTYSBURG CAMPAIGN (*b*) THE INVASION OF
PENNSYLVANIA 195

XI THE GETTYSBURG CAMPAIGN (*c*) THE BATTLE . 225

XII APPOMATTOX — COLONEL MARSHALL'S STORY OF THE
SURRENDER 253

INDEX 283

ILLUSTRATIONS

CHARLES MARSHALL . . . . . . *Frontispiece*

EYEWITNESS SKETCH AT APPOMATTOX viii

JAMES L. MASON 10

JEFFERSON DAVIS 22

ROBERT E. LEE 30

STONEWALL JACKSON 52

J. E. JOHNSTON 58

J. E. B. STUART 82

A. P. HILL 92

BENJAMIN HUGER 106

WADE HAMPTON 112

D. H. HILL 124

JAMES LONGSTREET 140

LEE AND JACKSON IN CONFERENCE ON THE NIGHT
  BEFORE CHANCELLORSVILLE 168

RICHARD S. EWELL 200

J. A. EARLY 236

GEORGE E. PICKETT 240

THE SCENE IN MCLEAN'S HOUSE AT APPOMATTOX . . 270

LEE AND MARSHALL RIDING AWAY AFTER THE SURRENDER 274

"FAREWELL TO THE TROOPS." FACSIMILE OF LEE'S LAST
  ORDER 276

MAPS

REGION OF THE SEVEN DAYS' FIGHTING 118

POSITIONS OF AUGUST 28, 1862 136

ENVIRONS OF WARRENTON 142

ILLUSTRATIONS

EARLY POSITIONS IN THE GETTYSBURG CAMPAIGN . . 197

POSITIONS OF JUNE 28 221

POSITIONS OF JUNE 30 226

RELIEF MAP OF THE BATTLEFIELD OF GETTYSBURG . . 238

MARYLAND AND GETTYSBURG CAMPAIGNS 252

EYEWITNESS SKETCH AT APPOMATTOX

Robert E. Lee leaving the McLean house at Appomattox Court House on April 9, 1865. In this sketch made at the scene by Alfred R. Waud, Charles Marshall follows closely behind Lee. *Courtesy Library of Congress*

INTRODUCTION TO THE BISON BOOKS EDITION

Gary W. Gallagher

Alfred R. Waud waited in the yard of Wilmer McLean's house at Appomattox Court House, Virginia, on the afternoon of April 9, 1865. Inside the substantial red brick structure, Ulysses S. Grant and Robert E. Lee labored over details regarding the surrender of the Army of Northern Virginia. Lee appeared on the front porch between 3:30 and 4:00 P.M., called for an orderly to bring him his horse, and within a few minutes had mounted Traveller. Waud watched the scene intently. A native of London and an accomplished artist, he had sketched many famous episodes of the American conflict. None had exceeded in importance or interest this final scene of the war in Virginia, and Waud rapidly captured the action as Lee departed. Two figures dominate his study—a grim-visaged Lee on Traveller and, trailing slightly behind, Col. Charles Marshall of the general's staff. Waud's eyewitness sketch would be reproduced in numerous books about the war, and a more polished version appeared as an engraving in the Century Company's famous Battles and Leaders series. Because of Waud's presence at Appomattox, generations of readers formed a visual image of Marshall as the only Confederate officer at Lee's side in a moment of high drama.[1]

Marshall's presence at the McLean house capped three years of unbroken service as a member of Lee's inner circle of staff officers. Commissioned a lieutenant on March 22, 1862, he joined Lee in Richmond during the latter's stint behind a bureaucratic desk as principal military advisor to Jefferson Davis. Promoted to major of cavalry on April 21, 1862, Marshall held that rank for nearly two years before receiving a lieutenant colonelcy as Lee's assistant adjutant general on February 25, 1864. He remained a lieutenant colonel until the surrender at Appomattox.[2]

Marshall could boast of distinguished Virginia roots, but he spent most of his adult life in Baltimore. Born at Warrenton, Virginia, on

October 3, 1830, the son of Alexander John and Maria R. Taylor
Marshall, he counted among his family a grandfather, Col. Thomas
Marshall, whose exploits at the battles of Brandywine and Germantown
during the Revolutionary War prompted Virginia's House of Burgesses
to vote him a sword. A more distant ancestor, Capt. John Marshall of
the British army, had established the family in America in the mid-
seventeenth century. Chief Justice John Marshall, a great uncle, easily
qualified as the most illustrious relative. Charles Marshall received his
early education at Warren Green Academy in Warrenton before enroll-
ing at the University of Virginia in 1846. A good student who, in a
friend's words, "bore off the highest honors of the University," Marshall
left Charlottesville with a master's degree in 1848, taught mathematics
at the University of Indiana between 1849 and 1852, and then studied
law and opened a practice in Baltimore. He married twice: in 1856 to
Emily Rosalie Andrews, daughter of Col. Timothy Patrick Andrews of
the United States Army, and in 1866 to Marylander Sarah R. Snowden,
with whom he reared their daughter and five sons. Except for the period of his Confederate service, Marshall practiced law in Baltimore
from the late antebellum years until his death on April 19, 1902. His
"distinguished abilities . . . famous ancestry and memorable associa-
tions," noted one account, enabled Marshall to occupy "a prominent
position" in Baltimore.[3]

Marshall's principal duties at Lee's headquarters consisted of drafting official reports and other documents and helping to manage an enormous flow of correspondence. Yet he was not merely a bland paper
shuffler. Various witnesses left glimpses of a man who faced danger on
battlefields, possessed a temper that flashed in reaction to perceived
incompetence, and enjoyed a good-natured association with Robert E.
Lee. A cavalryman attached to Lee's headquarters described "some pretty
heavy shelling" at the battle of Spotsylvania on May 18, 1864, during
which "Colonel Marshall was slightly wounded above the eye" by a
round that "knocked the glass out of his spectacles." Undoubtedly al-
luding to the same incident, a Georgia newspaper reported "the wound-
ing in the face of . . . Lieut. Col. Marshall" as evidence that Lee and his
staff had been exposing themselves to Union fire during the Overland
campaign. Marshall's temper showed during the last winter of the war
when a group of officers met at Lee's quarters. With Col. Joseph C. Ives
of Jefferson Davis's staff present, Marshall unburdened himself about

shortages of food in the army. "I remember the fierce attack that Colonel Marshall made on the commissary situation," recalled one of those present, "and Colonel Ives's attempted defense."[4]

An incident from the autumn of 1862 helps illuminate the nature of Lee's wartime relationship with Marshall. Edward Porter Alexander, the able Confederate artillerist and memoirist, recalled an evening at Lee's headquarters when he and another officer conversed about a mathematical problem. Marshall "cared little" for the topic (despite having taught mathematics before the war) and "produced a demijohn & proposed a drink." The others said they would join in a round presently and told Marshall to go ahead. "He took a glass in his left hand & the demijohn by the handle in his right," remembered Alexander, "raising it up so as to rest it behind his right shoulder. Then, raising his elbow, the neck of the demijohn came down over his shoulder, & the whiskey poured into the glass." As Marshall began to pour "a pretty stiff one, & looked the very quintessence of toughness, Gen. Lee opened the tent fronts & looked in"—whereupon Marshall immediately began to worry about the impression he had made. The next morning Marshall complained of a tender head, prompting Lee to make a gentle joke at his expense: "Too much application to mathematical problems at night, with the unknown quantities x & y represented by a demijohn & tumbler," stated the general, "was very apt to have for a result a head ache next morning."[5]

Like many other Confederate officers, Marshall took an active postwar interest in how the conflict would be interpreted for future generations. He gathered information for a projected study of Lee and the Army of Northern Virginia and delivered addresses on aspects of the 1862 campaign for Richmond, the Gettysburg campaign, and the surrender at Appomattox. Several of his speeches were published as pamphlets or in periodicals, and he was widely considered an authority on southern military operations in Virginia.[6] A number of former Confederates requested copies of official papers in Marshall's possession. In the spring of 1875, for example, Jubal A. Early asked for items relating to Gettysburg. "I have the papers to which you refer I think," replied Marshall, "but I am now having copies made of papers for Longstreet & Beauregard & cannot have yours copied for a week or two." Aware that Early hoped to use the requested material to attack Longstreet, Marshall sarcastically added that the latter had shown "agility" in crafting a defense of his performance at Gettysburg.[7]

Marshall paid close attention to what other major Confederate actors wrote about the war. For example, he pronounced Joseph E. Johnston's thick 1874 memoir, titled *Narrative of Military Operations*, an especially bad example of special pleading. Responding to a northern officer who had written a pamphlet on the battle of Fair Oaks, or Seven Pines, Marshall observed that Johnston had expended "much unnecessary labor, and inaccuracy of statement to explain . . . his failure" at that battle in late May 1862. "If books as large as Genl J's 'Narrative' are to be written to explain why things were *not* done," groused Marshall, "what room will be left in our libraries for the lives of those who actually did something deserving of record, and needing no apology or 'agility' of explanation?"[8]

Robert E. Lee stood at the top of Marshall's list of those "who actually did something"—a fact the general and his family recognized. After Lee's death in 1870, his children looked to Marshall to help create a satisfactory record of Southern military affairs in the eastern theater. An episode in 1880 underscored their good opinion of him. Former Confederate general Marcus J. Wright was working in Washington as an agent of the U.S. government charged with collecting Confederate documents for publication in the *Official Records*. Wright learned that Marshall had "a number of official letters, reports, telegrams &c of General Lee, which are of great value and importance in a history of his military operations." The captured Confederate archives then housed in Washington lacked copies of this material, and Wright asked George Washington Custis Lee, the general's oldest son, for help in gaining access to whatever Marshall held. Lee refused to assist Wright, apparently believing that Marshall would put the papers to better use. "I have informed him that I did not think it would be convenient for you to have your papers copied until you were done with them," Lee explained to Marshall, "and that I was not willing to add to your labors and troubles [by] my making the request that he wishes, &c."[9]

Marshall considered his old commander a model regarding postwar sectional relations. He thus separated himself from diehard ex-Confederates who sought to perpetuate hatred toward the North. The example of Appomattox remained a powerful influence on him, and he accepted an invitation to give a Memorial Day address in New York City at Grant's grave in 1892. Speaking at a time when reconciliation had supplanted sectional antagonism across much of the nation, Marshall nonetheless risked alienating at least some old comrades with his comments. "It is not easy to express the thoughts that the scene before me inspires in my mind, and in the mind of every man who understands the full meaning of this occasion," he remarks. "Men who were arrayed against each other in deadly strife are now met together to do honor to the memory of one who led one part of this audience to a complete and absolute victory over the other, yet in the hearts of the victors there is no feeling of triumph, and in the hearts of the vanquished there is no bitterness, no humiliation." As for Grant, Marshall suggested that "his crowning glory was as a peacemaker, and that to him belongs the blessing promised the peacemakers."[10]

However much Marshall admired Grant's behavior at Appomattox, Lee was his great hero, and *Lee's Aide-de-Camp* represents a major contribution to the literature on the Confederate commander. Among the first round of scholarly reviews that it received, one spoke of "the great value and importance" of the material and another termed the book "indispensable to all students of the war." A more restrained critic stated that the sections of the book "vary greatly in their character and value" but applauded Maurice's decision "to edit papers so intimately connected with one of the greatest of American soldiers."[11] Later opinion echoed these early reviews. Douglas Southall Freeman, Lee's most influential biographer, lamented the unfinished character of Marshall's book but called it "a major authority for the incidents covered" that "contains much useful material." James I. Robertson Jr. similarly labeled it a "[f]ragmentary and somewhat disjointed" work that "nevertheless is a valuable source for the hierarchy of the Army of Northern Virginia." A recent annotated bibliography singled out the section on Appomattox as "particularly valuable."[12]

Some elements of the book place Marshall firmly within the Lost Cause interpretive tradition. For example, he occasionally inflates the strength of Northern armies and underestimates Lee's numbers. He also presents Lee as an unmatched general who almost never made a mistake. But he does not engage in the bashing of James Longstreet at Gettysburg and other battles so popular among Lost Cause writers. Moreover, he offers a thoughtful critique of several Confederate icons, including "Stonewall" Jackson at the Seven Days and "Jeb" Stuart during the 1863 Pennsylvania campaign. He also points to slaveholders' selfishness as a negative influence on the Confederate government's effort to mount a successful war for independence.

The principal strength of Marshall's book is that it almost certainly reflects Lee's thinking about major questions and personalities. Marshall was so close to his commander for so long and so intimately involved in writing official reports that he better than almost anyone else could speak authoritatively about Lee's opinions, decisions, and reactions to events. His description of Lee's strategic thinking underscores its breadth and appreciation of both military and nonmilitary factors. Many of Lee's modern critics argue that he relentlessly sought to fight aggressive battles in Virginia with little thought about the rest of the Confederacy or the broader political context of the war. Marshall's analysis leaves little doubt that Lee understood the degree to which he and the Army of Northern Virginia functioned as the Confederate people's most important national rallying point—as well as the greatest potential threat to Northern civilian morale. By denying the initiative to more numerous Federals, believed Lee, he could dictate events, keep a larger enemy off balance, inspire the Confederate people, and possibly dampen enthusiasm for the war among the Northern populace.[13]

Movements north of the Potomac promised especially rich dividends. In his discussion of planning for the march into Pennsylvania in June 1863, for example, Marshall alludes to possible political effects. "Yet another important consideration was the moral effect of a victory north of the Potomac upon the people of the North," he notes. "A victory over the Federal Army in Virginia would have tended to strengthen the peace party in the North, only in so far as it would have tended to assure the Northern people that they could not succeed. They would not have been impressed by our consideration for their peace or comfort in keeping the war from their homes and firesides. The 'copperheads' were never weaker than when the Federal armies were successful, and the arguments for peace in the North would have been much more convincing if victory had placed Washington, Baltimore or Philadelphia within our reach than if gained in Virginia" (186–87).

Marshall's discussion of Lee's support for a national conscription act and other measures that empowered the Confederate government to muster Southern resources contradicts the notion that Lee was a localist concerned only with Virginia. "He thought that every other consideration should be regarded as subordinate to the great end of the public safety," wrote Marshall, "and that since the whole duty of the nation would be war until independence should be secured, the whole nation should for the time be converted into an army, the producers to feed and the soldiers to fight." Before passage of the type of national draft advocated by Lee in early 1862, the "efforts of the Government had hitherto been confined to inviting the support of the people. General Lee thought it could more surely rely upon their intelligent obedience, and that it might safely assume to command where it had as yet only tried to persuade." Put another way, Lee sought to give the central government sweeping coercive powers in a republic theoretically dedicated to the idea of state rights (32).

Marshall renders pointed judgments about famous Southern generals that readers, with some confidence, should accept as Lee's judgments as well. "But for Jackson's delay at White Oak Swamp," he writes of June 28, 1862, during the Seven Days battles, "General Lee would have this day inflicted on General McClellan the signal defeat at which his plans aimed" (109). In the section on Gettysburg, Marshall focuses on Jeb Stuart's failure to keep Lee informed of Union movements. He describes a period in the days preceding the battle when Lee feared that Joseph Hooker's Union army had not followed him across the Potomac and might be advancing against Richmond: "I heard General Lee express this apprehension more than once while we lay at Chambersburg, and the apprehension was due entirely to his hearing nothing from Stuart" (218). In these instances and elsewhere, Marshall's text conforms to other evidence, including Lee's comments in a series of postwar conversations at Washington College.[14]

No passage in Marshall's book yields more insight into the source of Lee's success than the description of May 3, 1863, at Chancellorsville. The situation is well known. Several hours of hard offensive fighting that morning had allowed two wings of the Army of Northern Virginia to reunite in a clearing near the Chancellor house. Recoiling from brutal assaults, Union troops withdrew toward the Rappahannock River as Southern artillery pounded them. "In the midst of this awful scene, General Lee, mounted upon that horse which we all remember so well, rode to the front of his advancing battalions," wrote Marshall. "His presence was the signal for one of those outbursts of enthusiasm which none can appreciate who have not been there." Thousands of Confederates raised their voices in victorious salute: "One long, unbroken cheer, in which the feeble cry of those who lay helpless on the earth blended with the strong voices of those who still fought, rose high above the roar of battle, and hailed the presence of the victorious chief." Marshall watched Lee "in the complete fruition of the success which his genius, courage, and confidence in his army had won" (172–73). Nothing in the literature on Lee better captures the profound bond between him and his soldiers—the reciprocal belief in each other that produced magnificent results on many fields but also led Lee to ask too much of his veteran infantry at Gettysburg.

Students of the Civil War should welcome this first paperback edition of Marshall's book. Enhanced by Sir Frederick Maurice's introduction and generally helpful annotations,[15] the text sheds considerable light on Lee, his campaigns from the Seven Days through Antietam, Chancellorsville, Gettysburg, and Appomattox. Marshall's testimony is essential for anyone who would understand the Confederacy's premier officer and his famous army.

NOTES

1. For the various versions of the sketch, see Frederic E. Ray, *Alfred R. Waud: Civil War Artist* (New York: The Viking Press, 1974), 180–81. The engraving appears in Robert Underwood Johnson and Clarence Clough Buel, eds., *Battles and Leaders of the Civil War*, 4 vols. (New York: Century, 1887–88), 4:743. Douglas Southall Freeman's *R. E. Lee: A Biography*, 4 vols. (New York: Scribner's, 1934–35), 4:142–43, includes details about Lee's departure from the McLean house.

2. Compiled Service Record of Charles Marshall, M331, roll 163, National Archives, Washington DC.

3. Lyon Gardiner Tyler, ed., *Encyclopedia of Virginia Biography*, 5 vols. (New York: Lewis Publishing Company, 1915), 3:74, 5:1037; Bradley T. Johnson, *Maryland*, vol. 2 of *Confederate Military History*, Clement A. Evans, ed., 12 vols. (1899; reprint in 17 vols. with 2-vol. index, Wilmington NC: Broadfoot, 1987), 2:354–55; Frederick M. Colston, "Efficiency of General Lee's Ordnance. Recollections of the Last Month in the Army of Northern Virginia—the End," *Confederate Veteran* 19 (1911): 25; [DeVere Schele], *Students of the University of Virginia. A Semi-Centennial Catalogue, with Brief Biographical Sketches* (Baltimore: Charles Harvey & Co. Publishers, [circa 1878]), [96]; Edward Warren, *A Doctor's Experience in Three Continents* (Baltimore: Cushings & Bailey, 1885), 295. Sir Frederick Maurice's introduction to this book incorrectly gives October 2, 1830, as Marshall's birthdate and 1849 as the year he left the University of Virginia.

4. Typescript of a letter by T. G. Lupton (39th Va. Cavalry Battalion) dated May 23, 1864, supplied to the author by Robert K. Krick of Fredericksburg VA; *Augusta Daily Constitutionalist*, May 31, 1864 (quoting from an article on the fighting at Spotsylvania by the correspondent of the *London Herald*); Colston, "Efficiency of General Lee's Ordnance," 23.

5. Edward Porter Alexander, *Fighting for the Confederacy: The Personal Recollections of General Edward Porter Alexander*, Gary W. Gallagher, ed. (Chapel Hill: University of North Carolina Press, 1989), 156–57.

6. Marshall's publications include *Address Delivered Before the Lee Monument Association, at Richmond, Virginia, October 27th, 1887, on the Occasion of Laying the Corner-Stone of the Monument to General Robert E. Lee* (Baltimore: J. Murphy & Co., 1888; reprint, J. William Jones et al, eds., *Southern Historical Society Papers*, 52 vols. [1876–1959; reprint, with 3-vol. index, Wilmington NC: Broadfoot, 1990–92]) 17:215–45 (hereafter cited as *SHSP*); *Address of Col. Charles Marshall . . . Before the Va. Division of the Army of Northern Virginia, at Their Third Annual Meeting, Held at the Capitol in Richmond, Va., October 29, 1874* (Richmond: Gary's Steam Printing House, 1875; extract reprinted in *SHSP* 1:408–13); *Appomattox. An Address Delivered Before the Society of the Army and Navy of the Confederate States in the State of Maryland, on January 19th, 1894, at the Academy of Music, Baltimore, Md., by Colonel Charles Marshall* (Baltimore: Press of Guggenheimer, Weil & Co. for the Society, 1894; portions reprinted in *SHSP* 21:353–60); "Events Leading Up to the Battle of Gettysburg. Address of Colonel Charles Marshall, Before the Confederate Veteran Association of Washington, D.C., in Celebration of the Birth-Day of General R. E. Lee, January, 1896," *SHSP* 23:205–29; "General Lee's Farewell Address to His Army," in *Battles and Leaders of the Civil War*, Robert Underwood Johnson and Clarence Clough Buel, eds., 4 vols. (New York: Century, 1887–88), 4:747; "The Last Days of Lee's Army," *Century Magazine* 63 (April 1902): 932–35; "Occurrences at Lee's Surrender," *Confederate Veteran* 2 (1894): 42–46; "The Sword of Lee. It Was Not Offered to General Grant at Appomattox. Colonel Marshall's Testimony. He Corrects an Oft-Repeated Misstatement that is Without the Slightest Foundation—What General Grant Wrote About the Matter," *SHSP* 29:269–73.

7. Charles Marshall to Jubal A. Early, April 10, 1875, Jubal A. Early Papers, Library of Congress, Washington DC.

8. Charles Marshall to G. W. Mindil, April 26, 1875, transcription from a copy of the original letter supplied to the author by R. E. L. Krick of Richmond VA (copy in the collections of the United States Military History Institute, Carlisle Barracks PA; original in the collections of the Post Library, Fort Monmouth NJ). For the pamphlet that triggered Marshall's response, see George Washington Mindil, *The Battle of Fair Oaks, a Reply to General Joseph E. Johnston* (New York: American Church and Press Co., 1874).

9. Marcus J. Wright to G. W. C. Lee, August 3, 1880, and G. W. C. Lee to Charles Marshall, August 24, 1880, Marcus J. Wright Papers, #10841, Special Collections, Alderman Library, University of Virginia, Charlottesville.

10. "A Confederate at the Tomb of Grant," *Confederate Veteran* 1 (1893): 45. Privately Marshall almost certainly harbored ill will toward the victorious North for some time after the surrender (as did Lee). He gave evidence of this in a letter containing his recollection of finding the badly wounded Union general James S. Wadsworth along the Plank Road in the Wilderness on May 6, 1864. Marshall referred to Union forces as "the enemy," prompting him to note in the final sentence of his letter that "in using the term 'enemy,' I refer to the past, and endeavor to avoid circumlocution." (Charles Marshall to John Lee Carroll, November 27, 1865, folder "May–November 1865," container box 6, James Wadsworth Family Papers, Library of Congress, Washington DC.)

11. Unsigned review in *American Historical Review* 33 (October 1927): 159–60; unsigned review in *Virginia Magazine of History and Biography* 35 (July 1927): 322–23; Oliver L. Spaulding Jr., review in *Mississippi Valley Historical Review* 14 (September 1927): 258–59.

12. Freeman, *Lee* 4:567; Freeman, *Lee's Lieutenants: A Study in Command*, 3 vols. (New York: Scribner's, 1942–44), 3:816; Allan Nevins, James I. Robertson, Jr., and Bell I. Wiley, eds., *Civil War Books: A Critical Bibliography*, 2 vols. (Baton Rouge: Louisiana State University Press, 1967, 1969), 1:128; David J. Eicher, *The Civil War in Books: An Analytical Bibliography* (Urbana: University of Illinois Press, 1997), 98.

13. For a selection of negative and positive assessments of Lee's generalship, see section 2 of Gary W. Gallagher, ed., *Lee the Soldier* (Lincoln: University of Nebraska Press, 1996).

14. For Lee's postwar comments about various lieutenants (as recorded by former Confederate staff officers William Allan and William Preston Johnston), see Gallagher, ed., *Lee the Soldier*, 3–34. On attitudes toward Jackson during the Seven Days, see Alexander, *Fighting for the Confederacy*, 96–97, 569 n. 9. After the war, wrote Alexander, Walter Taylor of Lee's staff told him that Jackson's tardiness had been an issue at headquarters: "Nothing was said of it in a general way, although there was quiet talk of it at the time, because we were so elated at raising the siege & there was no disposition to find fault." Marshall apparently took a particularly hard view of Stuart's conduct during the Gettysburg campaign. "At a dinner of gentlemen after the war," recorded one contributor to *Confederate Veteran*, "Colonel Marshall exclaimed in connection with his comments on Gettysburg: 'I thought Stuart should have been court-martialed.' 'What! Jeb Stuart?' was the astounded cry around the table. 'Yes, Jeb Stuart.'" (John Witherspoon DuBose, "Maj. Gen. Joseph Wheeler," *Confederate Veteran* 25:462.)

15. Some of Maurice's editorial comments are misleading, as when he describes Lee (42 n. 11) as "no supporter of slavery." Lee held quite conventional

views about slavery for one of his class and time. He can be considered an opponent of slavery only if one applies the most generous definition of "opponent." Lee did express the hope that slavery would end some day, but he believed the process should be left in the hands of God rather than pushed forward by humans. Similarly, Maurice places the relative human resources of the opposing sides at "about 22,000,000" white Northerners against "about 5,000,000" white Southerners (68 n. 1). In thus attempting to correct Marshall's claim that the Confederacy had just one fifth of the potential manpower of the United States, he overlooks the fact that the presence of 3,500,000 slaves, who helped keep the Confederate economy running, freed an inordinate percentage of white Southern men to shoulder muskets. The United States put into the field roughly 2,100,000 men as opposed to 750,000 to 850,000 for the Confederacy—a ratio of about two and one half to one.

PREFACE

In the spring of 1925 I published *Robert E. Lee, the Soldier*. The appearance of that book brought me a letter from one of the sons of Colonel Marshall, in which he was good enough to compliment me on the skill with which I had divined Lee's intentions at various phases of the Civil War. He told me that my suggestions agreed very exactly with what his father, who had been Lee's military secretary, had told him, and that there was much to the same effect in his father's papers, which he kindly offered to send me. I naturally accepted so interesting an offer. As soon as I had time to examine the papers in detail, I found that many of them were of great historical value, and I so informed my correspondent, who then invited me to edit them for publication.

The circumstances in which they were prepared and the sources of Colonel Marshall's information are sufficiently explained by myself in the Introduction and by Colonel Marshall in the first part of Chapter IX.

The papers fall roughly into three parts: those that were intended for a projected life of Lee, those that were intended for an account of the campaign of

Gettysburg, and those which consisted of notes on events of the war, of which some were used for lectures and addresses. Marshall's special position on Lee's staff from March 1862 until the end of the war gave him opportunities for getting to know what was in his chief's mind, which no one else enjoyed to a like degree; and as Lee never fulfilled his intention of writing his memoirs, these papers constitute the most authoritative defense of Lee's generalship that has yet appeared.

I had deliberately limited the scope of my *Robert E. Lee, the Soldier*, because I had learned that a life of Lee based upon his papers was in contemplation; but I could not refuse on such grounds the invitation to edit Marshall's papers, as they seemed to me to be indispensable to a complete life of his chief. There is hardly one of the twelve chapters in which I present these papers which will not be found to contain important and authoritative information upon some question which has been a matter of dispute amongst historians, or to throw new light upon matters which have been obscure. The first two chapters give the most complete and candid description of the reactions of political exigencies in the Confederacy upon military plans and actions which I have ever read. The third gives an excellent exposition of Lee's military policy. The fourth and fifth throw new light upon the facts and causes of Jackson's delays in the "Seven Days." The

sixth makes it clear that Lee never planned to fight
the second Manassas, but that that battle was brought
on by Stonewall Jackson. The seventh throws grave
doubt upon the stories — generally accepted — that
Lee was informed by a friendly citizen of Frederick
that McClellan had found the famous lost order of
South Mountain. The eighth should settle definitely
the question whether Lee or Jackson devised the flank
march round Hooker at Chancellorsville. The Gettysburg chapters contain much the fullest account yet
published of the fateful orders issued to Stuart. The
last chapter of all is the only account from a Southern
witness of the historic scene in McLean's house at
Appomattox.

One half of these contributions to history would
have justified the publication of Marshall's papers;
the whole makes an unique presentment from the
Southern side. It is only necessary to read Marshall's
graphic description of the surrender of the Army of
Northern Virginia to realize that he wrote "with malice
toward none," but, as he himself says more than
once, with a sincere desire to arrive at the truth. The
Union of North and South which, as Marshall says,
was made indissoluble at Appomattox, was dramati-
cally portrayed in the war with Spain, when a son of
Colonel Marshall performed for a son of Grant the
same functions which from 1862 to 1865 the father
had performed for Lee.

The Introduction is from my pen. I have intervened in Chapters VII and VIII to fill gaps in Colonel Marshall's papers, and have added to Chapter XI an interesting memorandum of a conversation with Lee, which Colonel Allan sent to Marshall. The remainder is wholly Marshall's, though I am entirely responsible for the selection and arrangement and for the notes. When there are differences in British and American nomenclature, I have retained the American; for example, "advance guard" for the "advanced guard" of the British Army.

Thanks are due to the Century Company, who have allowed the reproduction of many of the illustrations in this volume from their *Battles and Leaders of the Civil War*. All the maps are from this source except that of the Environs of Warrenton. The map of the Seven Days' Fighting and that of the Maryland and Gettysburg campaigns have been redrawn to suit the needs of this book; the Confederate entrenchments and further territory have been added to the former, and details have been omitted in both.

F. MAURICE

November 1926

INTRODUCTION

Colonel Charles Marshall, the writer of these papers, was born at Warrenton, Fauquier County, Virginia, on October 2, 1830. His great-grandfather, Thomas Marshall, commanded the Third Virginia Regiment in the Revolutionary War. Thomas Marshall's eldest son, John Marshall, was Chief Justice of the United States and Charles Marshall's great-uncle — he being descended from a younger brother. Charles graduated from the University of Virginia with the degree of M.A. in 1849, and for a few years was a professor at the University of Indiana. He then began to study law, and had established a practice in Baltimore when the Civil War broke out. He went at once to Virginia, but as he was in a very poor state of health he had considerable difficulty in finding a place in the Confederate Army. At the beginning of 1862, however, his health improved, and as he tells us, he was appointed Aide-de-Camp to General R. E. Lee on March 21 of that year.

Of the little group of five officers which Marshall then joined, the senior, Colonel Long, was at first Lee's military secretary, and he has given us his experiences and views of his beloved chief in *Memoirs of R. E. Lee*. Another, Major Taylor, wrote *Four Years with General*

INTRODUCTION

Lee, and yet another, Major Venable, contributed his quota to *Battles and Leaders of the Civil War.* Now at last we have the papers of a fourth.[1]

Colonel Marshall's point of view is different from that of any of the others. When he first joined Lee in Richmond, the great problem was to raise an army adequate to meet McClellan's threatened invasion. This required legislation, and legislation of a kind suited to the exigencies of the military situation. Lee made use of Marshall's legal training in the drafting of measures to be submitted to the Confederate Congress, and he was thus brought into close touch with that assembly and acquainted with the feelings and opinions of its members. He is therefore able to give us a very complete picture of the political difficulties, jealousies, and interests which prevented the complete adoption of Lee's proposals, and of the consequences of the changes Congress found it necessary or convenient to make. This is a story which, as far as I have been able to ascertain, has not been told by anyone of like authority, and it is a story full of valuable lessons for governments, soldiers, and people.

When Lee became Commander of the Army of Northern Virginia, Marshall with the remainder of the personal staff followed the chief to the field. In the intervals between campaigns Marshall's principal task became the collection and collation of material for Lee's dispatches, and the preparation of the drafts of these dispatches.

[1] Long became Brigadier General of Artillery in September 1863. Taylor, Venable, and Marshall became Lieutenant Colonels and Assistant Adjutant Generals in November 1864.

"It was," he says, "my duty to prepare the reports of General Lee under his directions. To do this as he required it to be done, I had first to read all the reports made by the different commanders of forces, who always forwarded the reports of all their subordinates, down to company commanders. From all these I prepared a statement in great detail, of course using such information as I possessed from my personal knowledge and observation as a staff officer and from orders and correspondence.

"One of the most difficult things I had to do was to reconcile the many conflicting accounts of the same affair. Sometimes this was impossible; and when the matter was important enough to warrant it, I was required to visit the authors of the conflicting accounts, or they were brought together and required to reconcile or explain their respective narratives. After exhausting every means to attain entire accuracy, a more general report of the whole was prepared and submitted to General Lee, who made such corrections as he thought proper and directed the omission of such things as he deemed unnecessary for a clear understanding of the subject. The report thus verified and corrected was then written for his signature.

"Some of the war stories I have heard remind me of an anecdote General Lee told me of General Zachary Taylor.[2] I was in General Lee's tent one day just before the battle of Chancellorsville, when an officer who had been with a scouting party came in with a

---

[2] General Zachary Taylor was Jefferson Davis's father-in-law, and commanded the United States forces in the battles of Monterey and Buena Vista in the Mexican War.

report. The report was not a little affected by the excitement that usually begins to be felt when an engagement is pending, and did not in the least understate the number of the enemy that the scouting party had seen. General Lee listened very quietly and attentively to the narrative, which bore on its face the evidence of its own want of probability, though the narrator may have believed it to be accurate. When the officer left the tent General Lee said in his grave way: 'That report reminds me of something I heard General Taylor say when I was with his army in Mexico, before I joined General Scott. As we advanced into the interior of the country there were rumours of the approach of General Santa Anna with an overwhelming force, and there was more or less excitement and anxiety on the subject. No considerable force of Mexicans had in fact been seen, and the alleged army of Santa Anna was left to the imagination, which always exaggerates the unknown and the unseen. One day a cavalry officer came to General Taylor and reported that he had seen 20,000 Mexicans with 250 pieces of artillery. General Taylor said to him: "Captain, do you say you saw that force?" The captain asserted that he had seen it. Thereupon General Taylor remarked, "Captain, if you say you saw it of course I must believe you; but I would not have believed it if I had seen it myself."'

"Narrators do not always restrict themselves to what they did themselves, but are much disposed to include in their reports what they think was done, or omitted to be done, by others. I remember a striking illustration of this which occurred during the battle of Fredericksburg. Fighting in that battle took place on the right and left of the Confederate Army; the centre had hardly been engaged at all. General Longstreet on the Confederate left had repulsed the repeated attacks made on the troops posted at the foot of Marye's Hill and General Jackson had repulsed the assault made on our right near Hamilton's crossing. The distance between the two scenes of combat was between three and four miles.

"In the afternoon I was sent to the right by General Lee with an order to General Jackson, and while looking for him I came across General D. H. Hill, who commanded a division in Jackson's corps. As soon as he saw me, General Hill exclaimed: 'Well, it is just as usual. This corps does all the fighting. Those fellows on the left have not fired a shot all day, except some little artillery firing.' I offered, with great respect, to bet the General a very large apple that 'the fellows on the left' could show two dead in their front for every one the fellows on the right could show. Nearly fifteen hundred Federal dead lay in front of Marye's Hill, and General Hill did not know that there had been any fighting there."

It is obvious that the preparation of Lee's dispatches must not only have given Marshall exceptional opportunities for ascertaining facts, but have made him very well acquainted with the opinions of his chief during the various phases of the campaigns. The dispatches were not finally approved without discussion, and indeed, Marshall says he was often disappointed and pained when an arduously acquired piece of information, showing clearly that the responsibility for some failure rested with a subordinate commander who had acted injudiciously or failed to act judiciously, was struck out by Lee. In vain Marshall would protest that in justice to himself Lee should include such passages. The answer invariably was: "The responsibility for this army is mine." Failures were accounted for in the fewest possible words, and never in a public dispatch did the commanding General blame anyone under his command.

Naturally enough, as soon as the war ended Marshall burned to use the special knowledge that he had acquired in the course of his duties, to enhance the reputation of his chief. Not only had he had — from the circumstances of his employment — a more complete and general knowledge of the facts and of Lee's intentions and opinions at various phases of the long war than anyone except perhaps the General himself, but for more than three years he had lived with the man, whom above all other men he loved and admired, in the closest association. Lee's staff was always small, remarkably small when compared with the numbers of officers on the headquarters staffs of European armies of similar size. The states of the Confederate armies show that at the time of the battle of Fredericksburg, when the army numbered over 80,000 men, there were twelve officers, including the General commanding, at headquarters. In July 1863, on the eve of Gettysburg, when the army comprised three army corps and a cavalry division, the number was sixteen, and of this number the military secretary and the four aides-de-camp formed the inner circle around the Commander.

The life which this little band led was very simple and the circumstances naturally drew them closely together. General Long, in his diary of June 4, 1862, — that is, the day after Lee assumed command of the Army of Northern Virginia, — gives us an idea of the life at "Dabb's House," where Lee was established : —

"Our headquarters are very comfortable. The front room on the house floor is the Adjutant-General's office. The General's private office is in the rear of this. There all the confidential business of the army is transacted, the General's usual attendant being the military secretary or some other member of his personal staff. In the front room the general business of the army is transacted by the Adjutant-General and his assistants. General Lee and his household mess together. The mess arrangements are not very ostentatious. Our meals are served and dispatched without any very great ceremony. The General is always pleasant at meals, and frequently hurls a jest at some member of his staff."[3]

Such were the surroundings of Lee and his military family in the immediate neighborhood of Richmond. But from the time when the Army of Northern Virginia first drove McClellan down the Peninsula until, yielding stubbornly to Grant's succession of hammer blows, it once more found itself engaged in the close defense of the capital, only the urgent entreaties of his staff, moved to insistence when their chief was sick, would induce Lee to seek the shelter of a roof. A foreign visitor marked by the scars and experiences of four campaigns came to Lee's camp in the autumn

[3] Long: *Memoirs of R. E. Lee*, p. 166.

of 1862, and has left us a description of what he then saw, which is worthy of rescue from the obscurity of an anonymous article in a magazine: —

"In visiting the headquarters of the Confederate generals, and particularly those of General Lee, anyone accustomed to see European armies in the field cannot fail to be struck with the great absence of all the pomp and circumstance of war in and around their encampments. Lee's headquarters consisted of about seven or eight pole tents, pitched with their backs to a stake fence, upon a piece of ground so rocky that it was unpleasant to ride over it, its only recommendation being a little stream of good water which flowed close by the General's tent. In front of the tents were some three or four wagons, drawn up without any regularity, and a number of horses roamed loose about the field. The servants — who were, of course, slaves — and the mounted soldiers called couriers, who always accompany each general of division in the field, were unprovided with tents, and slept in or under the wagons.

"Wagons, tents, and some of the horses were marked *U. S.*, showing that part of that huge debt in the North had gone to furnishing even the Confederate generals with camp equipment. No guards or sentries were to be seen in the vicinity, no crowd of aides-de-camp loitering about, making themselves agreeable to visitors and endeavoring to save their generals from those who had no particular business. A large farmhouse stands close by, which in any other army would have been the General's residence *pro tem*, but as no liberties are allowed to be taken with personal property in Lee's army, he is particular in setting an example himself.

His staff are crowded together two or three in a tent, none are allowed to carry more baggage than a small box each, and his own kit is but very little larger. Everyone who approaches him does so with marked respect, although there is none of that bowing and scraping and flourishing of forage caps which occurs in the presence of European generals; and whilst all honour him and place implicit faith in his courage and ability, those with whom he is most intimate feel for him the affection of sons for a father."[4]

The direction of the complex affairs of an army in the field in these simple circumstances must have been no easy matter. The troops always suffer if the staff work at headquarters is not efficiently performed, and there are good reasons for making the conditions under which that work has to be done as easy as possible. Of greater importance still is the health of the commander; more than one vital battle has been lost because the chief was in failing health, and Lee's own staff attributed to an untimely illness of their chief the fact that the chance was lost of dealing Grant an effective blow on the North Anna in May 1864.

There can be little doubt that the austere life which Lee elected to lead in the field affected his health. But it was from no desire to parade simplicity that Lee chose the simple life. Nor was it only that Lee, as Colonel Wolseley suggests, wished to set an example of respect for private property, though upon that he set great store. Indeed, marauding of any kind was one

[4] "A Month's Visit to the Confederate Head Quarters," *Blackwood's*, January 1863. The writer was Colonel Wolseley, afterward Field Marshal Lord Wolseley, Commander-in-Chief of the British Army.

of the few things which moved him to fierce anger
against his own men. Lee, as an experienced soldier,
who had served on the headquarters of an army in the
field in Mexico, knew well the suspicions and jealousies
of the staff at headquarters, which in all armies to a
greater or less degree are entertained by the men at
the front. He knew also that he had to create in his
army a type of discipline suited to the character of his
men, and that the circumstances of the Confederacy
would make it unusually difficult and often impossible
to provide these men with reasonable subsistence and
shelter. He set himself deliberately to bind his men
to him by ties of respect and affection.

Strange as it may appear now, even respect was not
won without considerable effort. As Marshall tells
us, when Lee assumed active command he was regarded
militarily as a failure. His predilection for entrenchments — an outstanding feature of his methods —
was looked upon as the hobby of the engineer, and was
resented by the men who had to dig and were unused
to "niggers' work." So as a part of his policy Lee
chose to live as nearly as possible the life of his men.

During a recent visit to Winchester, in the Valley,
a survivor of the Army of Northern Virginia told me a
story which illustrates the extent to which this was in
Lee's mind, and its effect upon the individual soldier.
It happened that one day in the Valley Lee had gone
into a house for a midday meal. He had just sat down
at table with General Wade Hampton when a weary
soldier in search of refreshment opened the door.
The man's embarrassment, when he suddenly found
himself in the presence of two generals, may be imag-

ined, and that embarrassment was not diminished when a moment later he recognized the Commander of his army. Lee promptly rose, and saying to Hampton, "Come on, General, this man needs this food more than we do," made way for the private — who from that moment would have gone anywhere and done anything at a nod from his chief. We may believe that this story quickly made the round of the camps, and with others of a like kind created a spirit which no hardship or adversity could quell.

Marshall gives a more serious account of the effect upon his men of Lee's methods. "While the army was on the Rapidan, in the winter of 1863–4, it became necessary, as was often the case, to put the men upon very short rations. Their duty was hard, not only on the outposts during the winter, but in the construction of roads to facilitate communication between the different parts of the army. One day General Lee received a letter from a private soldier informing him of the work he had to do, and saying that his rations were hardly sufficient to enable him to undergo the fatigue. He said that if it was absolutely necessary to put him upon such short allowance he would make the best of it, but that he and his comrades wanted to know if General Lee was aware that his men were getting so little to eat; he was sure there must be some necessity for it. General Lee did not reply direct to the letter, but issued a general order,[5] in

[5] The order ran : —

"General Order No. 7.   *Jan.* 22, 1864

The commanding general considers it due to the army to state that the temporary reduction of rations has been caused by circumstances beyond the control of those charged with its support. Its welfare and comfort

which he informed the soldiers of his efforts on their behalf, and that he could not then relieve their privations, but assured them that he was making every exertion to procure sufficient supplies. After that there was not a murmur in the army, and the hungry men went cheerfully to their hard work."[6]

The absence of any elaborate equipment at Lee's headquarters necessarily made the system of staff work simple. It was the business of the adjutant-general's staff to relieve him as much as possible of army routine. One of Marshall's colleagues, Colonel Taylor, says: "He had a great dislike to reviewing army communications. This was so thoroughly appreciated by me that I would never present a paper for his action unless it was of decided importance and of a nature to demand his judgment and decision."[7]

Another of the functions of the personal staff is described by Colonel Venable: —

are the objects of his constant and earnest solicitude, and no effort has been spared to provide for its wants. It is hoped that the exertions now being made will render the necessity of short duration, but the history of the army has shown that the country can require no sacrifice too great for its patriotic devotion.

Soldiers! You tread with no unequal step the road by which your fathers marched through suffering, privations, and blood, to independence. Continue to imitate in the future, as you have in the past, their valor in arms, their patient endurance of hardships, their high resolve to be free, which no trial could shake, no bribe seduce, no danger appal; and be assured that the just God who rewarded their efforts with success will in His own good time send down His blessing upon yours.

R. E. Lee
General"

(*Official Records*, vol. XXXIII, p. 1117)

[6] Address before the Lee Monument Association at Richmond, Virginia, October 1887.

[7] Taylor: *Four Years with General Lee*, p. 77.

"While he was accessible at all times, and rarely had even an orderly before his tent, General Lee had certain wishes which his aides-de-camp knew well that they must conform to. They did not allow any friend of soldiers condemned by court-martial — when once the decree of the court had been confirmed by him — to reach his tent for personal appeal, asking reprieve or remission of sentence. He said that with the great responsibilities resting upon him he could not bear the pain and distress of such applications, and to grant them when the judge advocate-general had attested the fairness and justice of the court's decision would be serious injury to the proper discipline of the army. Written complaints of officers as to injustice done them in regard to promotion he would sometimes turn over to an aide-de-camp, with the old-fashioned phrase: ''Suage him, Colonel, 'suage him,' meaning thereby that a kind letter should be written in reply. But he disliked exceedingly that such disappointed men should be allowed to reach his tent and make complaints in person.

"On one occasion in the winter an officer came with a grievance, and would not be satisfied without an interview with the commanding general. He went to the general's tent and remained some time. Immediately after his departure General Lee came to the adjutant's tent with flushed face, and said warmly, 'Why did you permit that man to come to my tent and make me show my temper?' The views which prevailed with many as to the gentle temper of the great soldier, derived from observing him in domestic and social life, in fondling of children, or in kind expostulation with erring youth, are not altogether correct. No man could see the flush come over that grand forehead and the temple veins swell on occasions of great trial of patience and doubt that Lee had the high strong temper of a Washington, and habitually under the same control.

"Cruelty he hated. In that same early spring of 1864 I saw him stop when in full gallop to the front — on report of a demonstration of the enemy against his lines — to denounce scathingly and threaten with condign punishment a soldier who was brutally beating an artillery horse."[8]

The chief reason why Lee desired that this kind of business should be kept from him was not merely that he did not wish a tender heart to be wrung. He was, as regards the plans and operations of his army, in a great measure his own chief of the staff. He but rarely issued elaborate written orders for operations; when he did, he usually drafted them himself and gave them to his personal staff to make the necessary copies. In the field his preliminary orders were usually given direct to his divisional and corps commanders, subsequent orders being delivered verbally by his aides-de-camp.

This absence of detailed orders struck another foreign observer, Colonel Freemantle, who was with Lee at Gettysburg. Speaking of the second day of that battle, he says: "So soon as the firing began, General Lee joined Hill just below our tree, and he remained there nearly all the time, looking through his field glass, sometimes talking to Hill and sometimes to Colonel Long of his staff. But generally he sat quite

[8] *Battles and Leaders of the Civil War*, vol. II, p. 240.

alone on the stump of a tree. What I remarked especially was that during the whole time the firing continued
he only sent one message and only received one report.
It is evidently his system to arrange the plan thoroughly
with his three corps commanders, and then leave to
them the duty of modifying and carrying it out to the
best of their abilities."

There is no doubt that Lee's reliance upon verbal
explanations and messages was sometimes carried to
excess, and at Gettysburg in particular led to mistakes
which were one of the causes of failure. His reason
was probably his keen appreciation of the importance
of secrecy, and of the difficulty of preserving it in a
war in which both sides spoke the same language.[9]
If we may judge from events, he was probably confirmed
in his practice by his knowledge of the effect on his
plans of the mischance which brought a vitally important order into McClellan's hands before the battle
of Sharpsburg. Be this so or not, Lee's method has
left us with less than the usual apparatus for judging
of a commander's thoughts and intentions when he
formed his plans. This gives peculiar value to Colonel
Marshall's papers, for though Lee was usually reticent
with his staff about his plans and intentions, he had to
discuss them, during and soon after the event, with
the man who drafted his dispatches; and that man
has, in the papers which follow, told what he believed
those intentions to have been.

[9] Stonewall Jackson adopted the same practice with the object of
ensuring secrecy, and one of his subordinates, General Taliaferro, says
of it: "This extreme reticence was very uncomfortable and annoying to
his subordinate commanders and was sometimes carried too far; but it
was the real reason for the reputation for ubiquity which he acquired."

As I have said, it was natural that Marshall, having lived for three years in circumstances of great intimacy with Lee, having special knowledge of his chief's mind, and feeling that Lee had often, from motives of chivalry, failed to do himself justice in his dispatches, should desire to write the life of his hero. He had served with Lee to the very end, and been the only one of his staff to accompany him to the surrender of Appomattox. Therefore in the years which immediately followed the war he began to elaborate the contemporary notes which he had made for the dispatches, and to insert in them his recollections of the reasons why Lee had acted as he did. Having drafted the dispatches himself, he took these as the basis of his work, and the reader will recognize a number of passages which appear over Lee's signature in the Official Records. But after the war Marshall had no longer the facilities which he had had in camp of meeting and questioning the chief actors in the events. Speaking in 1875 at a reunion of Confederate Veterans, he said : —
"I have been engaged for two or three years, as some of you may know, in trying to write an account of the life and achievements of the great leader of the Army of Northern Virginia, and conscious of my inability to rise to the height of that great achievement, I have spared no labour to make what I have written accurate, however in other respects it may fall below the dignity of the subject. . . .

"The Secretary of War saw fit to deny my request, preferred by a distinguished Senator of the United States who honoured me with his confidence and friendship, to be permitted to examine the captured records of the Confederate Government, of the contents of which some Federal officers, more fortunate than myself, have from time to time given what lawyers call 'parole testimony.' I have thus been thrown back upon other sources of information; and while I am most grateful for the assistance I have received from officers, both Federal and Confederate, to whom I have applied, candour compels me to acknowledge that the seeker after truth has a hard time of it when he undertakes to describe with anything like minuteness any of the great battles of the war."

Seeking, above all, accuracy, Marshall determined to await the publication of the Official Records; but by the time these had appeared the pressure of an expanding legal practice prevented him from resuming his task. In the interval he had written his reminiscences of his experiences at Richmond in the spring of 1862, had expanded a number of the dispatches, and had written a study of the Gettysburg campaign. These, with several addresses delivered on memorial occasions and the original drafts of some of the dispatches and some correspondence with persons prominent in the war, constitute the papers which have been placed in my hands. It is a proof that Marshall sought earnestly to follow his great chief's example in endeavoring to heal the wounds and remove the bitterness of war, that the greater part of the last chapter, in which he describes, as an eyewitness, — I may add, the only Southern eyewitness to do so, — the memorable scene at Appomattox, was prepared for an address delivered at Grant's tomb.

With this prelude, I give way to Colonel Marshall.

LEE'S AIDE-DE-CAMP

I

PREPARATION FOR WAR IN THE CONFEDERACY

On the 21st of March 1862, I became a member of the personal Staff of General Robert E. Lee, who had just been appointed to the general command of the Armies of the Confederate States, subject to the direction of the President. Congress passed a law creating the office of General-in-Chief, which President Davis returned without his signature. His objection was that the law was unconstitutional inasmuch as it clothed the General-in-Chief with the power of a Commander-in-Chief, and that by the Constitution, he, Mr. Davis, was Commander-in-Chief of the Army and Navy.[1]

This law grew out of the conviction that had become very general among the people of the Confederate States, that Mr. Davis was not competent to direct the

---

[1] This incident is not mentioned by Jefferson Davis in his *Rise and Fall of the Confederate Government*, nor is there any reference to it in the voluminous correspondence contained in *Jefferson Davis, Constitutionalist; His Letters, Papers, and Speeches*, while it appears to have escaped the notice of Lee's biographers, except for a brief reference in Long's *Memoirs of R. E. Lee*. The *Journal of the Congress of the Confederate States of America*, 1861–1865, shows (vol. II, p. 34) that on March 5, 1862, the House of Representatives reported to the Senate "An Act to create the office of Commanding General of the Armies of the Confederate States." Five days later, on March 10, there is a reference to a bill with the same title (vol. II, p. 47). As the bill, vetoed by the President, did not become law, it is not included in *Public Laws of the Confederate States of America*, passed at the first session of the first Congress.

operations of the Armies. Some voted for the law, not
with any intention of reflecting upon the President, but
because they thought that the military affairs of the
country were enough to absorb all the time and attention of its most skilful and experienced officers, and that
it was too great a task for one man to assume their sole
direction while burdened by the cares of civil administration.

It was not the intention of Congress, nor was it the
effect of the law itself, to infringe upon the constitutional powers of the President as Commander-in-Chief.
Officers had to be assigned to the command of each
army and of extensive districts. It was impossible that
the President should exercise a personal command over
all the armies, and Congress only created a new grade in
the service, which no more interfered with the constitutional power of the President than the assignment of an
officer to the command of an army or department
would do.[2]

The President was obliged to act as Commander-in-
Chief through the officers at the head of the various
armies. The law already provided for officers for that
purpose, but there was no provision to enable the Presi-

[2] After the fall of Forts Henry and Donelson, anxiety in the Confederacy gave rise to much criticism of Davis. On March 13, 1862, Davis
wrote to W. M. Brooks, circuit judge of Alabama, defending himself in a
long letter against charges of carrying on the war on a purely defensive
system; of keeping his generals in leading strings; and of treating the
Secretary of War as a "mere clerk." (See *Jefferson Davis, Constitutionalist*, vol. V, p. 222.) It was the uneasy feeling that there was something
wrong with Davis's methods of conducting war that stirred Congress to
action. Colonel Marshall here indicates the chief defect in the war organ-
ization of the Confederacy — the lack of means of coördinating the
operations of the several armies. This defect became much more pronounced when Lee ceased to be the President's adviser.

dent to exercise his power over all the armies through an officer of competent rank, just as he exercised his power over any particular army. The law was designed to supply that deficiency, but the President considered it an infringement of his rights and powers. This was not the only instance in which Mr. Davis manifested an extreme jealousy of any encroachment upon his prerogative by Congress, and defended his constitutional rights with no less zeal and with more success than he defended the country itself. This is said in no spirit of hostility to Mr. Davis, but as it is my purpose to point out as far as I can the causes that led to the failure of the Confederacy, I shall speak plainly on all subjects that seem to me to have a bearing on the matter I have in hand.

Mr. Davis, soon after his refusal to approve the law, assigned General R. E. Lee to the command of the armies of the Confederate States, subject to the direction of the President. The only difference in the position of General Lee under this order and that which he would have held had he been appointed General-in-Chief under the law above referred to, was that he had no increase of rank by the order. His legal authority was the same, and in either case he could have had no legal power which would not have been subject to that of the President.[3]

The action of the President indicated very plainly his purpose to be an active agent in military affairs, and his indisposition to leave them in the hands of the officers

---

[3] The order ran: "General Robert E. Lee is assigned to duty at the seat of Government, and under the direction of the President is charged with the conduct of military operations of the armies of the Confederacy." March 13, 1862. See *Official Records*, vol. V, p. 1099.

of the army, subject to his general constitutional control. He showed that he wanted to be Commander-in-Chief not only in law but in fact. It was most natural, therefore, that General Lee, coming into command in such circumstances, with so pointed a declaration on the part of the President of the limits within which the powers of a General-in-Chief should be confined, and so distinct an avowal that he was under the actual and immediate direction of the President, should have observed very carefully the wishes and views so expressed, and submitted his judgment in all things to that of his superior. Of all men in the Confederate Army, none had a greater deference for authority or was more scrupulous in manifesting due subordination to superiors.[4] It was natural then that General Lee became nothing but an adviser of the President. He was in fact an assistant Secretary of War. All papers relating to military matters of any sort received by the President, or by any member of the Cabinet, were referred to him to be answered, no matter how unimportant or purely personal might be their nature. I have had to answer great numbers of letters thus referred, which no more belonged to the province of a commander to answer than the most private personal letters. But as to military movements General Lee never did more than advise. He never on any occasion during the period of which I am speaking, so far as I can remember, ordered the movement of any part of the army without first submit-

---

[4] See Lee's letter to his wife, July 12, 1861: "I have never heard of the assignment to which you refer of commander-in-chief of the Southern Army, nor have I any expectation or wish for it. President Davis holds that position."

ting it to the President. And many and long were the conferences they held in the office of the President over movements recommended by General Lee or suggested by other officers.

I have heard the General say, after interviews of several hours' duration with the President, that he had lost a good deal of time in fruitless talk. Not that he ever uttered a word that was disrespectful to the President. On the contrary, from first to last, I have never known him speak of that functionary in any other terms than those of official and personal respect and kindness. What I mean to convey is that the country was very far from enjoying the benefit of the ability and skill of General Lee in the manner that was contemplated by the law of Congress. The President continued to exercise direct control over army movements.[5] General Lee did not take actual command of the armies of the Confederacy, but became the adviser of the President; nor was his advice uniformly followed.

After the order of March 13th 1862 appeared, Congress passed a law creating a staff for the officer on duty at the seat of Government under such an order.[6] He was allowed a military secretary with the rank, pay, and

[5] After his appearance on the field of the first battle of Manassas, at the close of the battle, Davis but rarely interfered with the actual operations of his generals in the field, though he did interfere in matters of administration and personnel. His were sins rather of omission than of commission. He failed to see that he needed expert assistance if the operations of armies were to be maintained effectively, with the result that too often they were not maintained.

[6] An Act to provide a staff and clerical assistance for any general who may be assigned by the President to duty at the seat of Government. March 25, 1862. See *Public Laws of the Confederate States of America*, Richmond, 1862.

allowances of a colonel of cavalry, and four aides-de-camp with the rank, pay, and allowances of majors of cavalry. To the former position Colonel A. L. Long, formerly of the U.S.A., was appointed. The aides were Majors W. H. Taylor, who also acted as Assistant Adjutant General, T. M. R. Talcott, C. S. Venable, and Charles Marshall. Four of these officers were from Virginia, the fifth from Maryland, though born and educated in Virginia where his family resided.[7]

At the time when General Lee entered upon the discharge of his duties in Richmond, the condition of affairs was most unpromising for the Confederacy. The enemy had effected a lodgment on the coast of North and South Carolina at points whence he threatened the lines of railway from Richmond to the South, thus rendering it necessary to employ a part of our force to guard those roads and prevent him from penetrating into the interior.[8]

In the west the fall of Forts Donelson and Henry, and the subsequent evacuation by General Albert Sidney Johnston of Kentucky and most of Tennessee, together with all the posts on the Mississippi to Memphis inclusive, had not only inflicted a great material injury upon us by depriving us of the supplies of a large and productive region in which were many manufacturing establishments of the utmost importance to the

[7] Not all these officers were appointed at the same time. Marshall was, as he tells us, appointed on March 21, 1862, in anticipation of the Act of Congress. Long afterwards Brigadier General A. L. Long, the author of the *Memoirs of Robert E. Lee*, the best contemporary life of Lee, was appointed on April 19. This little group formed the nucleus of Lee's military family. Marshall was the fifth, from Maryland.

[8] The Federals captured Roanoke Island on February 8, 1862.

western armies, and placing a great number of people friendly to the South and willing to aid a prosperous cause, beyond the reach of our recruit-agencies, but it had done us a still more irreparable moral injury. The confidence and enthusiasm inspired by the issue of the first battle of Manassas were sensibly impaired, while the Northern people were elated in a corresponding degree. A powerful expedition was already to move against New Orleans, by land and water; in Virginia the force under General J. E. Johnston at Manassas was known to be inferior in numbers and equipment to that which General McClellan was preparing to move from Washington, and the people saw plainly that they had indulged in a false confidence as to the strength of our armies. Upon no subject had the public less accurate information both at home and abroad, and when the Army of Kentucky retreated, such had been the exaggerated estimate of its strength, that there was at first a general disposition to attribute the disaster to incompetency on the part of its able and faithful commander. It will be remembered how expression was given on the floor of Congress to this opinion by some who watched current popular feeling most closely, and were ever ready to avail themselves of it to obtain influence and popularity.

The politicians of the South had been influenced in initiating the secession movement largely by the expectation of foreign intervention, and with fatal tenacity these politicians adhered to this original error, to the neglect of those measures of defence which, taken in time, might have proved successful. I am fully aware of the advantage he possesses who speaks of what is

past in the light of experience, over him upon whom de-
volves the duty of preparing to meet the unknown future. The critic can see in what has occurred what no
human sagacity could have anticipated. But with
reference to the subject about which I am about to
speak, no such reply can be made by the political leaders
of the South. There was at the time a division of
opinion among them, and the majority, when adhering
to the opinions upon which they acted in the beginning
of the movement, had full warning of the consequences
they might expect, and deliberately staked the issue
upon the soundness of their views.

A gentleman who was certainly entirely in the confidence of the original secession leaders, and who played
a most prominent part in the events of the day, told me
in conversation that the war might continue during one
campaign, but certainly would end before the spring
of 1862. This conversation took place in May 1861,
and the remark was made in reply to my question as to
the probable duration of the war which was then just
beginning. He said that accurate information had been
obtained as to the quantity of cotton then in Europe,
that the supply in the general course of business would
be exhausted by the beginning of the ensuing February,
and that then intervention would be inevitable.

As there is no violation of confidence in giving the
name of my informant, I will state that it was the Hon.
James M. Mason, late Confederate Commissioner in
Europe. I dined with him in Winchester on my way
from Baltimore to Richmond the Sunday after the
people of Virginia had voted on the ordinance of secession (Sunday, May 26th). It may well be supposed

JAMES L. MASON

that Mr. Mason was informed of the opinions of those with whom he had been so long acting in concert during the agitations that culminated in secession, and his subsequent selection to represent the views of the Confederate Government abroad justifies the belief that, in speaking of so important a subject as the duration of the war and the means by which it was to be brought to a close, he uttered not only his own views, but those of the Southern political leaders with whom he had been so intimately associated.

The Confederate Congress which assembled at Montgomery made but little preparation for war. In fact at that time and until after the battle of Manassas on the 21st July 1861, few persons, North or South, really believed that there would be a war, or that, if hostilities should occur, they would be either of great extent or long duration. Congress proceeded therefore to organise an army on a very limited scale, and when the preparations made by the United States for the first campaign rendered it necessary to make more extensive provision to meet them, a law was passed allowing the President to accept the services of volunteers for one year. The enthusiasm of the people, it was thought, would supply a force adequate to repel that which the United States Government was then preparing, and no further steps were taken. I think that in the circumstances this policy is no reflection upon the sagacity and foresight of the Confederate Congress. The want of preparation on the part of the United States at the time justified the Confederate authorities in the belief that they could concentrate at any place that might be threatened as rapidly as the enemy, and rendered it unnecessary to do more than collect an adequate force in front of that which the enemy was preparing. At that time, also, it was not difficult to know the intention of the enemy. Communication was comparatively open between the North and the South, and there was little effort made to conceal the plan of operations.

The Confederate Government was not therefore improvident in limiting its first preparations for war. But after the first battle of Manassas the aspect of affairs was completely changed. The Government of the United States appeared to be fully aroused. A call was made for men in numbers that amazed the world. At first the people and politicians of the South treated the subject with ridicule. It was believed to be impossible for the United States to assemble such a force as Mr. Lincoln summoned to the field. Calculations were made of the expense that would attend the formation of so vast an army, and it was confidently asserted that the credit of the United States would succumb. But as the season advanced those doubts were dissipated by events. Men came forward in such numbers and so rapidly that it was apparent that the large force called for by Mr. Lincoln would be raised.[9] The whole North resounded with the notes of preparation for war on a most gigantic scale. The credit of the government was unimpaired by its great efforts. The capacity of public and private dockyards was strained to the utmost to launch in the shortest possible time a powerful navy. Resort was had to the vast mercantile marine of the North to obtain the means of transporting troops

[9] Lincoln's answer to the first battle of Manassas was a call for 500,000 men for three years.

promptly to any point that might be selected for attack. The Atlantic and Gulf coasts of the Confederacy thus became as much exposed to attack as any part of the Northern frontier.   It was no longer sufficient to place an army in front of Richmond, as Nashville, Charleston, Savannah, Mobile, and New Orleans were equally exposed, and equally required means of defence.

The preparations of the United States were well known to our authorities.   In fact, they were made with so much ostentation as to raise a doubt in the mind of some whether it was not intended to intimidate our people by their very magnitude.   But one fact was most apparent, and that was that our force was wholly inadequate to cope successfully with that of the United States.   Yet during all the summer, autumn, winter, and part of the spring succeeding the battle of Manassas, the Confederate Congress did not pass a single law to raise an army except those to which I have referred as having been adopted at Montgomery.   Its apathy was astounding.   Volunteering had sensibly decreased since the summer of 1861, and nearly all the troops were enlisted for one year.   On the 11th December, 1861, a law was passed by Congress to encourage the volunteers to re-enlist.   A bounty of $50 and a furlough were offered to each man and the privilege of re-enlisting in his original or in any other command in any arm of the service which he might select.   The law went further and authorised the formation of new companies, battalions, and regiments, to be composed of new recruits and the original volunteers.   Authority to act under this law was given by the Secretary of War, and complaints began soon to be heard from the armies that the persons so authorised were canvassing the various commands to induce men to enlist in the new organisations they proposed to form.

Nothing could have been devised better calculated to disorganise the army and impair its efficiency than this law. Old regiments were to be broken up, the army to be thrown into a confused and disorganised mass, out of which, by the free action of the men, it was supposed that a new army would emerge at the expiration of the first year's term of service. This period would arrive about the time when active operations might reasonably be expected to begin in the spring of 1862, and this new army, the organisation of which would be such as the personal inclinations of the men might induce them to adopt, was to be opposed to the army that was being carefully formed and efficiently instructed. The Confederate Congress not only adopted no effective measure to increase the strength of the army, but, actuated by the sole desire to retain men in the service, it sacrificed the efficiency of such men as it had.

The Hon. J. P. Benjamin, who was first Attorney General and then Secretary of State in Mr. Davis' administration, writes to me of the effect of the legislation of Congress : —

As soon as war became certain, every possible effort was made by the President and his advisers to induce Congress to raise an army enlisted "for the war." The fatal effects of enlistments for short terms, shown by the history of the War of Independence against England, were invoked as furnishing a lesson for our guidance. It was all in vain. The people as we were informed by the members would not volunteer for the war, but they would rise in mass as volunteers for twelve months. We did not wish them to rise in mass nor in great numbers for any such short term, for the reason that *we could not arm them*, and their term of service would expire before we could equip them. I speak from memory as to numbers, but only a moderate force was raised (all that we could provide with arms) for twelve months service, and thus a *provisional* army was formed, but the fatal effect of the short term of service, combined with the painful deficiency of supplies, were felt long before the end of the year. While the Northern States after the Battle of Manassas were vigorously engaged in preparing for an overwhelming descent upon Virginia, our own army was falling to pieces. In February 1862, the President's message contained the following passages : —

"The active state of military preparations among the nations of Europe in April last, the date when our Agents last went abroad, *interposed unavoidable delays in the procurement of arms.*" [10]

"The policy of enlistment for short terms *against which I have steadily contended from the commencement of the war*, contributed in no immaterial degree to the recent reverse we have suffered (Roanoke Island and Fort Donelson), and even now renders it difficult to furnish you an accurate statement of the army . . . our high-spirited and gallant soldiers, while generally re-enlisting, are, from the fact of having entered the service for a short term, compelled in many instances *to go home* to make the necessary arrangements for their families during their prolonged absence. . ."

"I deem it proper to advert to the fact that the process of furloughs and re-enlistment in progress for the last month

---

[10] There were no exceptional military preparations in Europe in 1861, but the European armies had no large surplus stocks of arms available for sale.

has so far disorganised and weakened our forces as to impair our ability for successful defense, but this evil which *I had foreseen and was now powerless to prevent* may now be said to be substantially at an end."

The foregoing sentences (the italics are my own) will show the condition of the army and the causes of that condition.

The representatives of the people could not be persuaded to pass measures unpalatable to the people; and the unthinking multitude upon whose *voluntary* enlistments Congress forced us to depend were unable to foresee or appreciate the dangers of the policy against which we protested. It was only the imminent danger of being left without *any* army by the return home in mass of the first levy of twelve-month volunteers that drove Congress into passing a law for enlistments for the war, and in order to induce the soldiers under arms to re-enlist we were driven to the fatal expedient of granting them not only bounties but furloughs to return from Virginia to their homes in the far South, and if our actual condition had been at all suspected by the enemy they might have marched through Virginia with but the faintest show of resistance.

As to supplies of munitions I will give a single instance of the straits to which we were reduced. I was Secretary of War *ad interim* for a few months, during which Roanoke Island, commanded by General Wise, fell into the hands of the enemy. The report of that General shows that the capture was due in great measure to the persistent disregard by the Secretary of War of his urgent demands for munitions and supplies. Congress appointed a committee to investigate the conduct of the Secretary. I consulted the President whether it was best for the country that I should submit to unmerited censure or reveal to a Congressional Committee our poverty and my utter inability to supply the requisitions of General Wise, and thus run the risk that the fact should become known to some of the spies of the enemy of whose activity we were well assured. It was thought best for the public service that I should suffer the blame in silence and a report of censure on me was accordingly made by the Committee of Congress.

The *dearth* even of powder was so great that during the descent of the enemy on Roanoke, General Wise having sent me a despatch that he was in instant need of ammunition, I ordered by telegraph General Huger at Norfolk to send an immediate supply; this was done but accompanied by a despatch from General Huger protesting against this exhaustion of his small store, and saying that it was insufficient to defend Norfolk for a day. General Lee was therefore ordered to send a part of his very scanty supply to Norfolk, General Lee being in his turn aided by a small cargo of powder which had just run into one of the inlets on the coast of Florida.[11]

Another terrible source of trouble, disorganisation, and inefficiency was the incurable jealousy in many states of the General Government. Each State has its own mode of appointing officers, generally by election. Until disaster forced Congress to pass the Conscription law, all that we could do was to get laws passed calling for certain quotas of troops from the states, and in order to prevent attempts made to create officers of higher rank than the Confederate officers, who would thus have been placed under the orders of raw militia generals, we resorted to the expedient of refusing to receive any higher organisation than a regiment. But the troops being State troops officered by the State officers, the army was constantly scandalized by electioneering to replace regimental officers, and Confederate Commanders were without means of enforcing discipline and efficiency

[11] Lee was at this time (February 1862) in general charge of the coast defenses of the Carolinas.

except through the cumbrous and most objectionable expedient of Courts Martial. Another fatal defect was that we had no power to consolidate regiments, battalions, and companies. If a company was reduced to five men or a regiment to fifty, we had no power to remedy this. The message of the President of the 12th of August, 1862, showed the fatal effects of our military system, and a perusal of that message will shed a flood of light on the actual position of things and the hopeless helplessness to which the Executive was reduced by the legislation of Congress, and the restrictions imposed on his power to act efficiently for military success by the jealousy of Congress and the States. When I look back on it all, I am lost in amazement that the struggle could have been so prolonged, and one of the main, if not the main source of strength and encouragement to the Executive was the genius, ability, constancy, fidelity, and firmness of General Lee.

In short, Congress did not direct its efforts to a vigorous defence of the country by arms, but it looked to some other means of deliverance. The avowed intention of a large party at the North to control the action of Mr. Lincoln was discussed as if the issue were one of ordinary party politics. Most of all, the influence that the want of cotton would exert upon the chief manufacturing and commercial nations of Europe was looked to for a sure, speedy and satisfactory solution of the whole question. The Confederate Congress and a great part of the Southern people, encouraged by their representatives and by the press, were eager to adopt any theory that promised relief from the threatened danger other than recognition of the fact that their only safety lay in the vigorous use of the whole military resources of the country. In vain did event after event demonstrate the futility of those hopes of deliverance. They were adhered to with a tenacity which resisted at once the appeals of reason and the teachings of experience.

The long expected first of February 1862 arrived. The supply of cotton in Europe, according to all calculations, must now be exhausted, and intervention become inevitable. The increasing stringency of the blockade, aided by the efforts of the Confederate Government to prevent the exportation of cotton, soon began to make the want of that material felt, but before the end of 1861 the first Commissioners sent to Europe had returned and informed the people that cotton was no longer king.[12]

With February came the disasters on the coast of North Carolina, the loss of Kentucky, of the greater part of Tennessee, and the whole of the Upper Mississippi, and the approaching readiness of the large force on the northern border of Virginia to take the field as soon as the season for active operations should arrive.

The President issued a call for troops upon the Governors of the several States, but not until then. He too, like the Congress, had suffered the precious time for preparation to pass by, and made no effort to increase the army, except by obtaining volunteers, until the enemy, fully prepared, was advancing into the interior of the West, and threatening the capital itself. I should remark in this connection, that the State of Virginia, in which the reliance upon cotton had never been a controlling influence, impressed with the public danger, had

[12] For an explanation of why cotton was not king see Professor Channing's *History of the United States*, vol. VII.

already taken measures to bring her arm-bearing population into the field, and a law was passed on the 16th
February, superior in some respects to the Conscript
law subsequently adopted by the Confederate Congress.
The call of the President was however too urgent in its
nature to allow the troops to be assembled under the
law of the State, and the Governor ordered out the men
capable of bearing arms at once, endeavouring to comply as nearly as possible with the intention of the legis-
lature as indicated by the Act.

The actual strength of the Confederate armies in the
field, however much it might have been exaggerated
among the people and by the enemy, was well known to
the Confederate authorities. The force under General
J. E. Johnston at Manassas was known to be far inferior
to the army under General McClellan at Washington.
The army under A. S. Johnston in Kentucky was as
well known to be inferior to that which was preparing to
move against it, and was, moreover, stretched over a
large extent of country, from the Mississippi to the Virginia border. On each frontier the appearance of a
design to resist the enemy was kept up, and not only our
own people but the enemy and the world were deceived,
and there is reason to believe that the Confederate Government expected to attain its purpose by this show of
force and appearance of ability to meet the enemy at all
points of its frontier. Such a picture of affairs would,
it was hoped, justify foreign governments in recognising
the Confederacy, and it was confidently believed that
the exhaustion of the supply of cotton abroad would
induce them to avail themselves of any defensible pre-
text to adopt measures that would re-open the cotton

market of the South. The letter of General A. S. Johnston to President Davis, published after the fall of that
lamented officer at Shiloh, indicates very clearly the explanation that he had received of the policy of the Government. He had been impressed with the importance
in a political point of view of presenting a bold front to
the enemy in Kentucky, and of appearing to be able to
hold his own line.[13]

So also with General J. E. Johnston in Virginia.
These officers were not instructed to maintain their positions until they could be reinforced, for I have shown
that no adequate or efficient measures were adopted for
that purpose. But they were to impress the enemy and
the world with the belief that they would resist an advance and that they possessed the means to do it.
When the advance took place these impressions were
dissipated in a moment.

It cannot be supposed that the Confederate Government believed that the vast force that was being prepared would not be used against it. The solution is to
be found in the radical and fundamental error of those
who initiated the secession movement. . . . They
believed the Northern people would not unite in supporting the war. They saw them actually supporting
the war with singular unanimity. In fact the Government of Mr. Lincoln at the outset took efficient measures

[13] A. S. Johnston to Davis, March 18, 1862: "Believing it to be of the
greatest moment to protract the campaign, as the dearth of cotton might
bring strength from abroad and discourage the North and gain time to
strengthen myself by new troops from Tennessee and other States, I mag-
nified my forces to the enemy, but made known my true strength to the
Department and to the Governors of the States." *Official Records*, vol.
II, p. 259.

to deprive the South of this hope by the adoption of a policy which, whatever else may be said of it, was eminently wise in a military point of view. That Government threw aside the ordinary restraints upon its operations which were observed in times of peace. It did not stop to argue with those who opposed its measures, but forced them to acquiesce, or put it out of their power to offer effectual opposition. Southern politicians fell into the error of reasoning about the action of the Northern people as if the war had made no change. They continued to talk of parties, and to speculate about the probable action of their former political associates, as if those parties remained unchanged and possessed the power they had formerly exercised. The only exposition of the intentions and actions of the United States Government to which the South could look, and upon which it could safely form its own policy, were the declarations and measures of that Government, which had shown very plainly that it would tolerate no opposition from parties at home.

The other and principal cause of neglect to make adequate preparations was, as I have indicated, the confident belief that the want of cotton would compel foreign nations, particularly England and France, to intervene and stop the war. I have said that the time at which it was believed that such intervention would become inevitable had been designated by Mr. Mason as the month of February 1862. It is remarkable that Mr. Davis did not issue a general call for additional troops until this time, and it is equally remarkable that the enemy selected that month, unfavourable as it was in many respects for military operations, for the advance

JEFFERSON DAVIS

of his Western Army.   Both facts would seem to indicate that each party was influenced by the same
motive.[14]

Mr. Davis had found that he had waited for intervention until it would be unsafe to wait any longer; the
time had arrived when the cause upon which he relied
should have produced its full effect, and yet there were
no indications of foreign aid.   The North, on the other
hand, knowing that the pressure upon foreign governments would reach its maximum about that time, and
that the continuance of the semblance of ability on the
part of the Confederacy to defend its frontiers would
afford encouragement and justification to England
and France to act under the pressure, was desirous of
demonstrating that the South could not cope with her,
and of deterring the governments of these countries
from involving themselves in the contest by a display of its power to bring the war to a successful
conclusion.

It will be remembered how anxiously both sides
awaited news from Europe during the period of which I
am speaking.   Not a skirmish took place that the people of the North and South, especially the latter, did
not listen, *erectis auribus*, for the English and French
comments upon it.   Every utterance of the press of
those two countries was quickly republished, eagerly
read, and anxiously commented upon by both.

I remember when the news from Europe would absorb

[14] This is the best explanation of which I know of Lincoln's action in
issuing, on January 27, 1862, his much criticized War Order No. 1.   In
this order he fixed Washington's birthday, February 22, as the day "for
a general advance by the land and naval forces of the United States."

the attention of all parties in the Confederacy to the exclusion of important military events at home.[15]

The communications of Mr. Davis to Congress will be found to be devoted more largely to the subject of foreign recognition than to the war itself. Every man who observed the course of events in the South during this period is aware how entirely our people had accustomed themselves to look for intervention, and discuss the probability of its occurrence. I conclude then that the failure of the Confederate Government to make timely and adequate preparation for the campaign that opened in 1862 proceeded from its confidence that foreign nations would intervene before that campaign should open, and that the Northern people themselves would not unite in supporting the war.

It will doubtless be said that the people of the South were not then prepared to make the exertions and sacrifices which the full development of their military resources would have demanded; that they were only brought subsequently to make those exertions and sacrifices by the presence of imminent danger and the policy of the Northern Government. I am aware that throughout the whole war there was manifested by the Confederate Government a reluctance to try the patience and zeal of the people. It was often said during the war that the people were always in advance of the Government. Everyone remarked how the people

[15] One of the first acts of the Senate of the first Congress of the Confederacy was to pass a resolution: "That the President be requested to communicate to the Senate in secret session if not incompatible with the public interest, the instructions to and correspondence with all the Commissioners to this Government now in Europe." March 3, 1862. *Journal of the Congress of the Confederate States of America*, vol. II, p. 30.

clamoured to be taxed to save the country when a timid Congress was hesitating to impose taxes. This indisposition to exert its power, so often manifested by the Confederate Government, was a natural consequence of the theory upon which that Government was formed. Recognising no power to coerce a state, holding that any state might nullify a law of Congress, and that the league rested entirely in the consent of the parties composing it, the Confederate Government endeavoured to shape its policy so as to conciliate the States and secure their acquiescence in its measures. This was an inherent weakness of the theory of the Government, but there can be no doubt that it was carried further than was necessary by the Government of Mr. Davis. The people would have done more than the Government required of them, and had Congress boldly thrown itself on their patriotism at this time, they would have responded most cheerfully.

But if it be true that they were not prepared at the time for the exertions they subsequently made, and would not have patiently submitted or cheerfully supported any measures deemed necessary for the common defense, the Government itself was the cause of such a state of feeling. It had in every way sedulously fostered the belief that the war would be short, and intervention certain. In fact, the party in the Southern States which desired separation as a positive benefit, independently of any cause for such a measure (and that party was small), always regarded it as certain that the South would shape the policy of the manufacturing nations of Europe by means of cotton alone. They never believed that the war would ensue upon separation, and when it came they could not be persuaded for a long time that it would be of long duration. Unfortunately, as those who entertained this very mistaken opinion had been most active in trying to effect a dissolution of the Union, they acquired a fatal influence in the early management of the affairs of the Confederacy, and imparted into its councils that blind confidence in their views as to the effect of secession and the influence of cotton, which paralyzed the efforts of the Southern people at the beginning of the war.

Strange as it may appear, the influence of these narrow theories did not cease to be felt long after events had demonstrated that the South must rely upon her own efforts exclusively. After the fall of Corinth [16] a proposition was made by persons within the Federal lines, who asserted that they acted under the authority of a notorious military character in the U. S. service, to exchange several millions of pounds of provisions and flour for cotton, the provisions, etc., to be delivered within our lines on or near the lower Mississippi River. They furnished such evidence of their ability to do this without interruption from the Federal authorities, if not by their direct connivance, that the proposition was submitted to and considered by the Confederate Government. But it was rejected by the President, because it would be a departure from the principle he had laid down that it was impolitic for us to permit our cotton to go out of our lines, especially when it was to go directly to the enemy. The cotton was afterwards burned or captured.

In confirmation of the fact that the parties who made

[16] May 30, 1862.

the proposition could have carried it into effect, I can state that during the autumn of 1864 and the winter of 1865 quite a large traffic of the same kind took place, to some extent under my control, by order of General Lee, to whom the matter was entrusted. The persons engaged on the Federal side professed to act under the authority of the same person who had previously given his consent to the Mississippi traders. Their operations were conducted quite openly by means of steamers ascending the Blackwater and Chowan Rivers.

II

GENERAL LEE ATTEMPTS REFORMS

I HAVE briefly alluded to the posture of affairs when I joined General Lee's staff on March 21st, 1862. Manassas had been evacuated, and General J. E. Johnston lay behind the Rappahannock, awaiting the development of the plans of General McClellan. General Jackson had retired up the Valley, Winchester and Front Royal being in possession of the Federal forces under General Banks.[1] It was known that General McClellan did not intend to pursue General Johnston or attempt to advance upon Richmond from the north, and it was quite certain that he would transfer his forces to the Peninsula or James River line of approach.[2] General Magruder held the Peninsula with a small force, and it was believed that the Virginia or Merrimac would prevent the enemy from using the line of the James, and compel him to advance up the Peninsula, using the York River for his supplies. The enemy on the North Carolina coast had made no formidable attempt to penetrate into the interior. A movement was made in the direction of Norfolk from Roanoke

[1] Jackson evacuated Winchester on March 11, 1862.
[2] It is remarkable how much of the Federal plans was known at this time at Richmond, and how little of the Confederate plans was known at Washington. This may be in part due to the fact, at which Colonel Marshall hints plainly, that until the end of March 1862 the only Confederate plan was to make a display of strength wherever possible — in other words, bluff.

Island, but was foiled at South Mills by Colonel, after-wards Brigadier General, Wright, with less than a regiment of infantry and part of a battery. The troops south of the James River were therefore held in readiness to move to the assistance of General Magruder, except those at Norfolk, which were not withdrawn until some time afterwards.

In the West, General Albert Sidney Johnston had been compelled to evacuate Kentucky and a large part of Tennessee, and the Federal Army, after advancing some distance south of Nashville, turned towards the Tennessee River at Pittsburg Landing. New Orleans fell,[3] the upper Mississippi was abandoned, and there appeared to be no reasonable probability of our being able to oppose successfully the large army of General Buell, advancing southward through Tennessee, except by concentrating the troops that, in pursuance of the policy of making a front against the enemy at every point, had been scattered over a vast extent of country. Our weakness was but too evident, and to add to our trouble, the expiration of the term of service of the greater part of our troops was approaching. Many had not re-enlisted, and large numbers of those who had would, under the operation of the law of December 11th, 1861, to which I have referred, leave their original commands to unite with other entirely new organisations. The recruits obtained under the call of the President upon the Governors of the States did not come forth in adequate numbers, and those that did were not placed in existing organisations, but were permitted to form or assist in forming the new commands authorised by that

[3] April 26, 1862.

law which was disorganising the troops we had in the field.[4]

Such was the unpropitious aspect of affairs. Towards the last of March the army of General McClellan began to arrive at Fortress Monroe, and General J. E. Johnston proceeded to the lines at Yorktown to support General Magruder. As the plans of the enemy were more fully developed, the troops south of the James River were also ordered to join those engaged in holding the Peninsula at Yorktown, but the combined army was scarcely one-third as strong as that of General McClellan.[5] In these circumstances it became evident that some more efficacious means must be taken to obtain men than the process of calling upon the Governors of the several States.

About April 1st, or perhaps a few days earlier,[6] General Lee directed me to prepare a draft of a bill for raising an army by the direct agency of the Confederate Government. His instructions were to provide that the whole population between the ages of eighteen and forty-five should be placed in the service of the Confederate States for the duration of the war. The President was authorized to call out such parts of the popula-

[4] See Lee to Mrs. Lee, March 22, 1862: "Our enemies are pressing us everywhere and our army is in fermentation of reorganisation. I pray that the Great God may aid us, and am endeavouring by every means in my power to bring out the troops and hasten them to their destination."

[5] Colonel Marshall has somewhat antedated the development of McClellan's strength on the Peninsula. McClellan landed at Fortress Monroe on April 2nd, and on the 3rd had disembarked 53,000 men.

[6] It must certainly have been "a few days earlier," as the bill was presented to the Senate by Mr. Wigfall from the Committee on Military Affairs on April 1st, and was read a first and second time on that day. *Journal of Congress of Confederate States*, vol. II, p. 114.

ROBERT E. LEE

tion rendered liable to service by the law, as he might deem proper, and at such times as he saw fit. The bill further provided that the recruits thus obtained should be used in the first instance to fill existing organisations to their complement, and empowered the Government to form new commands, if necessary, whose officers were to be appointed by the President, with the advice and consent of the Senate. It repealed the act of December 11th, 1861, took from the volunteers the right conferred by that act of organizing and electing their officers, and retained in service for the war the men already enlisted. The men thus made subject to military duty, and not drafted into existing commands or used to form new organisations, were to constitute a reserve and were to be drilled in camps of instruction.

This measure completely reversed the previous military legislation of the South. It was inspired by General Lee's views of the real nature and object of the war on the part of the United States, and of the corresponding duty of the Southern people. Convinced himself of the rectitude and justice of the Southern cause, ready to make any sacrifice to ensure its triumph, he deprecated the apparent reluctance of Congress to throw itself upon the patriotism and earnestness of the people. The efforts of the Government had hitherto been confined to inviting the support of the people. General Lee thought it could more surely rely upon their intelligent obedience, and that it might safely assume to command where it had as yet only tried to persuade.

He believed that independence could only be achieved by the vigorous use of all the resources of the country, and that the people would support any measures wisely devised to secure the blessings of success, and to avert the incalculable ills of failure.   Without disregarding the possible aid to be derived from dissensions among the people of the North, or from European intervention, he maintained that an energetic policy would increase the probability of assistance from those sources. The North, he thought, would be less united in the prosecution of the war in proportion to the difficulties of success, and foreign powers would be more ready to intervene on behalf of a strong and well-prepared people than in favour of those who failed to show that they were able to defend themselves.   Therefore he insisted that the South should be prepared, to the extent of its resources, to defend itself without relying upon foreign assistance, and he held it to be a capital error to count upon contingencies, however probable, if the means of success, independently of those contingencies, were not used.   He thought that every other consideration should be regarded as subordinate to the great end of the public safety, and that since the whole duty of the nation would be war until independence should be secured, the whole nation should for the time be converted into an army, the producers to feed and the soldiers to fight.[7]

I accordingly drew up a paper embodying the foregoing provisions and General Lee took it to the President.   After a long consultation, the General informed me that the paper had been placed in the hands of Mr. Benjamin, then Secretary of State, to be put in proper

[7] This plan of Lee's for the utilization of man power in war, formed in April 1862, was substantially that adopted by the United States on its entry into the World War in 1917.

form to be recommended to Congress for adoption. I did not see the bill as drafted by Mr. Benjamin, but understood that it did not differ much in its main provisions from that written by me under the direction of General Lee. It was more detailed, contained some special provisions as to the mode of enforcing the law, and I believe repealed the law of December 11th, as General Lee's paper had proposed.

The bill was laid before Congress early in April, and debated by that body in secret session until about the 15th, when it was adopted,[8] with certain grave and most hurtful alterations, the effects of which we felt to the end of the war. I do not hesitate to assert, and I appeal to every officer of experience in the Confederate service to sustain me, that the provisions of the bill as it passed Congress did more to weaken the army, to impair its efficiency, and in fact to prepare the way for disaster, than any single cause.

The whole army was reorganised by the law. It retained the men then in service, for three years or the duration of the war. It gave all those who had received authority to raise new commands under the act of December 11th, 1861, thirty days within which to complete their organisations. It expressly repealed that Act, and placed the arms-bearing population between 18 and 35, with certain exemptions, in the service of the Confederate States for three years or the duration of the war, to be called into the field by the President, and provided that the Secretary of War should devise the mode of compelling their attendance. So far, save

[8] The Act was entitled, "An Act to further provide for the public defence," and was approved on April 16, 1862.

for some of the exemptions, to which I shall presently allude, the law was as good as could reasonably have been expected; but it contained the following fatal defects: It provided that the men of the existing commands retained in service should elect their field and company officers, within a certain short time before the expiration of their first enlistment. It further provided that men before enrolment might enlist in any command and in any arm of the service that they might elect, and that vacancies in the lowest grade of commissioned officers should continue to be filled by election by the men. Thus by the provisions of this law the armies in the immediate presence of the enemy, like that of General J. E. Johnston, on the Peninsula, were authorized to change all their officers by a popular election.

Comment on such a law is unnecessary, but I will state that the worst consequences anticipated by the opponents of the elective system were realised. Some of the best field and company officers, who had been in command a year, had acquired experience in their duties, and whom the men were accustomed to obey, were removed, and their places filled with raw and untried men, many of whom possessed no military merit, and only enjoyed the doubtful qualification of personal popularity with the electors. Of course those officers who had been most stringent in enforcing discipline were most unpopular, and not infrequently those men who had required the greatest restraint at their hands were their successors. Encouragement was given to those who wished to retain their commissions to seek favour for popularity at the expense of discipline. I doubt whether a more perilous experiment could have been devised at a moment of such critical danger. Some of the effects of it were visible in the army long after it passed under the command of General Lee. Nothing but the fine spirit and fighting qualities of those who composed the first army and the ability of their superior officers, saved it from total disorganisation and ruin. The elections in General J. E. Johnston's army actually took place in the Yorktown trenches, and men had to come from the skirmish line to decide by their votes whether the officers who placed them there should continue to command them.

But this was not the worst. Except for a clause authorising promotion for valour and skill, which was interpreted in such a manner by the Department as to render it almost useless and to remove the stimulus to exertion which it was designed to give, the law provided no means for maintaining the supply of officers except by election. When a vacancy occurred in any but the lowest grade of commissioned officers, the promotion was by seniority, but to supply the lowest grades, from which during the progress of the war the higher grades of company and field officers had to be filled, the process was by election by the men. The supply of officers thus depended ultimately upon election, and that fatal feature continued to characterize the service, notwithstanding representations of its baneful effects, until just before the campaign of 1865 opened, when it was repealed, but too late.

It is unnecessary to point out all the ill consequences of this measure, but there is one upon which I have frequently heard General Lee remark with great earnestness, and which was often brought to his attention.

That was the effect of the elective system upon the non-commissioned officers. Those officers are, as it were, the hands of military authority; with them the superior officer lays hold upon the men and compels the execution of orders and attention to duty. In camp, on the march, and in battle, good non-commissioned officers are equally essential to an army. They are in immediate contact with the men, and more apt to incur their ill-will than any other class of officers. Under the elective system, it is apparent that these officers not only had no encouragement to do their duty faithfully, but if they desired promotion, they were positively encouraged to neglect it. Strictness with the men would certainly debar them from promotion by their votes, and to gain popularity, they were tempted to tolerate conduct subversive of discipline, or to great indulgence inconsistent with the efficiency of the army. The evils of this state of affairs were much augmented by the fact that the immediate superiors of the non-commissioned officers owed their promotion to the same system to which the latter had to look for advancement, so non-commissioned officers seeking for popularity were only doing what their superiors had done before them, and were not apprehensive of being held to strict account. The consequence was that good non-commissioned officers frequently saw worthless but more popular men elevated over them to fill vacant posts, and in some instances the best non-commissioned officers, whose tried courage and experience qualified them for advancement, remained non-commissioned officers during the war.

I will sum up the matter with the assertion, based

upon the experience of many of the most accomplished
and able officers in the Confederate army and upon a
personal observation which my position enabled me to
make extensive, that such discipline as we had, we had
in spite of the operation of this law of Congress, and
that it was of all the laws passed by that body the
most injudicious and hurtful to the efficiency of the
service.

When the law was first made public, I asked Mr.
Wigfall of Texas why that provision had been incorpo-
rated in it. He told me that the friends of the Conscript
Law in the Senate were obliged to make the concession
in order to get the law passed at all by that body. It is
incredible that any body should have fallen into so griev-
ous an error, especially when menaced by such pressing
danger. At that moment it was evident that the sole
hope of the country was its army, and the utmost
efficiency of the army, it would seem, should have been
the first object of legislation. If those representatives
of the Southern people had read anything on the subject
of military organizations, they must have known that
the law which they were enacting was in opposition to
the experience of the most warlike of modern nations,
contrary to the judgment of the greatest masters of the
art of war, and unsupported by reason, even without
military knowledge. It is difficult to account for their
course. They were doubtless influenced to some extent
by the consideration that the Conscript Bill contained
provisions which might appear harsh and rigorous to
the first volunteers, who were retained in service, and
they were therefore disposed to give them the privilege
of electing their officers by way of compensation. They

probably reasoned in the same way as to the new recruits to be brought into the field by the operation of
the law.   In short, these popular features of the law
proceeded from the inherent defect, for military purposes, of the theory of the Southern Confederacy.[9]
The Confederate Government was always careful to
conciliate, rather than to command, the States and the
people. Its theory of a league between consenting but
independent sovereignties compelled it to pursue this
course. Such stringent measures as it was forced to
adopt were, when practicable, and often to the emascu-
lation of the measures themselves, accompanied by
provisions tending to reconcile the people to them.
Congress was always timid of legislating to meet the
extraordinary emergencies of the situation, and rarely
anticipated the popular voice in its action.

[9] It is also probable that the same reasons which induced Congress to
send the President a bill for the creation of the office of commander-in-
chief influenced that body when it was considering the Conscript Law.
As I have pointed out, the failure of the Confederate arms had naturally
enough been a cause of criticism of the President, and to this feeling was
added some resentment of what was held to be his autocratic action under
martial law which he had proclaimed in and around Richmond.   Congress may therefore have desired to clip his wings by taking the appoint-
ment of officers out of his hands.

Colonel Marshall has here exposed clearly the defects of the military
measures of the Confederate Congress which came under his notice, but
it must be remembered that the Federal commanders were often even
more hampered than were their Confederate opponents.   A Conscription
Act in the North did not become law until March 3, 1863, nearly a year
after the Confederate Act was passed.   Its application was accompanied
by serious disturbances, and even after it was in force Grant's operations
were seriously prejudiced in 1864 by the necessity of discharging large
numbers of experienced men whose period of service had expired.   The
Confederate Act at least provided for a regular supply of recruits, and for
the preservation of existing regiments.   In the Northern armies regiments
with established reputations were often allowed to expire, and their places
were taken by new formations with no knowledge of war.

The members of the first Congress under the permanent Government of the Confederacy, inaugurated on February 22nd, 1862, were generally men who had sat in the Federal Congress. The best capacity of the country — I say it without disparagement to Congress — was in the army. The representatives were generally of the class I have before mentioned, who did not anticipate a long war and were confident of European intervention. They had been long accustomed to the peculiar party tactics and legislation of the old Government, and feared for their personal popularity when called upon to enact laws the mere mention of which by any public man before the separation would have sealed his political fate.

I will only notice that one of the exemptions which was most odious to the army and to the people and demonstrates most clearly the spirit and feelings of Congress. It is very certain that the immediate cause of the political agitation which culminated in the dissolution of the Union was the institution of slavery. The controversy arose between the extreme advocates and opponents of that institution, and the moderate people of both sections were drawn into the dispute. While the war raised other issues more vital to the Southern people than the continuance of slavery, there can be no doubt that they were fighting to maintain slavery or prevent its overthrow by the hands of their enemies. It was to be supposed, therefore, that the slaveholders would have been at least as zealous as any other part of the population in supporting the war, and there were reasons why they should have been ready to bear even more than an ordinary proportion of its burdens. At the beginning of the struggle the slave owners did recognize this obligation and strive most nobly to meet it. It was with feeling stronger than surprise therefore, that among the numerous exemptions from the operation of the Conscript Law were found the owners of fifteen slaves.[10]   It is true that only one able-bodied man was exempted on each plantation for this cause, and that when there was no white person not subject to military duty living on the plantation; but these facts do not relieve the provision from the charge of being partial in its operation and conferring a special privilege upon a favoured class.   Apart from other objections, the law of April 16th, 1862, allowed substitution in the army, and it might well be supposed that the owner of fifteen slaves would be able to relieve himself from conscription if he wished to do so by employing a substitute.   Other persons of smaller means, whose circumstances rendered it very onerous for them to leave their families or their affairs, could only avoid being conscripted by purchasing the services of a substitute at a price which they were much less able to pay than the owner of fifteen slaves, and it was thought to be unjust that the latter should be placed in a more favourable position under the peculiar circumstances of the case than the former.   Why was this peculiar privilege conferred upon this particular class?

It was said in defence of the law that it was necessary to leave at home at least one able-bodied white man to fifteen slaves to direct their labour and preserve order. But this does not explain why the owner should be left rather than anyone else.   It is well known that in the

[10] This exemption became law on October 11, 1862.

South the owner of that number of slaves generally employed an overseer, and it would seem that he might still have done so from among the large number of persons exempted from conscription by reason of their age or for other causes. So far as the preservation of order among negroes was concerned, the neighbours of the owner were as much interested in that, and quite as able to exercise the necessary control over the negroes as the owner. In no aspect is the measure defensible on the grounds of expediency. Its explanation is to be sought, I think, in the controlling influence that circumstances had given to the owners of slaves in the management of affairs in the Southern States. They represented a very large proportion of the wealth of the country, were generally better educated, and had more leisure to devote to public affairs than the non-slaveholders, as a class. Besides, the whole community was interested in the preservation of order among the negroes and the maintenance of due subordination, and for these purposes submitted to legislation which if attempted with respect to any other class would not have been tolerated. I refer now to the rigorous provisions contained in the Southern codes with reference to negroes, and the indulgence always conceded by the law and by public opinion to the exercise of the authority of the master.

But the influence of slavery went further. It not only claimed important modifications of the common law governing social relations in favour of slavery, regarding the institution not only as conferring a benefit upon the owner but as something the whole people were bound to support; it claimed and was allowed many

privileges. Slaves were represented in the State legis-
latures in all the States, being treated as persons for this
purpose, while for other purposes, when the interest of
the owner required it, they were regarded simply as
chattels. They were not taxed as other property, but
an arbitrary value was set upon them, without reference
to their actual value. All other kinds of property were
taxed according to value. The habit of regarding slaves
as a peculiar kind of property was fixed in Southern
legislation, and the special exemption recognized this
in the Act of which I am speaking.[11]

The effect of the measure upon the army and upon
the people was however very injurious. The Federal
Government sedulously endeavoured to inculcate the
idea that the war was a slaveholders' war, in which the
non-slaveholding people of the South had no interest,
while it was generally agreed by the people of the South
that the object of the war was to defend slavery. It
may well be imagined that, in these circumstances, they
viewed with surprise, not to say indignation, the exemption of a part of the class of slaveholders from the common burden of the country. This provision of the law
was severely commented upon in the army. I heard
the remark made that the slaveholders would have to
be taught that they owned naught but their slaves, and
that they could not stay at home and send their countrymen to fight their battles. In several applications

[11] It is evident from this that Marshall, like his chief, was no supporter
of slavery. He fought for those " other issues more vital to the Southern
people " and in other papers not published here was wont to dwell upon
the large proportion of the Southern people who were opposed to the
institution of slavery and to point out how inconsiderable was the number
of officers and soldiers in the Confederate Army who were slaveholders.

for indulgence of different kinds forwarded to head-quarters, I have seen allusions to this exemption, the applicants referring to the fact that they had not the good fortune to own fifteen slaves and therefore had to ask as a favour what was accorded to the more fortunate slaveholders as a right.

Under the operation of this law, troops began to come forward in considerable numbers, but they were drafted into the existing organizations, and in some cases formed new ones in the midst of an active campaign. They were, of course, without either discipline or experience, and it will ever be regarded as one of the most remark-able facts of the struggle that the first law, passed by the weaker party to provide an army, was adopted after the war had continued for a year and the enemy was in the field with a numerous force, which he had been organizing and drilling within sight almost of the Con-federate lines for more than eight months.

I now turn to the history of military events after I joined the staff of General Lee. I have mentioned the movement of General J. E. Johnston to the Peninsula, and must now say a word about the policy of that com-mander in falling back from Manassas. He certainly had not at his disposal the means to hold the long line from the Blue Ridge to the Potomac. The position could be readily turned by landing troops below his right flank on the Potomac, or even by landing them entirely in his rear on the Rappahannock. It was not to be expected therefore that he would attempt to retain so advanced a position, with a long line of communica-tions consisting of a single railroad; for, abundant in supplies as was the country accessible to the army at Manassas, the Commissary Department decided to feed the army from Richmond. This fatal policy exhausted the supplies in the rear of the army, to which it was bound to resort if compelled to abandon the lines of Centreville, and left the stores of the fruitful regions, accessible to it while holding these lines, to fall into the enemy's hands when it retired. The wheat, corn, and meat of the lower Valley, and of the rich counties of Fauquier, Warren, and Loudoun were thus lost to us.[12]

While on this subject, it should also be mentioned, as a remarkable illustration of the blind confidence of the Commissary Department in the ability of our Army to maintain its position, or of the want of judgment and practical foresight that characterised the operations of that Bureau, that a depot for salting meat was established near Thoroughfare Gap within a few miles of Centreville and close in the rear of the army. Many of the animals slaughtered at this depot were driven great distances from the interior of the country, and the salt had also to be brought from Richmond to Manassas and thence by the Manassas Gap road to the Thoroughfare Gap. A large quantity of meat was accumulated at this depot which was destroyed when Centreville was abandoned. I have been informed by the Chief Commissary of the Army of General J. E. Johnston that this measure was adopted by the Commissary Department against the remonstrances of that officer. It

[12] One of Lee's first acts after he was summoned to Richmond by Davis was to endeavor to get this policy reversed, and to make the supplies in these districts available for the army, or at least to prevent them from falling into the hands of the enemy.

would seem not to be justifiable on any consideration of expediency or economy. It was inexpedient to assume, when the assumption was not justified by any circumstances, that the army could retain its position, and the depot would surely have been safer if located farther in the rear. It was not economical, for all the animals slaughtered at the depot could as easily have been driven to Gordonsville or to some safer point in the rear, and many of them were nearer to Gordonsville than to Thoroughfare Gap, while the salt and material used in packing the meat had to be carried a greater distance.

This extraordinary measure has never been satisfactorily explained. The suggestion that the depot was located at such an exposed place to suit the convenience of officers and agents of the Commissary Department residing in the vicinity and desiring to remain at home while discharging their duties, reflects too strongly upon those officers and agents to be accepted without strong evidence. It is, however, the only advantage the depot at Thoroughfare Gap possessed over the safer and equally if not more eligible places in the interior.

The explanation of the policy of refusing to supply the Army at Centreville from the region accessible to it is better known. It arose from a difference between the Commissary General and the producers of that region as to the price that the latter should receive for their grain, flour, and other commodities. It was explained to me by the officer to whom I have above referred, who informed me that he had frequently asked to be allowed to purchase supplies from the country around the army. He told me that the Commissary

General considered that, as the farmers of the country
referred to had been deprived of their usual market in
Alexandria, Washington, and Baltimore and compelled
to send their produce to Richmond, they were only entitled to receive for that produce, when sold to the army,
the Richmond price less the cost of sending it to Richmond from the place of production. He argued, for
instance, that as the miller in Loudoun, if he sent his
flour to Richmond, would have to pay, say, one dollar
per barrel for the carriage, he should be content to sell
it at Manassas or Centreville for the Richmond price,
less that charge. The farmers, on the other hand, contended that they were entitled to some benefit for having supplies so near the army. They said that if they
took a barrel of flour to Richmond and paid a dollar for
carriage, the Commissary Department buying that
flour in Richmond would have to pay the same price to
get it back to Manassas, and that the Departments
would lose nothing if it paid at Manassas, for a barrel
of flour delivered there by the neighbouring producer,
the full Richmond price, inasmuch as it would thereby
save the cost of transportation from Richmond to
Manassas. The Commissary General unfortunately
adhered to his views, and the consequence was the loss
of great quantities of valuable supplies. He was a man
of no experience in business, but of great self-conse-
quence. He said to my informant, pointing to the large
mills in Richmond, "Here are my magazines; I will
bring those gentlemen to terms." Having never seen
as large mills as those in Richmond, he perhaps naturally
over-estimated their capacity to control the markets
of the country. The interests of the Richmond mills

were clearly promoted by the arrangement, but I have seen no proof that this consideration had any weight in determining the policy of the Department.

I shall have occasion to refer again to other singular theories that were put in practice by the Commissary Department during the war to the great loss and injury of the country. I shall do so because it is part of the history of this time, and from no desire to injure the officers concerned, for many of whom I entertain the highest esteem and regard.

But to return to the evacuation of Manassas by General J. E. Johnston. I have already said that his long line was untenable with the force at his disposal, and that to retire was a necessity as soon as the enemy chose to avail himself of his vastly superior numbers by a direct advance, and of his ability to turn the position, or of both advantages at once.

Accordingly, when the army of General McClellan was about to advance, General Johnston fell back without delay behind the Rappahannock, his army extending from Fredericksburg along the south bank of that river to Culpeper Court House. His movement was rapid, and considerable quantities of stores were abandoned or destroyed. It had all the appearance of a hasty retreat. It is well known that immediately after this retreat General McClellan induced the President of the United States to consent to the transfer of the greater part of the Federal Army to the Peninsula, with the design of moving on Richmond by that route. General Johnston immediately proceeded to the support of General Magruder at Yorktown with nearly his whole army, leaving a small infantry force at Fredericksburg and Ewell's division on the upper Rappahannock. Jackson remained in the Valley, watching the superior forces of General Banks.

It has been remarked of these movements of General Johnston that they were probably too rapid. The President of the Confederate States was of opinion that the movement of McClellan to the Peninsula might have been delayed, if not prevented, by a judicious use of the intense regard manifested by the Federal Government for the security of its capital.[13] That anxiety, it was argued, would prevent any considerable diminution of the force around Washington as long as it was thought to be in danger of attack by General Johnston. And it was thought that if, as soon as General McClellan began to transfer his army to the Peninsula, General Johnston had made a demonstration towards Washington, it would have checked that movement and led to the recall of such troops as had already been sent.[14]

Be this as it may, it is quite certain that the Federal

[13] Johnston began his retirement from Manassas Junction on March 7, and it resulted in the abandonment of the meat-packing establishment at Thoroughfare Gap, of a number of immobile heavy guns, and of a large amount of stores. Johnston had warned Davis on February 26 that his position could be turned whenever the enemy chose to advance, but he was not furnished with sufficient rolling stock to enable him to get his stores away. The meat-packing establishment had been located without consultation with him, and the heavy guns were sent to him against his wishes. These things had been done before Lee came to Richmond, and were the result of the absence of expert advice at the Headquarters of the Confederacy. Davis was indignant at the loss of the stores, and this consequence of Johnston's retreat was one of the causes of the friction between the two. The chief responsibility for the loss must rest with Davis.

[14] It was to provide for this very contingency that Lincoln insisted on McClellan making adequate provision for the defense of Washington, and when he was not satisfied with this he retained in Northern Virginia McDowell's corps of McClellan's army, much to the latter's indignation.

Government always, and especially in the early part of the war, made provision for the defence of Washington rather in proportion to the importance of holding it than to the force which menaced it. General McClellan contends that the promised results of the Peninsula campaign were sacrificed to this extreme sensitiveness, which caused a large part of the troops with which he expected to operate to be detained to meet an imaginary danger. It is equally certain that the prompt and rapid retreat of General Johnston from Manassas on the advance of McClellan enabled that officer to obtain the consent of the Federal authorities to the transfer of his army to the Peninsula, instead of adopting the plan of President Lincoln of moving directly on Richmond from the north, keeping Washington always covered by the advancing army.[15]

If General Johnston's position at Manassas was untenable, the Yorktown line was even more difficult to hold. Two wide and deep rivers, the James and the York, offered opportunities to the Federal commander to turn either flank. The passage up the York was defended by the works at Yorktown and Gloucester Point. That up the James was guarded by the works at Jamestown Island and other points higher up, but chiefly by the steamer Virginia, formerly the Merrimac, which made her appearance in Hampton Roads coming out from Norfolk on March 8th, and sunk the U. S. frigates Congress and Cumberland.

[15] This is not correct. Lincoln authorized the Secretary of War to procure vessels for the transport of McClellan's army on February 27, eight days before Johnston began to retreat. It is probable, however, that the President's final approval of McClellan's plan was hastened by the retirement of the Confederate forces from Manassas.

The presence of the Virginia in James River, it seems, determined General McClellan to advance by the York, and accordingly he sat down before the Confederate troops at Yorktown and began his approaches before the arrival of General Johnston. General Magruder held the Yorktown lines with his original command of about 7000 men, to which on the approach of McClellan were added some troops from the south of the James.

The history of General Johnston's operations on the Peninsula is before the public in the official reports. I remember that it was known that General Johnston intended to evacuate Yorktown several days before the movement actually took place. But the notice received by General Lee of the evacuation was not more than twelve hours. As soon as he was advised of it, he telegraphed to General Johnston to know if he could not hold his lines a little longer, to enable proper preparations to be made for the removal of the valuable stores from Norfolk. The necessity of concealing the intention of evacuation rendered it impossible to make the necessary preparations for leaving Norfolk until the last moment, but had the notice been extended a short time, the valuable stores lost in Norfolk might have been saved to some extent.

I remember a despatch from General Johnston to General Lee, after the gunboat Galena and her consorts had passed up James River, in which he said that the approach of the gunboats to Richmond made him anxious for the city and desirous to be nearer to it.[16] I pass over the approach of General McClellan to the

[16] Johnston began his retreat from Yorktown on May 3 and on May 5 fought a rear-guard action with McClellan at Williamsburg.

Chickahominy, and the establishment of his army on the north of the stream.

When General Johnston fell back upon Richmond, the Confederate Government hastened to reinforce him with all its available troops. But the presence of the enemy at various points along the Atlantic coast, endangering an important line of railway between Richmond and the South, and the pressure of superior numbers upon the Confederate army in the Southwest, left the army of General Johnston greatly inferior in numbers to his adversary.

When the battle of Seven Pines was fought,[17] General Johnston had received all the accessions that could be made to his army, but his force, exclusive of cavalry, did not exceed 53,000 men. The army at this time was suffering from sickness, the immediate effect of the Conscript Law, as has been before remarked, having been to bring into its ranks as volunteers many who were unwilling to be enrolled under its provisions. The trying service during the latter part of April and the month of May told severely upon this class of troops, unaccustomed to the exposure and privations of military life. General Johnston states that his strength had been reduced, between the time his army went to Yorktown and the battle of Williamsburg on May 5th, by more than 4000 alone from sickness. This was at a time when his whole force, exclusive of cavalry, was only about 50,000 men, and before the operation of the Conscript Law had begun to be much felt.

General McClellan on May 14th, when urging Presi-

[17] The battle of Seven Pines or Fair Oaks was fought on May 31 and June 1.

dent Lincoln to send him reinforcements, and when it cannot be supposed that he exaggerated his strength, states that after all deductions for "casualties, sickness, garrisons, and guards" he could "bring into actual battle against the enemy not more than 80,000 men at the utmost." But in addition to the army under General McLellan, General McDowell was at Fredericksburg within two days' march of Richmond with between 35,000 and 40,000 men, and May 26th was appointed for the beginning of his movement to unite with the army of General McClellan.

Nor in estimating the dangers at this time threatening the Confederate capital should the armies of General Frémont advancing from northwestern Virginia, and of General Banks moving from Winchester, be disregarded. The success of those expeditions would have greatly increased the difficulty of defending Richmond. It would have aided General McClellan in the same way, and probably in no less degree than the subsequent successes of General Sheridan in the same quarter assisted the operations of General Grant in the campaign of 1865. In these circumstances nothing was left to General Lee but to endeavour to prevent the junction of the armies of Generals McClellan and McDowell, and so frustrate the movements of the enemy in the Valley. The execution of this purpose was entrusted to General Jackson.

General Lee had been in constant correspondence with General Jackson during his campaign in the Valley after the battle of Kernstown. He had ordered General Ewell from the Rappahannock, through Swift Run Gap, to join Jackson. It was explained to the latter that he

STONEWALL JACKSON

must endeavour by all means to prevent the advance of McDowell from Fredericksburg. About that time, Jackson being at Swift Run Gap, the expedition under Milroy [18] was approaching the Valley from the northwest by way of McDowell,[19] Banks was at Winchester and its vicinity, and it was supposed would advance to co-operate with Milroy. General Jackson submitted his views. He said that he could attack either, but that he preferred to move against Milroy first. To reach Banks he said he wou d have to cross the Massanutton Mountain, and in case of disaster the entrance of Milroy into the Valley in his rear might be ruinous. He expressed the opinion that he could fall upon Milroy and drive him back, and then turn on Banks before the latter could make much progress up the Valley. It was left to his discretion which course to pursue, but the importance of making such a demonstration towards the Potomac as would excite the easily-aroused apprehensions of the Federal authorities was impressed upon, and fully appreciated by him.

General Jackson with his own division, aided by the brigade of General Edward Johnson, first checked the advance of the enemy from western Virginia towards Staunton by defeating the command of General Milroy on May 8th at McDowell. Being thus relieved of immediate apprehension of the enemy penetrating the Valley in his rear General Jackson turned rapidly upon General Banks, who had advanced as far up the valley as Strasburg.

---

[18] Milroy commanded the advance guard of Fremont's force coming from western Virginia.
[19] The village, not the man.

On the 23rd May a detachment from the army of
General Banks was totally defeated at Front Royal, and
the main body retreated rapidly towards Winchester.
It was vigorously pursued and attacked at that place
on the 25th and driven in confusion through the town.

General Jackson, in obedience to his instructions to
produce the impression that he intended to cross the
Potomac and thus act upon the excessive anxiety with
which the Federal Government watched the slightest
approach of danger to Washington, drove Banks in the
utmost disorder with heavy loss into Maryland. This
movement produced the desired result. On May 24th
President Lincoln notified McClellan that, owing to
the critical position of Banks, the movement of Mc-
Dowell had been suspended. Immediately afterwards
part of McDowell's force was sent to Harper's Ferry
by way of Washington, and another part under General
Shields moved from Fredericksburg to enter the Valley
from the east in the rear of Jackson, and co-operate with
the army under Frémont, now rapidly advancing from
the west.

It is well known with what consummate skill and
courage Jackson extricated his army from these dangers,
and by the brilliant actions at Port Republic and Cross
Keys,[20] frustrated the designs of the enemy, and prevented the union of the forces of Frémont and Shields.

The consequences of the success of Jackson in the
Valley were even more important and far-reaching than
the immediate relief afforded to the army engaged in
the defence of Richmond, great as that relief was. It
not only prevented the concentration of an overwhelm-

[20] Fought June 8th and 9th.

ing force against Richmond and raised the drooping spirits of the Southern people, but it may with truth be said that it controlled the plan of military operations subsequently adopted by the contending armies in Virginia. On the one hand, it secured the final rejection by the Federal Government of the advice of McClellan and caused its adherence during the war to the plan advocated by Mr. Lincoln, while on the other it demonstrated that the Confederate Army could most effectually defend Richmond and relieve the country of the presence of the enemy by availing itself of the sensitiveness of the authorities at Washington with reference to the safety of that city.

McClellan was of opinion that the most certain way to render Washington safe, and the surest means of taking Richmond, were to be found in the use of the easy and secure water communication between the two cities, by which the Federal Government could bring such a powerful naval and land force to bear as would compel the concentration of all the Confederate troops in Virginia for the defence of the capital. This policy would have deprived Richmond in a degree of the military advantages of an interior position, and would have relieved the attacking force of the difficulties and dangers of a long overland march. The opposite policy of Mr. Lincoln, which assumed that the army operating against Richmond should never leave Washington uncovered, enabled the Confederate army to enjoy some of the advantages for manœuvre which the distance between the two capitals afforded, while the sensitiveness of the Federal Government to a threat against Washington, as evinced by the results accomplished by Jackson's

small force, influenced in a great measure the plans of
the leader into whose hands the defence of Richmond,
and the protection of the vast interests which depended
upon its tenure, were about to pass.

McClellan, finding himself deprived of the co-operation of McDowell, undertook to accomplish his designs
with the force at his disposal. Part of his army had
crossed the Chickahominy, and the remainder lay on
the north of that stream. The old bridges were repaired, and several new bridges were constructed to
connect the two wings of the army. McClellan, with a
view to opening a way for the expected movement of
McDowell, had extended his right wing north of the
Chickahominy, had defeated the brigade of General
Branch near Hanover Court House, and succeeded in
breaking the Virginia Central Railroad connecting
Staunton with Richmond, and also in seizing the railway
between Richmond and Fredericksburg. The communication by rail between Richmond and northern Virginia was thus interrupted, but McDowell not coming
to his assistance, McClellan recalled the troops which
had been operating on these roads. During the day
and night of May 30th a heavy fall of rain occurred,
which it was supposed would carry away the bridges
over the Chickahominy and sever the communications
between the Federal troops on the right and left banks
of the river. General Johnston therefore availed himself of the opportunity to crush the force south of the
Chickahominy, and on the following day, May 31st,
the indecisive battle of Seven Pines took place.

During the battle I was at General Johnston's headquarters on the Nine Mile road, while the attack of

Longstreet on the Williamsburg road was progressing. General Johnston, General Lee, and President Davis were at a small house on the right of the Nine Mile road, and the troops which were intended to co-operate on that road with Longstreet's attack were halted on the road in front of those quarters.

We heard the sound of the battle further to our right, but the troops on the Nine Mile road did not begin to move forward for several hours after Longstreet had become engaged. Johnston stated that he was waiting to hear the sound of musketry on Longstreet's front.[21] I remember perfectly, while this delay continued, that I conversed with Surgeon Gailard of General G. W. Smith's division, and with several other officers. I had never heard the sound of musketry before, and as we stood on the opposite side of the house from that on which General Lee and General Johnston were, I heard the sound for the first time and was told by the other officers that it was musketry. We heard it very distinctly, and conversed about its apparent direction and progress, with a view to forming an opinion as to the result of the attack. This was at least an hour and a half before the troops on the Nine Mile road advanced, and General Johnston himself rode to the front. It was unfortunate that it was not known to us that this was to be the signal for the advance of the troops under

[21] The failure of Johnston, who had caught McClellan in an embarrassing position astride the Chickahominy, to gain a more complete success on May 31, was due to a series of delays in the movements of his troops. Here Colonel Marshall accounts for one such delay. The Confederate generals in the early part of the war had a predilection for making the sound of firing by one body of troops the signal for the advance of other bodies. As an expedient, it almost always failed.

G. W. Smith on the Nine Mile road. I am confident that numbers of officers who were present heard the musketry as soon as I did.

General Johnston was severely wounded towards the close of the action, and the command of the army devolved upon General G. W. Smith. On June 1st some severe skirmishing took place, but it being evident that the Federal troops south of the Chickahominy had been reinforced from the north side of the river, attack was abandoned, and the Confederate army withdrew to its former position.

The state of General Smith's health was such that on June 2nd President Davis directed General Lee to take command, and on the following day he removed from Richmond and assumed the immediate direction of the movements of the army. The order of March 13th was not rescinded, but General Lee was assigned to the command by the Secretary of War on the verbal order of the President.[22] He took with him only the small personal staff he had had in Richmond, and nothing could have been less imposing than his introduction to the position which he was to render so illustrious.

The circumstances in which General Lee found himself thus suddenly called to the foremost place in the great contest are full of instruction to those who would form a just estimate of his character and genius. It has been seen that the campaign of 1862 had hitherto been attended with almost uninterrupted success for

[22] The order ran: "June 2nd, 1862. By direction of the President, General Robert E. Lee, Confederate States Army, will assume the immediate command of the armies in Eastern Virginia and North Carolina. By command of the Secretary of War — JOHN WITHERS, Assistant Adjutant General."

J. E. JOHNSTON

the Federal arms. The services in which he had previously been engaged had afforded him no opportunity to justify the expectations which his great reputation as an officer in the Federal army had created among the Southern people. At the beginning of the war his duties had detained him at Richmond, and the value of his services was known only to the few with whom he shared the labour and cares of preparing for the contest. From Richmond he had gone to western Virginia, and thence to the southern coast, where the same comparative obscurity and the same impossibility of accomplishing great and striking results awaited him. A whole year had passed, and his name was not yet connected with a single great event. Comparisons injurious to his reputation were made between the part he had taken in the struggle and the achievements of others who had occupied more conspicuous positions, and the opinion generally entertained with reference to the operations in western Virginia had produced in the minds of many an actual distrust of his military capacity. His silence under this censure had confirmed the belief that it was merited, and its injustice was known only to a few who had witnessed the campaign, and to President Davis, to whom alone General Lee had explained its real character. These circumstances had produced such an unfavourable impression that when he was transferred to the southern coast, Mr. Davis deemed it necessary to ask for him the support and co-operation of the authorities and people of South Carolina, by assuring the Governor of that state, in a private letter, of his own unabated confidence in the merit and capacity of the new commander.

It is a remarkable fact, illustrating the effects of alarm and excitement upon the minds of people generally moderate and just in their judgment, that the three men who rendered the most distinguished se vice to the Confederacy and attained the highest place in the love and gratitude of the country, were each at one time almost universally regarded as unfit for command. The strongest influence ever brought to bear upon the President to induce him to remove the commander of an army occurred in the cases of Albert Sidney Johnston, Stonewall Jackson, and Robert E. Lee. Among all the services rendered by President Davis to the Southern people, none were perhaps greater or more honourable to him than his refusal to yield to that impatience which recognizes success as the only test of merit, and his steadfast support of these great men in the midst of misfortune.

The Southern people were greatly depressed, and their reverses had inspired painful doubts of their ability to cope with their powerful adversary. One after another, the hopes of succour upon which they had relied had been disappointed, and the conviction that they could depend upon them vanished at a moment when they seemed to have reached the crisis of their fate. All eyes were turned to the impending struggle for the possession of Richmond. The army engaged in its defence was inferior in numbers to that of the enemy and imperfectly supplied with arms and equipment. It had been retreating almost continuously since it left Centreville and had now reached a point beyond which it could not retire without the loss of the Confederate capital and the sacrifice of those vital interests which depended upon its possession. It had just undergone a change of officers, and its ranks were filled with raw and inexperienced recruits. Weak in everything but the spirit, intelligence, and patriotism of the men who composed it, it was made weaker by the infirmities of its own organisation. At a time when it most needed all that confidence in its commander could impart, a leader who possessed and deserved that confidence had been stricken down.

It was at this extreme moment, when the exultant North was eagerly and confidently expecting the reward of its great efforts, and the despondent South regarded its cause as almost lost, that a man as yet comparatively unknown caught the standard as it fell from the stricken hand that had carried it so bravely, and bore it resolutely to the front. But it was not only the unpromising condition of affairs or the imminence of the public danger that rendered the position of General Lee difficult and embarrassing. He did not shrink from the grave responsibilities and arduous labours which he knew must be encountered to relieve his country from its danger, but to enable him to perform the task with hope of success he greatly needed the confidence of the people and of the army. It cannot be denied that when he first took command at Richmond he had yet to acquire both.

General Lee had submitted to the unjust judgment of his countrymen without repining. Aware of his ability to direct the greatest affairs, longing to share in the exciting events taking place around him, he never asked for service of his own choice, but was content to perform with all his energies such duties as were assigned to him.

His only desire was that the work should be done, he cared not by whom; and in this spirit he endured without a murmur enforced' obscurity and unmerited condemnation, and felt an unselfish pride in the exploits of his more fortunate brethren in arms. He pursued the path of duty with equal and unfaltering steps through the unseen labours of the office, and through commands sterile of opportunities for distinction.

Now that path led him to the foremost place in the eyes of his country. His patient waiting at last had its reward; the bloody drama had reached a stage worthy of his intervention; and in the midst of universal despondency, oppressed by the consciousness that he did not possess the confidence of the people or of the army, he entered modestly and humbly, but with unshaken resolution, upon the performance of his arduous task.

III

GENERAL LEE'S MILITARY POLICY

THE gloomy condition of the affairs of the Confederacy in the first months of 1862 made it apparent that the policy pursued by the Government during the first year of the war had not only resulted in serious losses, but permanently impaired its ability to maintain the contest.

This discovery was made when the real magnitude of the struggle and the fallacy of all expectations of relief, except by arms, began to be understood, and the need of men, arms, and munitions became most urgent. The present relief of Richmond was therefore only a part of the care which devolved upon General Lee when he assumed command, in the circumstances described in the last chapter. He might accomplish that object, but there remained the far more difficult task of devising a system of defence adapted not only to the immediate dangers, but to the inevitable demands which a protracted war on such a great scale would make upon the resources of the country.

Although experience had shown that the attempt made to defend every point exposed to attack had led to our most serious disasters, and although the necessity of concentrating our forces had become evident, there were reasons arising from the relations of the Confederate Government to the people themselves which rendered the adoption of that policy peculiarly difficult.

It has been seen that in the beginning of the secession movement its advocates had generally believed that it would be peacefully accomplished, or that, should hostilities ensue, they would speedily be brought to an end by foreign intervention and by dissensions in the North. This belief had become fixed in the minds of the people, who were taught to expect that the new Government would at once confer upon them a greater degree of safety and of liberty than they had enjoyed under the old.

When therefore it became impossible for the Government any longer to doubt that a war of invasion upon a large scale was certain, it attempted to reconcile the people to the disappointment of their hopes of peace by establishing confidence in its ability and readiness to extend to them ample protection. It sought to accomplish this by such a distribution of the forces of the South as would impart a feeling of security at every exposed point, and convince the people that the Confederacy would vigilantly guard them against the dangers of an unexpected war. Unwise as this course was, and disastrous as it proved to be, the peculiar position of the Southern people rendered it extremely difficult for the Government to close its ears to the cry for local protection. The presence of a large slave population exposed them to greater and more serious perils in time of war than those which usually attend invasion by a civilised enemy. The fear of the consequences that might result from the influence of Northern troops on the slaves was naturally keenly felt, and the necessity of a sufficient force to prevent the horrors of a servile insurrection contributed as much as any single cause to the unfortunate dispersion of the Confederate troops during the first year of the war.

Before General Lee left Richmond to take command of the Confederate army he had been made sensible of the strong influence of these considerations upon the minds of the people and their representatives. Repeated and urgent demands were made upon him by some of the most influential members of Congress to furnish troops to protect the people along the navigable waters of Virginia, who had been left exposed to the incursions of the enemy by the withdrawal of General J. E. Johnston from Manassas, and one of the chief objections to the Conscript Law (apart from some doubts as to its constitutionality) was that it would enable the Confederate Government to deprive the states of the means of providing for the safety of their own citizens. The mere existence of slavery gave the Federal Government a great advantage in the prosecution of the war and imposed additional cares and responsibilities upon those charged with the conduct of military operations in the South. It imparted consequence to movements of the enemy otherwise trivial, and enabled a small force to excite apprehension along the whole sensitive border of the South.

In such circumstances and under such influences as these, General Lee was called upon to devise a military policy which would enable the Confederate Government to meet at once the dangers of the present emergency, and allay the just apprehensions of the people. To concentrate the Confederate army, in sufficient numbers to resist the Federal army which threatened Richmond, required the withdrawal of troops detached to guard exposed localities; and to withdraw those troops would expose the Government to the charge of unwillingness or inability to protect the country. But fearful as were the dangers apprehended, the condition of affairs was such that General Lee had no alternative, and he did not hesitate to adopt a policy which in a great measure reversed the course previously pursued by the Confederate Government. This resolution not only brought against him the opposition of persons of influence connected with the Government, but subjected him to the severer trial of having to disregard the safety of those from whom he felt bound, for the public good, to withdraw the protection they so anxiously desired.

The families of the soldiers were among those who were to be exposed to perils in comparison with which the dangers of battle were lightly regarded, and the desire to protect their wives and children sometimes outweighed, even in the army, the sense of obligation to the cause of the whole country.

No man felt greater sympathy for the trials and dangers of the helpless and defenceless than General Lee. No one more earnestly desired than he to allay their fears and mitigate their sufferings. But having a more comprehensive view of the whole problem, directing his energies to secure what he regarded as the real object of the war, he did not permit himself to be diverted from his purpose by considerations which exerted so much influence upon those who perceived less clearly the lamentable consequences of defeat. Instead of sending troops to every exposed locality, he thought it wiser to compel the enemy to concentrate his own forces and thus deprive him of the means of making inroads. This could only be effected by such concentration on our part as would necessitate a like action on the part of the Federal authorities, and the event demonstrated the wisdom of his views. That part of the country which depended for its protection on the troops which he drew together to form the great Army of Northern Virginia was never more exempt from invasion than while that army retained its strength and efficiency. In its formidable presence the enemy did not venture to weaken his own army by detachments for harassing excursions, and the women and children of the South reposed securely under the terror inspired by its name.

To arrive at a correct understanding of the events which marked the history of the three years during which General Lee held command, it is necessary to consider them in relation to the policy of defence which he devised. The battles and strategic movements which attracted so much attention were not separate and distinct events, entirely independent one of the other, but formed parts of one plan of warfare, adopted by General Lee at the time he took command of the army, and steadily pursued until his means were exhausted.

It is neither just to him nor consonant with the truth to measure his success by the issue of each engagement, or to judge of his skill by the consequence of each movement. The war in Virginia with all its chances and changes was in fact one campaign. The battles on the Chickahominy and at Manassas, the invasion of Maryland, and the invasion of Pennsylvania, all had a common object. They were results of a plan of defence

based upon a survey of all the circumstances, a plan
deemed by General Lee to be the best adapted to meet
the necessities of this country, and to secure final
success. The necessities of the country required that
General Lee's measures should be adapted to its capacity to sustain a war of such magnitude, and that they
should neutralize the enemy's great superiority. The
population of the South available for military service
was less than one-fifth of that of the United States.[1]
From the former the negro population had to be de-
ducted, as the policy of the Government would only
permit the emplo ment of negroes in the army to a
limited extent, and those only in the capacity of non-
combatants and labourers.

The white population alone could be looked upon for
supplying losses by battle and disease, and so great was
the drain upon it to furnish a sufficient force to oppose
that of the United States in 1862, that very early in
the campaign of that year ability to keep the army up
to the standard of strength began to be doubted. General Lee thought that to expose our armies to the sacrifices of great battles the object of which was only to
disperse or destroy those of the enemy would soon
bring the Confederacy to the verge of exhaustion.
Even victory in such engagements might prove disastrous. The North could readily raise new armies,
while the means of the South were so limited that a few
bloody victories might leave it powerless to continue

[1] The white population of the 23 States of the Union was in 1861 about
22,000,000, and that of the 11 Confederate States about 5,000,000, so that
Colonel Marshall somewhat overstates the weakness of the South. The
total white population of the United States, according to the census of
1860, was 26,932,537.

the struggle, and the enemy might derive from our exhaustion the success that he could not win with the sword.

It was therefore desirable not to risk the irreparable losses except as and when battles might become necessary for the accomplishment of the general purpose. For this reason the plan of compelling the enemy to grant peace by a campaign of conquest was impracticable. A few general engagements in the North, however successful, would have soon left the invading army too weak to remain in the enemy country, and the South could not have furnished another.

On the other hand, it was equally imprudent to remain entirely on the defensive, and await the attack of the enemy. Such a policy would reduce the contest to a mere trial of strength and resources, and the issue of such a trial could be easily foreseen. The enemy, if uninterrupted, could bring to bear an overwhelming force upon any position that might be assumed by the Confederate army, and decide the conquest by mere stress of numbers. Especially was this true if Richmond should be the place to be defended, as the command of the large rivers by which it could be approached would enable the enemy to concentrate his troops and transport his supplies with entire safety and freedom from interruption, since his army would have the powerful support of his fleet.

Nor did the policy of retreating before the enemy and drawing him further into the interior of the country promise greater advantages. This system of warfare often practised elsewhere with success was attended with great and serious objections in the case of the

Confederate States. Its navigable rivers, penetrating in every direction, afforded the enemy an easy and rapid mode of transportation of troops and supplies into the heart of the country, and the attempt to defend those avenues of approach would require more men than the Confederacy could afford if it would defend them successfully, besides leading to the ruinous dispersal of its forces. Such a policy would give the enemy access to the slave population of the South, and expose more of its people to the dangers which I have already indicated as arising from the first retreat of Manassas. In the case of Virginia, the policy of retreating had in the spring of 1862 been pursued until it could be prosecuted no further without the loss of the whole State. The army was already at Richmond and the next retreat must take it south of the James river. The political consequence assigned by common consent to the capital of a country, and especially the capital of a country struggling for recognition, would doubtless have rendered any place the Confederate Government might have selected for that purpose a prominent object of attack; but Richmond had a value from a military point of view that far exceeded its political importance. The great region of country between the James River and the Potomac has become historic. It was the Flanders of the war, and it is no exaggeration to say that nearly a quarter of a million men perished in the fierce struggle for its possession in which the armies of the North and South were engaged for nearly four years.

This territory was of great use to the Confederacy, on account of the supplies it furnished to the army and the recruits whom its brave and patriotic population sent to our ranks. But it was not the supplies and the recruits which gave it its chief value. The effectiveness of any army of the Confederacy depended in a great measure upon its proximity to the enemy's country, and it soon became apparent that the same number of Confederate troops could not be placed where they would give occupation to so much of the vastly superior force of the enemy as in that region between the James and the Potomac, within reach of the sensitive southern frontier of the United States, where on the extreme border stood the city of Washington, for the safety of which the Federal authorities considered no preparation excessive, no sacrifice too great.

Valuable as Northern Virginia was to the Confederacy, its possession came to depend entirely upon our ability to defend Richmond. Here were established the depots and arsenals of the army operating in Northern Virginia, and through Richmond that army had its chief means of access to sources of supply further south. With Richmond in the hands of the enemy, it is evident that no large army could have been maintained in Northern Virginia. There was no other city in Virginia that had railroad connections with the South sufficient to furnish transportation for the supply of such an army in that part of the country. Lynchburg might have been connected with the railroads in North Carolina, and thus an interior line of communication with the South might have been provided less accessible to the enemy than any which Richmond furnished, but no such communication was made, nor does it profit now to enquire whether it could have been made.

Early in the second year of the war, the Confederacy was compelled to yield to the enemy great possessions on the James River to within a few miles of Richmond. From that time it was always possible for the Federal Government to transport troops from the North and land them within less than a day's march of the city, without the fear or even the possibility of interruption by us. The enemy had too the additional facilities of approach which the York River afforded. The place upon the safety of which so much depended was in fact almost as accessible from the North by water as the city of Alexandria. Its distance from the base of a Federal army operating against it gave it no advantage if that army could almost reach its gates by a safe and rapid water transportation. In attacking a city situated as it was, the powerful flotilla of the enemy was able to co-operate efficiently with his land forces, so that the defenders of Richmond had to resist the combined efforts of the Federal Army and Navy. Nor did Richmond possess any advantages of defence should the enemy, renouncing the facilities which the command of the water afforded him, attempt to approach the city by land.

In these circumstances there was but one course left for General Lee to pursue, if he would save Richmond from the peril which he knew would attend its investment by the large army of the enemy. He must give occupation to that army, and such occupation as would compel the largest concentration of its forces. By this means he might even induce the enemy to withdraw troops from other parts of the Confederacy, and thus obtain additional reinforcements for himself.

So the most marked influence which the situation of Richmond, and the necessity of providing for its defence, exerted upon the conduct of the war in Virginia, is seen in its connection with the expeditions of the Army of Northern Virginia beyond the Potomac. The great advantages which the enemy would have in besieging Richmond were so apparent that it was a saying of General Lee that Richmond was never so safe as when its defenders were absent. His meaning was that the safety of Richmond depended upon our ability to employ the enemy at a distance and prevent his near approach to the city. Such was the policy adopted by him, a policy which procured the comparative security of Richmond, from the time when the Army of Northern Virginia moved northward in 1862 to the time when, worn out with more than two years' exhausting war, it was forced to retire within the entrenchments of its capital.

It was only by acting upon the apprehensions of the enemy that the object of this policy could be obtained with the force under General Lee's command. Unwilling to incur the risks and losses of an aggressive war having for its object the destruction of the enemy, and regarding as equally unwise the policy of remaining strictly on the defensive or of retreating before his advance, General Lee adopted a plan by which he sought to attain some of the advantages of each of the others.

The Government at Washington seemed to be impressed with the importance of bringing the war to a speedy conclusion, and their preparations were directed to attaining that end. They dreaded the effect of protracted hostilities upon their own people, and perhaps were even more apprehensive of complications with other nations. The expenses incurred were so enormous that to put a stop to them became an additional and powerful inducement to make the war a short one. At first the enthusiasm of the people supplied all the demands of the Government for men and money. The troops were not enlisted for long terms of service, and both the army and the people were confident of speedy success. When, however, the first year ended and the North perceived that, notwithstanding the great advantages it had gained, much yet remained to be accomplished, the popular enthusiasm was somewhat abated, and the burden of supporting the war rested more exclusively upon the public credit, which began to show signs of feeling the pressure. As it was the manifest policy of the Federal Government to conclude the war speedily, and to feed the growing impatience of the people with successes which would give assurance of such a result, so on the other hand it became the policy of General Lee to disappoint these hopes and encourage the belief that the war would be of indefinite length.

The means to accomplish this end were to frustrate the enemy's designs; to break up campaigns undertaken with vast expense and with confident assurance of success; to impress upon the minds of the Northern people the conviction that they must prepare for a protracted struggle, great sacrifices of life and treasure, with the possibility that all might at last be of no avail; and to accomplish this at the smallest cost to the Confederacy.

In the opinion of General Lee, Virginia presented the most favourable theatre of war for this plan of operations. He considered that there were circumstances by the judicious use of which he could impart to his army an importance and influence greatly exceeding what was due to its actual strength and numbers. He appreciated fully the importance attached by the Government of Mr. Lincoln to the safety of the Federal capital. Affecting as that Government did to treat the war as the suppression of a rebellion, its inability to defend the city of Washington might have been accepted by other nations as an admission of the superior power of the South, and have justified the recognition of the Confederacy. But even if this consequence had not followed the loss of Washington, the overthrow of an administration which had shown itself unable to defend the capital would have been swift and certain. The disappointment of the promises so often repeated, of a speedy "suppression of the rebellion" would have been overwhelming, and the party headed by Mr. Lincoln would have been driven from office by an indignant and deceived people. As the party of Mr. Lincoln had made the war, its existence depended upon success. Danger to Washington threatened the supremacy of that party, and it was certain that Mr. Lincoln would sacrifice every other consideration to its safety.

General Lee had seen how even the supposed presence of a powerful Confederate army at Manassas, thirty miles from Washington, had detained the strongest army of the United States around the capital. He had remarked with surprise how the Federal Government had neglected for months the easy means of compelling the withdrawal of General Johnston from Manassas by transporting its own army to the vicinity of Richmond, and he had been confirmed in his views of the apprehensions of that Government for the safety of their capital by the effect produced upon its powerful armies by the advance of Jackson down the Valley, when he drove Banks beyond the Potomac and caused the recall of McDowell from Fredericksburg. These results were utterly out of proportion to the Confederate force employed, and satisfied General Lee that the Government of Mr. Lincoln would provide for the safety of Washington in proportion to the political importance attached to its possession, rather than in proportion to the real danger that threatened the city.

It will be seen how the blows struck by General Lee's army upon the northern border of Virginia, and beyond the Potomac, relieved the pressure of the enemy upon the whole Atlantic Coast, paralyzed his efforts in western Virginia, and even diverted troops from the remote regions of the lower Mississippi.

But the people could not foresee all the advantages of the successful prosecution of this system of defence, and regarded with dissatisfaction a policy which seemed to expose them to certain and immediate danger. These circumstances added largely to the difficulties and embarrassments of General Lee, but they did not deter him from pursuing steadily and in spite of all opposition the plan by which alone he believed the war might be prosecuted to a successful issue.

IV

THE SEVEN DAYS

(a) BEAVER DAM AND GAINES'S MILL

IMMEDIATELY upon taking command, General Lee established his Headquarters at "Dabb's House," about two miles from Richmond on the Nine Mile Road, and convened a council of his Division commanders to consider the plan of defence. This conference, held on June 3rd at a place called "The Chimneys," on the Nine Mile Road near the scene of battle of May 31st, was quite protracted, the first question discussed being whether the army should take a position nearer to Richmond and there await the enemy, or whether it should seek to resist his further advance. After the consultation was over I heard from General Lee that a number of officers were in favour of withdrawing nearer to Richmond. Our line where it approached the river was within reach of the enemy's artillery on the north side, and it was argued that the enemy could drive us from the position. General Lee said to me, "If we leave this line because they can shell us, we shall have to leave the next for the same reason, and I don't see how we can stop this side of Richmond."

The ground on our left was more favourable for us, as compared with the enemy's position, than any we could have taken between that point and Richmond, and possessed this other advantage, that as long as we held it General McClellan was forced to have part of his army north of the Chickahominy and part on the south, a circumstance which subsequently proved fatal to his campaign. I understood from others that Generals Longstreet and D. H. Hill agreed with General Lee. What General Johnston's purpose had been can only be conjectured from the fact that he had brought his army almost into the suburbs of the city, probably with the design of inducing McClellan to advance from the Chickahominy and fight with that river in his rear.[1] From what was subsequently observed of General McClellan's character I think it is extremely doubtful whether he would have accepted the challenge, unless he could have brought down McDowell and other large reinforcements.

General Lee immediately resolved to take up a line further from Richmond, and accordingly advanced the troops along the Williamsburg and Charles City Roads.[2] His plan was formed very soon after he took command. Indeed, the general features of it had been sketched before he left Richmond, and, as has been related, he had concerted with Jackson plans to bring about the

---

[1] Johnston says: "The army crossed the Chickahominy because the possession of James River by the enemy suggested the possibility of a change of base to the river. And it was necessary that we should be so placed as to be able to meet the United States Army approaching either from York River or along the James." — *Battles and Leaders*, vol. II, p. 207.

[2] Lee found it very necessary to show a bold front in order to revive the spirits of his army. Davis arrived at "The Chimneys" while the conference was in progress and says: "The tone of the conversation was quite despondent, and one especially pointed out the inevitable consequence of the enemy's advance by throwing out bayoux and constructing successive parallels." There are few things more demoralizing to troops than having to await passively the slow advance of a superior enemy, and Lee, to avoid that, decided to be as aggressive as possible.

withdrawal of General McDowell from Fredericksburg. When, however, it became apparent that no movement of Jackson's small force could effect any result which would induce the recall of General McClellan's army, General Lee turned his attention to other means of dislodging that army, and formed the plan of operations which resulted in the Seven Days' Battles round Richmond, and the retreat of McClellan's army to the James.

He immediately ordered a line of earthworks to be constructed along our front, extending from the Chickahominy above New Bridge, across to the Charles City Road and beyond. These works were very slight. Some heavier fortifications for artillery were erected along the ridge just south of the Chickahominy from the Nine Mile Road towards our left, and the guns from these batteries replied with good effect to those of the enemy on the north side in the vicinity of New Bridge, Hogan's and Gaines's houses. The erection of these works met with great opposition, not only among some officers in the army, but among the press and politicians of Richmond. It was considered that General Lee was merely an engineer, and that the troops under him would be more familiar with a spade than a musket. I remember hearing an officer of some rank speak very contemptuously of this "digging," as he called it. The progress of the works was very slow. The men were unused to such labour, and it was not until June 21st that they began to approach such a state of forwardness as to enable General Lee to proceed with the other measures he contemplated. He bore the abuse and ridicule which were heaped upon him by the press of

Richmond and the South (with few exceptions) in silence. Nothing diverted him from the execution of his purpose. He visited the lines almost daily in person, and sent members of his staff constantly to observe the progress of the work.

General McLellan's army lay then part on the north and part on the south of the Chickahominy, the two wings connecting by New Bridge and several other bridges below. His line of communication was the York River Railroad, his depot of supplies being at the White House on the Pamunkey. Lee's plan was to use the line of works which he had constructed so as to enable him to hold the direct approaches to Richmond with part of his army, while with the remainder, to which Jackson's force was to be added when the proper time arrived, General Lee resolved to cross the Chickahominy and fall upon the enemy's right wing.[3] His idea was that by directing the movement so as to threaten the York River Railroad he would draw the whole of McClellan's army to the defence of that line, if it was the purpose of that officer to retain his connection with the White House and continue to use that depot.

General McClellan selected the left bank of Beaver Dam Creek as the extreme right of his line. Forti-

[3] Lee's great contribution to the military art was his use of entrenchments as an aid to manœuvre. He was the first to perceive the possibilities which improvements in arms combined with entrenchments afforded. In 1815, neither Blücher at Ligny nor Wellington at Waterloo, though both were on the defensive, considered with the weapons of their day the use of entrenchments in field warfare. In 1854, the Russians on the defensive at the Alma had provided entrenchments for some of their guns, but not for their infantry. The Seven Days, therefore, mark the beginning of an epoch in military history.

fications were erected at various points along the line, connected by rifle pits, the fire from which swept the open ground on the right bank of the creek over which troops advancing from the direction of Mechanicsville would be obliged to pass. The passage of Beaver Dam was difficult along the entire front of the Federal position, and impracticable for artillery except by the roads which were commanded by the guns of the works. Trees were felled along the right bank of the stream to impede the advance of infantry, and detain them under the fire of artillery and musketry at short range from the entrenchments on the opposite side.

The dispositions of General McClellan were well taken to defend himself from attack by the Confederate army around Richmond, but there was one weak spot of which General Lee proceeded to take advantage. There were other roads leading down the Chickahominy towards the York River Railroad, besides those commanded by the enemy's position on Beaver Dam.

These roads run along the narrow ridge between the waters of the Pamunkey and the Chickahominy and lie beyond the routes which General McClellan had undertaken to defend. Beaver Dam has its source on the south side of that ridge, and the Totopotomy and other small tributaries of the Pamunkey rise on its northern slope.

By moving along this ridge the right of the enemy's line on Beaver Dam could be turned, and, the position carried, the way would then be opened for a force crossing from the south side of the Chickahominy at Mechanicsville Bridge to reach the enemy's communications without going too far from the city.

While his works were slowly progressing, General Lee
took measures to ascertain the position and arrangement
of the enemy's forces on the north side of the Chickahominy. General J. E. B. Stuart, with a detachment
of cavalry, was directed to reconnoitre the country between the Chickahominy and the Pamunkey in the rear
of the enemy. This order was executed with great
skill and entire success. General Stuart, with 1200
men and a battery of horse artillery, on June 12th proceeded by way of Hanover Court House in the direction
of Old Church. Finding Hanover Court House in possession of the enemy's cavalry, Stuart proceeded down
the Pamunkey River, and, crossing the Totopotomy,
made the entire circuit of the Federal Army, returning on the 14th to the south side of the Chickahominy by way of Forge Mill.[4] He found that
the enemy's fortifications did not extend beyond the
right of his line on Beaver Dam, and that the dividing
ridge between the two rivers was unoccupied. From
all that he observed there was no indication of an intention on the part of General McClellan to change his
base of operations. Roads had been repaired and
opened to aid the railroad in supplying the army on the
Chickahominy, and immense stores were collected at
the White House. But the most valuable and important information obtained by General Stuart was the
fact that the enemy had neglected to fortify the ridge
between the head waters of the Beaver Dam Creek, a
small tributary of the Chickahominy which it enters
about two miles below Mechanicsville Bridge, and an
affluent of the Pamunkey. It was by the road running

[4] Six miles below Long Bridge.

J. E. B. STUART

along this ridge that General Lee expected to reach the enemy's communication and turn the strong position at Ellerson's Mill on Beaver Dam Creek. The character of these two streams was such as to make it very difficult to cross with troops and artillery, but the high ground lying between them, which forms the watershed between the Chickahominy and the Pamunkey, affords a practicable road to the York River Railroad.

General McClellan had fortified the left bank of the Beaver Dam Creek very strongly, so as to arrest any movement down the Chickahominy by the road from Mechanicsville to Cold Harbor, but a force moving along the ridge above referred to would turn the position of Ellerson's Mill, which barred the Mechanicsville road, and render it untenable. The reconnaissance of General Stuart indicated that the importance of guarding this avenue to his rear had escaped the attention of the Federal commander. General McClellan did not perceive the object of this bold reconnaissance; he supposed that the destruction of stores and "a little *éclat*" were its only results. He was soon to learn that it had a far more terrible significance. On June 14th at midnight he telegraphed to Secretary Stanton, "All quiet in every direction. The stampede of last night has passed away. Weather now very favourable. I hope two days more will make the ground practicable. I shall advance as soon as the bridges are completed and the ground fit for artillery to move." Within two days, guided by the information obtained by the expedition to which General McClellan attached so little importance, General Lee had sent the order which put Jackson in motion to take his part in the contest that was to bring to nought the hopes and designs of the Federal Commander.[5]

In order to mislead the enemy, rumours were diligently circulated that General Jackson was preparing to move northward, and to give weight to these rumours, Whiting's division and Lawton's brigade were sent to reinforce his. Lawton's brigade, then approaching from the coast of South Carolina, was ordered to turn aside at Burkesville and proceed by way of Lynchburg, as if to join Jackson. Whiting's troops took the cars by day in Richmond, and some appearance of haste was given to the movement, the object of which was not concealed. I was sent myself to the depot while the troops were being taken on the cars, with some orders to the officer in charge as to the necessity and importance of despatch if they were to be in time to help Jackson in his advance. These troops did not reach the Valley. When they arrived at Mechum's River, west of Charlottesville, they met the van of Jackson's army moving towards Richmond.

On June 23rd, on entering our headquarters after an absence of a few hours, I found indications among the staff officers present of something mysterious going on. Several general officers arrived, and General Lee was in his room upstairs in company with a number of his Division Commanders. I soon learned that a mysterious stranger had arrived, and that he was no other than the famous chieftain of the Valley. He had come very quietly and almost unattended. I had never seen

[5] The preliminary order to Jackson to be ready to move was dispatched by Lee on June 11th, the same day on which he ordered Stuart to make the reconnaissance. The final order to Jackson to come to the Peninsula was sent on June 16th. (See *O. R.*, vol. XII, part III, p. 913.)

him, and his presence was, I believe, unknown to any except those at General Lee's Headquarters. He departed with equal secrecy and the meeting broke up. At this meeting the general plan of operations was explained and discussed, and the several officers returned to their commands to prepare to put them into execution.

General Jackson expressed the belief that his army would all be at Ashland by June 23rd. General Lee allowed him extra time in case of any unlooked for delay, and formed his plans on the supposition that Jackson would not be ready to move from Ashland before June 25th. This was told me by General Lee.[6]

[6] This confirms the stories of D. H. Hill (*Battles and Leaders*, vol. II, p. 347) and Longstreet (*From Manassas to Appomattox*). Both these generals were present at the conference. Hill says that Longstreet suggested that Jackson, having the longest march to make, should fix the hour for the beginning of the attack, and that Jackson answered, "Daylight on the 26th."

Longstreet says that Jackson first fixed the morning of the 25th, and that when he pointed out that the roads would probably be obstructed and Federal pickets met, Jackson altered the hour of attack to daylight on the 26th. To attack on the 25th, Jackson must have had all his force at Ashland Station on the 23rd. Jackson had halted his leading division for their usual Sunday rest day at Frederickshall on the 21st. Frederickshall is 38 miles by road from Ashland Station, and, judging from his experiences in the Valley, Jackson might well have supposed that his force would march that distance in two days. Lee's order required Jackson to halt on the night of the 25–26th near Merry Oaks Church, 5 miles east of Ashland Station, so that, to get there at the required time, he would not have had to leave Ashland till the afternoon of the 25th. Lee therefore allowed Jackson an ample margin.

Henderson's elaborate defense of Jackson (*Stonewall Jackson*, vol. II, p. 22 *et seq*) will not stand close examination. He blames Lee's staff for requiring Jackson to do the impossible, and for drafting a "foolish order." Colonel Marshall here tells us that Lee drafted the order himself, and that his personal staff merely made the necessary copies, and Lee in that order gave Jackson twenty-four hours longer than the latter, in his second opinion, held to be necessary. The fact seems to be that Jackson had rightly acquired a reputation for great speed of movement in the Valley, but

The General remained in his room nearly all day after the meeting, of which I have spoken, broke up. In the interval between that time and the beginning of the movement, he made a thorough examination of the defensive plan once, and possibly twice. On June 24th he gave to his staff the confidential order of battle, with instructions to prepare copies themselves, and forward them at once to the several division commanders.

Those orders were substantially as follows: The army was disposed with Huger's division on the Charles City Road extending over towards Darbytown Road on the right, and towards the Williamsburg Road on the left; Longstreet's and D. H. Hill's divisions were on the same wing, but did not occupy the lines. Magruder's command, consisting of D. R. Jones' division, McLaw's division, and Magruder's own division under General Griffith, connected with Huger's left, and extended

that he underrated the difference between moving three or four thousand men quickly and a force of nearly 19,000. Jackson's command had been largely increased, and now consisted of ten brigades, but his staff had not been increased, and he made a mistake due to inexperience of the time and means required to get a force of that size closed up and deployed for battle. It is also possible that Jackson overrated the use the railway would be to him. He had had no experience of the time required to entrain and detrain a considerable force. In fact, owing to shortage of rolling stock and interruptions to the track by the enemy, the railway was of little service to him after he left Frederickshall.

During the fighting of the Seven Days, Jackson's command was further increased to nearly 25,000 by the addition of D. H. Hill's division, and this may also account for the slowness of his movements after he first came into action. Henderson suggests (vol. II, p. 25) that one reason for Jackson's delay was that he had not enough cavalry, "for Stuart's squadrons were on his left flank and not on his front." But a reference to Stuart's report shows that this was not so, and Colonel Martin, of Stuart's command, says definitely that he was in touch with Jackson's advance guard at Ashland Station on the afternoon of the 25th. — *O. R.*, vol. XI, part II, p. 528.

across the New Bridge on Nine Mile Road up the Chick-ahominy towards Mechanicsville. His line connected on the left with that of A. P. Hill, whose division cov-ered the Chickahominy from Mechanicsville Road, beyond Meadow Bridge. Branch's brigade of Hill's division was at Half Sink, near the crossing of the Fredericksburg Railroad. The cavalry was on our extreme left. Wise's brigade was on the James River in the vicinity of Chaffin's Bluff, supporting the river batteries, and there was cavalry on the New Market, or River Road, and the Darbytown Road, forming an imperfect connecting-link between the main body and the troops on the James.

General Holmes with about 6000 troops had come from North Carolina, and was encamped on the south of the James near Proctor's Creek. The orders assumed that Jackson would be ready to move from Ashland on the 25th. They directed him to march from Ashland on that day and encamp that night near and west of the Central Railroad, in the vicinity of Merry Oaks Church. From this point he was to move at 3 A.M. on the 26th, taking the road towards Pole Green church, where he was expected to halt at night. This route runs along the dividing ridge, to which I have referred, between the head waters of Beaver Dam Creek, and those of the Totopotomy. By moving on this road, General Jackson would turn the strong position held by the enemy on Beaver Dam Creek at Ellerson's Mill, about a mile east of Mechanicsville, and he was directed to do so in the orders.[7]

[7] The wording of the order ran: "General Jackson bearing well to his left, turning Beaver Dam Creek, and taking the direction toward Cold Harbor."

As soon as General Jackson's progress had begun, General Branch was to cross at Half Sink, and move down the north side of the Chickahominy, so as to open Meadow Bridge for the passage of A. P. Hill's division. Hill's movement was not to begin until he was apprised of Jackson being sufficiently advanced to be ready to turn Beaver Dam. Hill was then to cross the Chickahominy and advance directly upon Mechanicsville, opening Mechanicsville Bridge for Longstreet's and D. H. Hill's divisions. These were to be massed on the Mechanicsville Road, concealed from view of the enemy, early on the morning of the 26th, and were to cross the Chickahominy as soon as Hill's advance should have opened the way. After passing the river, D. H. Hill was to march to the support of General Jackson, and take position on his right, but somewhat in his rear. Longstreet was to take a similar position with reference to A. P. Hill, and the four columns were then to sweep down to Chickahominy in echelon, Jackson in advance extending well to his left, and moving so as to threaten the York River Road. General Stuart was to cover General Jackson's front and left, extending towards the Pamunkey, and as Jackson approached the railroad Stuart was to guard particularly against the advance of any troops from the direction of the White House.

Information had been received that about 10,000 troops had reached that point on their way to join General McClellan, and one object in making Jackson extend so far to the left was to cut off that force and prevent its junction with McClellan. The information turned out to be untrue, the force alluded to being only a part of one of McClellan's divisions, with perhaps some absentees returning to their commands. While these movements were progressing Generals Huger and Magruder were to hold the lines in front of McClellan's left wing, observe him closely, and upon any indication of withdrawal attack vigorously.

General Lee, in conversing with me about these operations, said, as the orders themselves clearly indicate, that his idea was to compel General McClellan to come out of his works and give battle for the defence of his communications with the White House. With this view, Jackson was to advance so as to threaten the railroad, and it was expected that if an engagement ensued, it would be brought on by him and D. H. Hill, so that Longstreet and A. P. Hill could fall upon the left of any force that might engage the former commands. It will be seen that this general idea controlled General Lee's movements in the important operations of Friday 27th.

If McClellan should abandon the railroad, General Lee expected that he would either attempt to cross the Chickahominy below the railroad bridge and move to the York to place his army under the protection of his gunboats, or that he would retreat to the James. General Lee also told me that he did not anticipate a battle at Mechanicsville or Beaver Dam. He thought that Jackson's march turning Beaver Dam would lead to the immediate withdrawal of the force stationed there, and did not intend that a direct attack should be made on that formidable position. General Lee selected the bridge at Mechanicsville as the place for the main body of the troops drawn from the Richmond lines to cross, and made his arrangements for a rapid advance against the enemy on the north side of the river. For it was expected that the rapidity of the intended movement would most effectually prevent the advance of the enemy towards Richmond. Should the troops sent across the Chickahominy promptly effect a junction with those of Jackson near Mechanicsville, and should the measure adopted to avoid the resistance at Beaver Dam prove successful, the enemy would be forced to give battle before he could carry our lines south of the Chickahominy, or to abandon his communications. On the other hand, should General McClellan refuse the battle and concentrate his whole army south of the Chickahominy for a rapid movement against Richmond, our troops could recross the river and attack him in the rear while he was assailing the entrenchments in his front.[8]

The perils attending the enemy if he adopted such a course of action were so great and so apparent that General Lee had little apprehension, or rather little hope, that it would be attempted by General McClellan. Although it cannot be denied that General Lee's plan was attended with some risk to Richmond, it was far safer than to remain inactive while the adversary was constantly increasing his strength, and far less hazardous than a direct assault upon the strongly fortified line of the enemy south of the Chickahominy.

[8] Lee's plan was to leave about 28,000 men in the lines south of the Chickahominy to confront McClellan's main army, while with about 59,000 he attacked the Federal right, north of the Chickahominy. He said to Davis, when the latter was anxious about the dangers to which Richmond would be exposed if McClellan attacked south of the Chickahominy: "I will be on McClellan's tail." As Marshall says, celerity of movement was the essence of the plan, and it may easily be imagined how greatly Lee's anxieties were increased when the man most famous for celerity proved for once to be slow.

Celerity of movement was one of the essential features of the plan of operation, not only that the enemy might be deprived of the opportunity for preparation, but also to diminish the danger that might arise from the absence of the troops engaged beyond the Chickahominy. For these reasons, General Lee desired to force a decisive engagement on the first day.

As I have said, General Jackson supposed his army would be at Ashland by the 23rd. His orders required him to move from Ashland to the Virginia Central Railroad near Merry Oaks Church, so as to be in a position to march thence at 3 A.M. on the 26th. Longstreet and D. H. Hill moved out on the Mechanicsville Road at an early hour on the 26th, and were cached behind the high hill just south of the bridge, and in the woods in rear of it, ready to take their respective parts. General Lee accompanied these troops in person, and all eyes were anxiously turned towards Meadow Bridge, watching for the movement of A. P. Hill upon Mechanicsville, by which the bridge would be opened for the passage of the troops of Longstreet and D. H. Hill. The enemy had some works on the north side at and to our left of Mechanicsville which covered the bridge and the road leading from it to the hamlet, but A. P. Hill's route would bring him upon the flank of this position, and it was thought would enable him to dislodge the enemy without difficulty.

The troops lay on their arms from about 10 o'clock A.M. until nearly 4 P.M., without any appearance of a movement from above. No one could account for the delay. At one time it was thought that the whole movement would fail, as if we then abandoned it, the enemy would get knowledge of the plan and of Jackson's approach, which would have thwarted the whole scheme. It turned out that General Jackson had been disappointed in his expectation of the arrival of his troops at Ashland. Instead of getting there in time to march to Merry Oaks Church on the 25th, he had to begin from Ashland the movement that was directed to be made against the Central Railroad on the 26th.[9] This was not made known to General Lee on the 25th, for what reason I never knew. Had it been, the whole movement would probably have been postponed until the 27th, as General Lee would not have counted on the co-operation of Jackson in turning Beaver Dam on the morning of the 26th if he had known that that officer would have to march from Ashland to reach his appointed position.

About 4 P.M. A. P. Hill's troops were seen approaching Mechanicsville from the direction of Meadow Bridge. They soon dislodged the enemy from his first position and pursued him towards Beaver Dam. An ineffectual attempt was made to drive him from his entrenched position at Ellerson's Mill. The position was very strong. Immediately in front was the milldam, which was impassable. Trees had been felled on the margin of the stream to keep the advancing troops under fire as long as possible. The creek could only be crossed at one or two points, and the bridge on the road from Mechanicsville had been torn up. General Hill threw a

[9] Jackson marched from Ashland early on the 26th, and the head of his column crossed the Central Railroad at Atlees Station at 9 A.M. so that he was six hours behind time. Jackson sent a report of this to General Branch commanding the left brigade of A. P. Hill's division. (See *O. R.*, vol. XI, part III), but this report was not passed on to Lee.

A. P. HILL

bridge across the creek on his left above the position of the enemy, but the troops attacking the enemy in front being repulsed, the brigade which was to have crossed by this bridge was recalled. The ground on the side occupied by the Federals rose from the stream. One field work with artillery and infantry, just to our left of the road leading up the hill from the stream, commanded the direct approach to the bridge from the direction of Mechanicsville and the slope of the hill on that side of the creek down which the assaulting party had to move. Another to our right of the road, also manned with artillery and infantry, had equal command of the opposite slope immediately on its front, and gave an enfiladed fire on troops approaching the bridge. A third work to the left of the one first mentioned also commanded the bridge. The cross fire from these three works swept the whole front along which the troops had to advance to cross Beaver Dam.[10]

The attempt was very injudicious, as night was approaching, and with morning Jackson might confidently be expected to turn the position. Indeed, at that time nothing had been heard of him, but before Longstreet and D. H. Hill crossed the Chickahominy, which they began to do as soon as A. P. Hill had gained Mechanicsville, the smoke of artillery had been seen beyond Mechanicsville, apparently on the road from Atlees to Pole Green Church, which was supposed to proceed from Jackson's guns. Had this been true, Jackson might still have been expected to turn Beaver

---

[10] The defenders of Beaver Dam Creek were the Pennsylvania Reserves of Porter's command. A. P. Hill, tired of waiting for Jackson, attacked on his own initiative.

Dam in time. It seems, however, that the firing alluded
to was done by General Stuart, who preceded Jackson
and occasionally shelled the woods in front of him as he
advanced.[11]

A. P. Hill's troops had pursued the enemy rapidly
from Mechanicsville towards Ellerson's Mill, and had
begun the attack on that position. General Lee
thought that, if he halted in front of Beaver Dam, General McClellan might reinforce that position, and as
Jackson was very far to our left, might accumulate on
him. He therefore considered it best to allow the
attack on this strong position to proceed, in order to
prevent troops being moved from it against Jackson
before communication had been opened between that
officer and the main body.

Such was certainly McClellan's best policy. Had he
held Beaver Dam in force in front of A. P. Hill, and
moved a strong body of troops to meet Jackson, he
would have effectually covered the right of his position at Ellerson's Mill and been able, with the force at
that point, to threaten the flank and rear of any troops
we might have sent from Mechanicsville to support
Jackson. Had he succeeded in driving Jackson back
towards Atlees, he could have fallen upon the left of our
position at Mechanicsville.[12]

The attack itself on Ellerson's Mill was not properly
conducted. It should not have been made directly, but
A. P. Hill should have followed up the partial movement
he made on the enemy's right, and thrown a strong force

[11] See Stuart's Report, *O. R.*, vol. XI, part II, p. 514.

[12] One reason why McClellan did not attempt these manœuvres was that
he believed as early as 12 noon on the 26th that he was being attacked by
Jackson, and that he was contending against "vastly superior odds."
See *McClellan's Own Story*, p. 394.

across Beaver Dam above Ellerson's, so as to take the works at that point in reverse.

It was evident that Jackson's movement had so far produced no impression, as the enemy was found to be still occupying his works in force at Beaver Dam, and he vigorously resisted every effort made to cross, but it being confidently expected that Jackson would soon be felt on his right, the attack was maintained with obstinacy, and a brigade of D. H. Hill's division was sent to reinforce A. P. Hill. It was now nearly dark. The bridges over Beaver Dam had been destroyed, and although the attacking force made its way to the bank under a most destructive fire from the works on the opposite side, it was found impossible to cross.

Jackson's prescribed march should already have made his presence felt on the enemy's right, unless he had encountered a serious opposition, and it was assumed that, had such been the case, it would have been made known.[13] His arrival being therefore momentarily expected, and its effect upon the enemy being regarded as certain, the efforts to find means to cross Beaver Dam were continued until nearly 9 P.M., and were attended with serious loss.

Attempts were, at length, made to find a practicable passage higher up the creek, and although the troops made their way up to the right bank under a destructive fire from the enemy's entrenchments, it was impossible to effect a crossing in the increased obscurity. The troops were accordingly withdrawn and the engagement ceased about 9 P.M.

[13] Jackson had halted for the night of the 26th at Hundley's Corner, about halfway between Shady Grove Church and Bethesda Church. He never came into action.

The troops behaved very bravely. They forced their
way through the fallen timber under the deadly cross-fire
from the three works I have mentioned, none of which
were more than 300 and two less than 300 yards from
the stream. The dead lay on the margin of the dam
and on the broken bridge immediately under the
works of the enemy. Our loss was heavy; that of the
enemy in this action could not have been large.

Thus the first, and one of the most important parts of
General Lee's plan miscarried from the outset. Instead
of uniting all of his forces north of the Chickahominy
in time to bring the enemy to a decisive engagement on
the 26th June, when that day closed he was still in front
of Beaver Dam and his communications with Jackson
were not yet established.

General Lee remained at Mechanicsville consulting
with Longstreet and the two Hills until about 11 P.M.,
when he rode back to the south side of the Chickahominy and remained for the night at a house near the
Mechanicsville Road, at the top of the hill overlooking
the bridge. He returned to Mechanicsville before sun-
rise on the 27th, and as we rode down the hill to the
bridge a sharp fire of musketry with some artillery
was heard for about half-an-hour in the direction of
the battle-ground of the previous evening. Preparations had been made to cross Beaver Dam above and
below Ellerson's, but before they were completed the
firing ceased, and soon after our arrival at Mechanicsville it was reported that the enemy had retreated.[14]
This was caused by the progress of Jackson on his right,

[14] Porter withdrew his troops to Gaines's Mill during the night, in accordance with orders from McClellan.

and demonstrated the correctness of the original plan. Had Jackson been able to turn Beaver Dam on the afternoon of the 26th, the loss at Ellerson's would have been prevented.

D. H. Hill had moved from Mechanicsville to support Jackson according to his orders, and about 8 A.M. on the 27th Longstreet and A. P. Hill began to cross Beaver Dam below Ellerson's, Longstreet being nearer the Chickahominy. The enemy retreated very rapidly,[15] abandoning the camps in rear of Ellerson's, and leaving a considerable quantity of stores, tools, etc. He fell back by the road to Gaines's Mill and burned a number of waggons as he retreated.

Longstreet and A. D. Hill pushed on rapidly, and by 12 noon arrived near Hogan's house, opposite New Bridge, which was found to have been partially destroyed. A force was immediately put to work to repair it, so as to open communications by that route with our troops on the opposite side of the Chickahominy. It was made passable during the afternoon, and was used for the removal of the wounded from the battlefield of Gaines's Mill that night.

Apart from the question of the danger to Richmond involved in General Lee's plan, which I have already discussed, there is the question of the risk incurred in placing the Chickahominy between the two wings of the army, and in leaving only Magruder's and Huger's divisions to oppose so large a force of the enemy on the south side of that river. Even before we had opened up New Bridge, we were not much further from Richmond by way of Mechanicsville than General McClellan

[15] They were only Porter's outposts.

himself. He could not have moved upon Richmond from the south side until he had forced the works held by Magruder and Huger, and it was supposed that they would resist him long enough to enable General Lee to rejoin them before McClellan could reach Richmond. After we got possession of New Bridge and held both sides of the Chickahominy at that point, immediate communication between our troops north and south of the stream was practically restored.

Besides, it must be remembered that General Lee had no other reasonable alternative to that which he adopted if he would act at all. He could not have attacked General McClellan's right without crossing the Chickahominy, and to have attacked his left, strongly entrenched with artillery in formidable works commanding every avenue of approach, and with the ground on each side of the roads rendered impassable for troops by the forests, which had been felled and left lying with tangled branches and trunks of trees, was a much more dangerous plan than that he adopted. No bold movement was ever made without assuming some risk, and in all the circumstances the movement for General Lee was attended with as little danger to the point he had to defend as could have been required by any prudence short of that which ventures nothing and gains nothing. Had he refrained from this movement he could have done nothing but await the action of General McClellan, who could have brought such a force upon him in time as to make the offensive impossible. The disparity between General Lee and his opponent could have been increased until the campaign of McClellan in 1862 would have been like that of Grant in 1864, when

General Lee's strength was so far reduced that he could only endeavour to extend his small numbers to oppose a thin line along an extended front to the overwhelming numbers of the enemy.

By noon on the 27th, it was found that the enemy had made a stand beyond Powhite Creek, which flows by Gaines's Mill to the Chickahominy, and General Lee decided to adhere to the plan of operations which I have explained. As Jackson, thrown well out to the left, was threatening to cut the York River Railroad, General Lee's expectation was still that McClellan, if he intended to hold that line of communications and retain his position on the Chickahominy, would move out to give battle. Finding the enemy in position behind Powhite Creek, General Lee supposed that Jackson's movement would cause McClellan to draw this force to its right to oppose Jackson, and so enable him to throw Longstreet and Hill upon its left and rear.[16] He and Jackson had a meeting near Walnut Grove about noon, and there General Lee explained his plans.

In accordance with this plan, it was not intended that Longstreet and A. P. Hill should advance until the

[16] McClellan very wisely, instead of attempting such a manœuvre, decided to change his base and retreat to the James. Lee was justified in assuming that his opponent would make use of his superior numbers in an effort to save his communications with White House, and he was unaware on the 27th that McClellan had, on the previous day, given orders for the abandonment of the York River Railway as a line of communication and of White House as a base; but he made a mistake in acting on the assumption before its correctness had been confirmed by information from the front, and in sending off on the 28th Stuart's cavalry and Ewell's division from Jackson's command on what proved to be a wholly unnecessary expedition to White House, which base McClellan had already abandoned. The absence of Stuart's cavalry was one of the main causes of the lack of information from which Lee suffered throughout the Seven Days.

enemy moved to meet Jackson's attack, but their troops found themselves engaged with the enemy as soon as they reached the vicinity of New Bridge, while Jackson's column far to the left had not yet reached the York River Railroad.

About 2.30 P.M., General A. P. Hill, pressing toward the York River Railroad, met the enemy near New Cold Harbor, and, hastily forming his line of battle, soon became hotly engaged with a superior force. Nothing had been heard of Jackson since noon, and for two hours General Hill with his single division encountered the greater part of the Federal troops north of the Chickahominy with conspicuous gallantry and courage.[17]

The battle raged fiercely and desperate efforts were made to force the enemy's position; three regiments, the 16th and 22nd North Carolina, and the 35th Georgia, carried the crest of the hill east of Dr. Gaines's house, and forced their way into the enemy's camp, but had to fall back before overwhelming numbers, and it was soon apparent that they could not do more than hold their own until help came. The enemy occupied a range of hills, his right resting in the vicinity of Mc-Gehee's house and his left near that of Dr. Gaines on a wooded bluff which rose abruptly from a deep ravine east of the house of Dr. Gaines; the ravine was filled with sharp-shooters to whom its banks gave shelter; a second line of infantry was stationed on the side of the hill behind a breastwork of trees, the branches of which made a strong abattis, while a third line of infantry

[17] Porter's force at the beginning of the battle of Gaines's Mill numbered about 27,000 men.

entrenched occupied the crest of the bluff, which was crowned with artillery. To approach this position, the troops had to cross the open plain about a quarter-of-a-mile wide, commanded by this triple line of fire and swept by the heavy batteries south of the Chickahominy. In front of the Federal centre and right the ground was generally open, bounded on the side of our approach by a wood of dense and tangled undergrowth, and traversed by a sluggish stream which converted the soil into a deep morass.

The attack expected to be made by Jackson was so long delayed by the difficulties he encountered on his march [18] that Longstreet was ordered to make a diversion in A. P. Hill's favour by a feint on the enemy's left; in the course of this demonstration the great strength of the position held by the enemy was discovered, and Longstreet perceived that to render the diversion effective, the feint must be converted into an attack. He resolved with characteristic promptitude to carry the heights occupied by the enemy by assault; his column was quickly formed near the open ground, and his preparations were completed when Jackson arrived, and his right division, that of Whiting, took position on the left of Longstreet; at the same time D. H. Hill formed on our extreme left, and after a short but bloody conflict, forced his way through the morass and obstructions,

[18] The chief cause of Jackson's delay is generally said to have been a collision on the Mechanicsville-Bethesda Church road between D. H. Hill's division moving from Mechanicsville on Cold Harbor and Jackson's columns coming south from Hundley's Corner. But in view of Marshall's suggestion that Lee at noon told Jackson that he expected McClellan to move to his right against Jackson, and that he, Lee, intended then to attack with A. P. Hill and Longstreet, it may well be that Jackson was waiting for a development which never took place.

and drove the enemy from the woods on the opposite side. Ewell advanced on Hill's right and engaged the enemy furiously; the first and fourth brigades of Jackson's own division filled the interval between Ewell and A. P. Hill; the 2nd and 3rd brigades were sent to the right to support Longstreet; the arrival of these fresh troops enabled A. P. Hill to withdraw some of his brigades, wearied and reduced by their long and arduous conflict.

The line being now complete, General Lee ordered a general advance; on the right the troops moved forward with steadiness unchecked by the terrible fire from the triple lines of infantry on the side of the hill, and the cannon on both sides of the river, which burst upon them as they emerged upon the plain. Their dead and wounded marked their intrepid advance; the brave Texans leading were closely followed by their no less daring companions.[19]   The enemy were driven from the ravine to the first line of breastworks, over which our impetuous column dashed up to the entrenchments on the crest; these were quickly stormed, 14 pieces of artillery captured, and the enemy driven into the fields beyond. Fresh troops came to his support, and he endeavoured repeatedly to rally, but in vain; he was forced back with great slaughter till he reached the woods on the banks of the Chickahominy, and night put an end to the pursuit. Long lines of dead and wounded marked each stand of the enemy in his stub-

---

[19] The 4th Texas of Hood's brigade of Whiting's division was the first to pierce the Federal line. The Confederate losses in the battle were about 8000, the Federal 6830. Porter, who had about 26,000 infantry against about 48,000 Confederate infantry, made a gallant fight to gain time for McClellan to prepare his retreat.

born resistance, and the field over which he retreated was strewn with the slain.

On the Confederate left, the attack was no less vigorous and successful. D. H. Hill charged across the open ground in his front, one of his regiments having first bravely carried a battery whose fire enfiladed his advance. Gallantly supported by the troops on his right, who pressed forward with unfaltering resolution, he reached the crest of the ridge and after a sanguinary struggle, broke the enemy's lines and captured several of his batteries, and drove him in confusion toward the Chickahominy, until darkness rendered further pursuit impossible. Our troops remained in undisturbed possession of the field covered by the Federal dead and wounded, and their broken forces fled to the river and wandered in the woods.

V

THE SEVEN DAYS

(b) WHITE OAK SWAMP TO MALVERN HILL

GENERAL LEE's plans now depended first upon whether General McClellan would retreat from the Chickahominy or not, and secondly upon the direction of that retreat. On the morning of the 28th it was ascertained that none of the enemy who had opposed us at Gaines's Mill remained north of the Chickahominy, but as he might yet intend to give battle to preserve his communications, the 9th Cavalry supported by Ewell's division was ordered to seize the York River Railroad, and General Stuart with his main body was ordered to co-operate. When the cavalry reached Dispatch Station the enemy retreated to the south bank and burned the railway bridge.

During the forenoon clouds of dust south of the Chickahominy showed that the Federal Army was in motion; the abandonment of the railroad and the destruction of the bridge proved that no further effort would be made to recover his communications with White House,[1] but the roads which led to James River would also enable General McClellan to reach the lower bridges over the Chickahominy and retreat down the Peninsula; if he adopted the latter course it was neces-

[1] McClellan had in fact decided to abandon White House from the time when he received news of Jackson's advance against his right, and Porter's fighting on the 26th and 27th had been to gain time to prepare the retreat to the James; but Lee did not know this.

sary that our troops should continue on the north bank of the river, and therefore until the intention of General McClellan was discovered it was considered injudicious to change their disposition.

For information as to what was happening on the south side of the Chickahominy, General Lee had to rely upon the vigilance of the troops charged with watching and reporting the movements of the enemy on that side of the river. Several orders were sent by General Lee enjoining vigilance, but the whole of June 28th was lost to the pursuit in waiting this intelligence. General Lee first learned of the retreat on the morning of the 29th, from information obtained by two officers belonging to General Longstreet's engineer corps, who had crossed from the battle field of the day before by way of New Bridge to the south side of the river. They discovered that the pickets of General Huger were in line in front of the enemy's entrenchments on the south side of the river, and communicated to those pickets the fact that they were watching the vacant fortifications of General McClellan. A very short examination revealed the fact that the whole line of General McClellan's works on the south side of the Chickahominy had been abandoned and that his retreat had already begun and had been carried on without interruption for a whole day.[2]

---

[2] Magruder and Huger have been much criticised for their failure to discover McClellan's retreat earlier, but this criticism must now be tempered by the knowledge acquired during the Great War of the ease with which troops can be withdrawn unobserved from behind entrenchments. The most notable examples are the withdrawals from Suvla Bay and Cape Helles in the Gallipoli campaign; and there were many examples of the same thing in the Western Front.

Pursuit was immediately ordered and the troops of Generals Longstreet and A. P. Hill were directed to recross the Chickahominy at New Bridge and move down the Darbytown Road towards the Long Bridge Road. Those of Generals Huger and Magruder were ordered to march, the former by the Charles City Road to take the Federal army in flank, and the latter by the Williamsburg road to attack its rear. General Jackson and his own division, accompanied by D. H. Hill's division, was ordered to cross the Chickahominy at Grape Vine Bridge and march by way of Savage Station in pursuit of the retreating enemy. General Magruder reached the vicinity of Savage Station about noon, where he came upon the rear guard of the retreating army. He mistook the resistance which he met for a renewal of the enemy's movement against Richmond. Under this belief, as soon as he encountered the enemy's rear guard at Savage Station he sent to General Huger, who was marching down the Charles City Road, for reinforcements, and two brigades of Huger's division were sent to his support. When it became apparent that the force on Magruder's front was only covering the retreat of his main body Huger's troops were sent back by General Lee's order, but valuable time was lost in the pursuit by this delay. Jackson's line of march led the flank and rear of the enemy at Savage Station across the Grape Vine Bridge, but the latter was delayed by the necessity of rebuilding the bridge. Magruder attacked the enemy at Savage Station late in the afternoon of the 28th, but entirely mistaking the character of the resistance to him, he attacked with only one division and two regiments of another. Owing to

BENJAMIN HUGER

the lateness of the hour and the small force employed by General Magruder the result was not decisive, and the enemy was enabled to continue his retreat under cover of darkness, leaving several hundred prisoners with his dead and wounded in our hands, but the time thus gained enabled General McClellan to cross White Oak Swamp without interruption, and destroy the bridge leading over it.[3]

Jackson did not reach Savage Station till early on the 30th. He was then directed to pursue the enemy on the rear road he had taken, and Magruder was ordered to follow Longstreet on the Darbytown Road. As Jackson advanced he captured great numbers of prisoners, and collected so many arms that he had to detach two regiments for their security. The enemy had, however, crossed White Oak Swamp before he came up. Longstreet and A. P. Hill, continuing their advance on the 30th, soon came upon the enemy strongly posted across the Long Bridge Road and about one mile northwest from its intersection with the Charles City Road. Huger's route lay to the right of the enemy's position, Jackson's to the rear, and the arrival of their commands was awaited to begin the attack.

Meanwhile, on the 29th General Holmes had crossed

[3] Magruder, who expected Jackson to come up on his left flank, only attacked with two brigades, and two battalions of another, against Sumner's army corps and was naturally repulsed. He had in fact surprised Sumner, but the premature opening of fire by a battery of Magruder's artillery gave the Federals sufficient warning to make them prepare for defense. Lee, much disappointed at the want of vigor of Magruder's pursuit, wrote to him that night: "General, I much regret that you have made so little progress to-day in the pursuit of the enemy. In order to reap the fruits of our victory the pursuit should be most vigorous. I must urge you then again to press on his rear, rapidly and steadily. We must lose no more time or he will escape us entirely."

from the south side of James River with part of his
division, and on the 30th, reinforced by General Wise
with a detachment of his brigade, he moved down the
River Road, and came upon the line of the retreating
army near Malvern Hill. Perceiving indications of
confusion among the enemy, General Holmes opened
upon his columns with artillery. He soon discovered
that a number of batteries advantageously supported
by an infantry force superior to his own, and assisted
by the fire of the gun boats in the river, guarded this
part of the line. Magruder, who had arrived at the
Darbytown Road from the direction of Savage Station,
was ordered to reinforce Holmes, but he did not reach
the latter in time to attack. General Huger reported
that his progress down the Charles City Road was
obstructed, but about 4 P.M. firing was heard in that
direction, which was supposed to indicate his approach.
Longstreet immediately opened with one of his batteries
to give notice of his presence. This brought on the engagement,[4] but Huger not coming up on the enemy's
flank, and Jackson having failed to effect the passage of
White Oak Swamp, Longstreet and Hill were without
the support they expected. The battle raged furiously
till 9 P.M.; by that time the enemy had been driven with
great slaughter from every position but one, which he
maintained until he was able to withdraw under cover
of darkness.[5]

[4] The Battle of Frayser's Farm.

[5] Huger was opposed by Slocum's division, but was hardly engaged.
Jackson and D. H. Hill were confronted by Franklin's division, but made
no serious attempt to cross White Oak Swamp. The brunt of battle was
borne by Longstreet and A. P. Hill, who were opposed by the four divisions of Kearny, McCall, Sedgwick, and Hooker.

At the close of the struggle nearly the whole field remained in our possession, covered with the enemy's dead and wounded. But for Jackson's delay at White Oak Swamp, General Lee would have this day inflicted on General McClellan the signal defeat at which his plans aimed. That Jackson could have crossed the Swamp but for some unaccountable delay on his part is shown by the following letter which I have received from General Wade Hampton : —

WILD WOOD
June 13, 1871

MY DEAR SIR,

In accordance with your request, I give you a few memoranda, which may aid you in preparing your Life of Lee. Where the field of operations was so large as it was during the late war, each actor on the scene could necessarily take in only such portion as came under his own observation, and it is only by comparing all the accounts given by those who participated in the events narrated that [an] historian can come to a correct conclusion. The first point to be considered in the preparation of an history of the war is the truth. To establish this you will have to consult all authorities, and I feel assured that in all cases the truth will redound to the credit of General Lee. Feeling this, I shall state frankly such incidents as I think may prove of value to you, giving you in all cases such facts as came under my personal observation, and within my own personal knowledge. My only interest will be to subserve the interests of truth and to vindicate General Lee, and I hope that you will not regard me as reflecting on any other officer, when giving my statement of what was accomplished and what was left undone.

Great as is General Lee's fame, and wonderful as were the results he accomplished, the former would have been if possible greater and the latter still more wonderful if his plans had always been carried out and his conceptions realised. I shall not venture to blame anyone because these results were not accomplished and I only propose to state the simple facts in regard to a few of the operations in which I had a part. This I give as my contribution, small as it may be, to the memory and the fame of our great chief. Should any of the facts be of value to you, you can use them as you think best.

Taking these few facts in chronological order, I begin at the Seven Days fighting around Richmond, where Lee delivered his first blow. Returning to the army, from which I had been absent some time, on account of a wound received at Seven Pines, just as these movements began, I was given command of two brigades of Jackson's corps. One of these had to be sent back to guard prisoners and I retained the other, the Taliaferro Brigade, to which the Hampton Legion had been attached, until the retreat of McClellan to Harrison's landing. This brigade was placed under my command on Saturday June 28th, the brigade being then in front of Grape Vine Bridge, near Cold Harbour. The enemy withdrew from our front on Saturday night, leaving only a small picket guard [at] the bridge. We were inactive all Sunday and did not cross till the night of that day. On Monday 30th about 10 A.M. or a little later the head of our column appeared before White Oak Swamp, where we found a battery of the enemy in position on the opposite side of the stream. General Jackson moved up some of [the] artillery and soon drove off this battery, dismounting one of its guns, which was left on the field. General Jackson then rode across the creek, taking some cavalry, Ashley's old brigade I think, and remained over some little time. The enemy, moving up with cavalry, recrossed the stream and I was ordered to repair the bridge.

In the meantime the artillery of the enemy was concentrated so as to command the bridge, and finding that many men would be sacrificed in rebuilding it, General Jackson ordered the work discontinued.   My brigade then took position on the crest of the hill, the right resting on the public road, the left extending down to White Oak Swamp.   While here we could readily hear firing at Fraser's [6] Farm above us, and I remember seeing Captain Fairfax who had been sent by Longstreet to ask for reinforcements.   It was practicable for us to have moved by the right flank and thus join Longstreet, for I made a movement with a division of cavalry between these two very points in 1864, coming from White's Tavern, down the White Oak Swamp, crossing where Jackson halted and turning the flank of the enemy who were stationed below.

There are various places too where the swamp can be passed.   While we were in position, I rode into the swamp in my front, below the road, and to my surprise found no difficulty in crossing it.   This I did and I came out on the opposite side, just in rear of the right flank of the enemy. Carefully reconnoitring them I recrossed and reported the results of my observation to General Whiting and afterwards to General Jackson.   The latter enquired if I could make a bridge across the stream, to which I replied that I could make one for infantry, but not for artillery, as in attempting the latter my presence would be detected, owing to the fact that we should have to cut down trees in order to clear a road for wheels.   General Jackson directed me to make the bridge, and taking a detail of 50 men I put it up in a very short time.   It may be well to state too that the stream here was so narrow and shallow that it offered in reality no obstruction to the passage of troops.

As soon as the bridge was constructed I made another

[6] Spelled on most maps Frayser's.

reconnaissance of the enemy, whom I found in the same position and totally unsuspicious of our presence, though I approached their line to within 100 or 150 yards. Returning I reported to General Jackson, stated to him the admirable position we should secure for an attack, and urged that an attack should be made. He sat in silence for some time, then rose and walked off in silence. We remained in position all night and in the morning the enemy had withdrawn. We encountered him next at Malvern Hill, and I believe that battle would never have been fought had we struck them on the flank and in rear in White Oak Swamp.

If you refer to Dabney's *Life of Jackson*, you will find mention made of the strange delay at White Oak Swamp, and various conjectures on the cause. What did cause it I cannot say, nor do I venture to criticise the great and good soldier who made it. I only state facts, facts which in justice to General Lee should be known. Doubtless some of General Whiting's staff are cognizant of these facts, and of my own staff who accompanied me across the stream I recall Major T. G. Barker, and Lieutenant Wade Hampton, Jr., the latter serving me temporarily, as his Chief General J. E. Johnston had been wounded and was absent. He has read this communication and his recollection agrees with mine as to everything stated herein. Doubtless Major Barker will also confirm all that has been said, and an examination of the ground will prove that I am correct as to its topography.

Yours very truly,

WADE HAMPTON [7]

[7] A somewhat similar letter from General Wade Hampton is given in Alexander's *The American Civil War*, p. 149 *et seq.* Henderson, in a long defense of Jackson, vol. II, p. 60 *et seq.*, maintains, first, that in attempting the crossing Jackson would have exposed infantry to undue loss, and secondly, that the crossing would from natural causes have been extremely difficult. In support of the latter statement he quotes a letter from Mum-

WADE HAMPTON

Early on July 1st Jackson reached the battlefield of the previous day, having succeeded in crossing White Oak Swamp where he captured a part of the enemy's artillery and a number of prisoners. He was directed to continue the pursuit down the Willis Church Road, and soon found the enemy occupying a high range extending obliquely across the road in front of Malvern Hill. On this position of great natural strength the enemy had concentrated his powerful artillery, supported by masses of infantry, partially protected by breastworks. His left rested near Crew's house, and his right near Binford's. Immediately in his front the ground was open for a width of from a quarter to half a mile, and sloping gradually from the crest was completely swept by the fire of his infantry and artillery. To reach this open ground our troops had to advance through the broken and thickly wooded country traversed nearly throughout its whole extent by a swamp passable in but few places and difficult at that. The whole was within range of the batteries on the heights, and of the gun boats on the river, under whose incessant fire our movements had to be executed.

Jackson formed his line with Whiting's division on his left and D. H. Hill's on his right, one of Ewell's brigades occupying the interval. The rest of Ewell's and Jackson's own divisions were held in reserve, and

ford. But Mumford says (Alexander, p. 149) that he later found a better crossing: "I know that I thought at the time that he could have crossed his infantry *where we recrossed*. I had seen his infantry cross far worse places, and I expected he would attempt it." Hampton here shows that there were other and easier crossings of which Jackson was informed. The fact seems to be that, whether from fatigue or from some other cause, Jackson forgot his own maxim, "Never let up in a pursuit."

Magruder was directed to take position on Jackson's right, but before his arrival two of Huger's brigades came up and were placed next to Hill. Magruder subsequently formed on the right of these brigades, which, with a third of Huger's division, were placed under his command. Longstreet and A. P. Hill were held in reserve and took no part in the action, their troops having been relieved in the first line by Magruder. Owing to ignorance of the country, to the difficulty of communication through the dense forests, and to the broken character of the ground, the whole line was not formed until late in the afternoon. The obstacles presented by the woods and swamps also made it impracticable to bring up a sufficient amount of artillery to oppose successfully the extraordinary force of that arm employed by the enemy, while the field itself afforded few positions favourable for its use and none for its concentration. Orders were issued for a general advance at a given signal,[8] but the causes referred to prevented concerted action among the troops.

D. H. Hill pressed forward across the open field and engaged the enemy gallantly, breaking and driving back his first line, but as a simultaneous advance of the

[8] This is another instance of the mistake of using a sound signal for an attack. Lee had told his generals that the signal for a general advance should be the famous rebel yell from Armistead's brigade of Huger's division. D. H. Hill believed he heard that signal, and so reported to Jackson, who directed him to attack. Lee appears not to have stopped the attack, because he took the retreat of the pickets in front of Armistead to be the beginning of a general withdrawal of the enemy. Perhaps also he was impatient at the loss of opportunities in the preceding days and had made up his mind to press the attack in any circumstances against an enemy whom he believed to be demoralized. The result was that a strong position was attacked piecemeal and the Confederates suffered a heavy repulse.

other troops did not take place he found himself unable
to maintain the ground he had gained. Jackson sent
to his support his own division and that part of Ewell's [9]
held in reserve, but owing to the increasing darkness
and the intricacy of the forest and swamp they did not
arrive in time to render the desired assistance. Hill
was therefore compelled to abandon part of the ground
he had gained after suffering severe loss and inflicting
heavy damage upon the enemy.

On the right the attack was gallantly made by
Huger's and Magruder's commands. Two brigades of
the former commenced the action, the other two were
subsequently sent to the support of Magruder and Hill.
Several determined efforts were made to storm the
hill at Crew's house, the brigades advancing bravely
across the open field raked by the fire of a hundred
cannon and the musketry of large bodies of infantry.
Some were broken and gave way, others approached
closely to the guns and drove the infantry back, compelling the advanced batteries to retire to escape capture,
and mingling their dead with those of the enemy. But
for want of concert among the attacking columns their
assaults were too weak to break the Federal line, and
after struggling gallantly, sustaining and inflicting great
loss, they were compelled successively to retire. Night
was approaching when the attack began, and it soon
became difficult to distinguish friend from foe. The
firing continued until after 9 P.M. but no decided result
was obtained; part of the troops were then withdrawn
to their original positions, others remained on the
open field and some rested within a hundred yards of

[9] Early's brigade.

the batteries that had been so bravely but so vainly assailed.

General Stuart with his cavalry, after seizing the York River Railroad, on June 28th had proceeded to the vicinity of the White House, and secured a large amount of property, including more than 10,000 stands of small arms partially burnt. Leaving one squadron at the White House, he in compliance with his orders, returned to guard the lower bridges of the Chickahominy. Moving off again on July 1st, after a long march he reached the rear of the army at Malvern Hill on that night at the close of the engagement.

On July 2nd it was discovered that the enemy had withdrawn during the night, leaving the ground covered with dead and wounded, his route exhibiting evidence of precipitate retreat. The pursuit was at once resumed, General Stuart with his cavalry in the advance, but a violent storm which prevailed throughout the day greatly retarded our progress. The enemy, harassed and closely followed by the cavalry, succeeded in gaining Westover on James River and the protection of the gun boats. He immediately began to fortify his position which was one of great natural strength flanked on each side by a creek, and the approach to his front commanded by heavy guns of the shipping in addition to those mounted in his intrenchment. It was deemed inexpedient to attack him and in view of the condition of our troops, who had been marching and fighting almost incessantly for seven days under the most trying circumstances, it was determined to withdraw in order to afford them the repose of which they were in so much need. Several days were spent in collecting arms and other property abandoned by the enemy, and in the meantime some artillery and cavalry were sent below Westover to annoy his transports. On July 8th the army returned to the vicinity of Richmond.

The Federal Army should have been destroyed. Its escape was due to the causes already stated, of which the most prominent was the want of timely and correct information. The character of the country enabled General McClellan to conceal his retreat, and added much to the difficulties which beset the march of our pursuing column. But if the enemy's army was not destroyed, the siege of Richmond was raised, and the object of his campaign, which had been prosecuted after months of preparation and an enormous expenditure of men and money, completely frustrated. More than 10,000 prisoners, including officers of rank, 52 pieces of artillery, and upwards of 35,000 stands of small arms were captured.

The stores and supplies of every description that fell into our hands were great in amount and value, but small in comparison with those destroyed by the enemy. His losses in battle exceeded our own [10] while his subse-

---

[10] These paragraphs are almost identical with General Lee's dispatch. When he wrote them, Colonel Marshall had not seen the official figures of the Federal losses. The actual losses were: Federal, 15,849, Confederate, 20,135. The number of Federal missing was 6053, so that the prisoners did not amount to 10,000. The description which Colonel Marshall gives of the constant lack of co-operation between the parts of the Confederate army shows clearly that besides lack of information there was lack of experience. The Confederate Generals were engaged for the first time in manœuvring a large army, while many of the men were, as Colonel Marshall explains, little more than recruits. The blunders were many and were due to more than one cause, but the lessons of the Seven Days were taken to heart by Lee and his generals, and soon bore fruit.

A curious and dangerous neglect of the War Department in Richmond

quent inaction shows in what a condition the survivors reached the protection to which they fled.

has never been explained. Though the Confederate forces had been for a long time in the Peninsula, no maps had been issued to the Army. Lee was fairly well acquainted with the Peninsula as a whole and had a very complete knowledge of that portion across which he had planned that Jackson's advance from Ashland Station should take place, for White House was his wife's property, and he had ridden many times from it into Richmond by Cold Harbour, Gaines's Mill, and Mechanicsville. Magruder too knew the ground well, for he had been for months in the Peninsula, but Jackson did not, and twice during the Seven Days his columns took wrong roads.

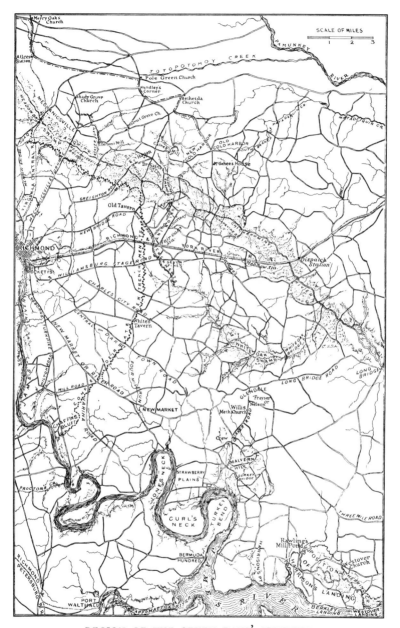

REGION OF THE SEVEN DAYS' FIGHTING

VI

THE CAMPAIGN AGAINST POPE

IT is noteworthy that the Army of Northern Virginia, though in 1861 it had for long been in sight of the Potomac, did not receive the name it was about to make historic until it had been withdrawn from Northern Virginia and become engaged in the defence of Richmond.[1] This would seem to be a proof that General Lee from his first assumption of the command of the army was inspired, even when he was engaged in the defence of the capital of the Confederacy, with the conviction that Northern Virginia was destined to become the principal scene of the operations of his troops. The concentration of the Confederate forces in Virginia and the Carolinas began when the troops under D. H. Hill, who had been stationed south of the James River, were drawn to Richmond, the policy was continued by bringing in Stonewall Jackson from the Valley in the manner described in the last chapter, and this was followed by summoning to the main body of General Lee's army such reinforcements as the withdrawal of General Burnside from North Carolina had made disposable.

[1] The first reference in the *Official Records* to the Army of Northern Virginia occurs in General Order No. 60, dated June 3, the day after Lee assumed command. That order runs: "Surgeon D. C. de Leon, in accordance with the instructions from the War Department, is announced as Medical Director of the Army of Northern Virginia." — *O. R.*, vol. XI, part III, p. 572

This movement of Burnside's troops was the first result of General Lee's plan for forcing the Federals to concentrate and for protecting the territory of the Confederacy much more effectively than by scattering troops in a number of states. As soon as General McClellan was in need of help General Burnside's corps was withdrawn from the South Carolina coast and the transports conveying his troops were sent to Hampton Roads.

After the retreat of General McClellan to Westover his army remained inactive for about a month. It was not known what his next move would be, and in the presence of so large a force as his it was necessary to take all precautions lest he should renew the movement against Richmond. It was a matter of grave responsibility for General Lee to decide how his army could be moved elsewhere while that of General McClellan was yet in the immediate vicinity of the city. Yet inaction was impossible, for another great army commanded by General Pope had begun its advance from Washington along the Orange and Alexandria Railroad, and its commander proclaimed his intention of making his way from the Federal capital to New Orleans.[2] It became necessary therefore for General Lee to prepare to meet this second army, while a larger force than his own lay still upon the James River at a comparatively short distance from Richmond. General Jackson's division was accordingly ordered to proceed towards Gordonsville on July 13th.

[2] On June 26, the opening day of the battles of the Seven Days, Lincoln had placed under Pope the armies of Frémont, Banks, and McDowell. Frémont thereupon resigned and his place was taken by Sigel. Shortly afterwards Lincoln brought General Halleck to Washington to direct the military operations of the Federal armies.

Upon reaching Gordonsville General Jackson learned that a force under General Pope, superior to his own, had reached Culpeper, but the uncertainty that surrounded the plans of General McClellan still rendered it inexpedient to send reinforcements from the army at Richmond.   General Jackson was therefore directed to observe the enemy's movements closely and to avail himself of any opportunity to attack them, assistance being promised from Richmond should the progress of General Pope put it in our power to strike an effective blow at his army without withdrawing our troops too long and too far from the defence of the capital.

Towards the end of July General Pope's advanced troops moving southward reached the Rapidan, and as General McClellan continued to manifest no intention of resuming active operations, General A. P. Hill was sent with his division on July 27th to reinforce General Jackson.[3]   At the same time, in order to keep General McClellan stationary, or at least to excite his uneasiness as to the security of his position at Westover, General D. H. Hill, who now again commanded the troops on the south side of James River, was ordered to shell the enemy's shipping in the James, and on the night of July 31st General French placed forty-three guns under Brigadier General Pendleton, chief of artillery, within range of the enemy's vessels and of his camp on the north of the river.   The guns were withdrawn before daybreak with small loss from the fire of the gun boats.   This attack caused General McClellan to

[3] Lee in his letter of July 27 to Jackson, announcing A. P. Hill's departure, says: "I want Pope to be suppressed."   He had perceived that Pope had ventured farther south than was safe, and wanted to take advantage of the fact.

send a strong force to the south bank of the James, which entrenched itself at Coggins Point opposite Westover, an indication that he intended to retain his position at Westover with the expectation of receiving reinforcements.

At this time General Burnside's troops still lay on transports in Hampton Roads. From that point he could easily ascend the James to reinforce General McClellan's army at Westover, or as easily move up Chesapeake Bay to reinforce the army of General Pope now advancing from the north. Until the destination of General Burnside became known it was difficult for General Lee to determine his plans, for, as it was not believed that General McClellan would resume action without reinforcements, much depended upon whether Burnside joined him or not.[4] The attention of General Lee was therefore fixed at the end of July upon the movements of General Burnside's corps. To settle the destination of that corps and also to hasten the withdrawal of General McClellan from the Peninsula, General Lee was determined to act upon the fears of the Washington Government for the safety of its capital by creating the belief that it was Jackson's purpose to advance northwards. With this object in view, Jackson was ordered to advance towards the Rapidan, which the main body of the Federal Army under General Pope was known to be approaching along the Orange and Alexandria Railroad. Jackson crossed the

[4] McClellan was at this very time beseeching Halleck at Washington to send him reinforcements for a resumption of the advance on Richmond. Halleck at first hesitated and then his mind was made up by Lee's action. Burnside was sent to Pope and McClellan withdrawn.

Rapidan on August 8th, and the next day attacked the advance of General Pope's army under General Banks at Slaughter's Mountain, sometimes known as Cedar Run. A determined battle ensued, the result of which was to leave Jackson for two days in possession of the battlefield. On the rest of Pope's army coming up Jackson retired south of the Rapidan, but his attack at Cedar Mountain had served its purpose in that it had strengthened the impression in Washington that he was advancing against that city and would endanger its safety, for news was shortly received that General Burnside's corps had been moved up Chesapeake Bay from Fortress Monroe.

This information made General Lee certain of the ultimate destination of General Burnside's command, and he immediately dismissed all fear that General McClellan would renew the attack on Richmond. He hoped that, if Jackson's force should be reinforced and move northward from the Rapidan, the result would be the recall of General McClellan's army from Westover to aid in the defence of Washington.

Meanwhile events in the Peninsula had confirmed these conclusions, for about August 4 General McClellan's intention not to renew seriously the advance on Richmond was further demonstrated by the fact that he then made a feeble advance from Westover to Malvern Hill and was found occupying the ground upon which the battle of July 1st had been fought; but as soon as he was challenged he retired, without delivering battle, during the night to his lines around Westover and offered little or no resistance to the advance of the Confederate force sent against him.

On August 13th, while Jackson was on the march back to Gordonsville, General Lee, having decided on his plan, sent Longstreet's command with the addition of two brigades under General Hood to join Jackson at that place; at the same time General Stuart was directed to move thither with the main body of his cavalry, leaving a sufficient force to observe the enemy still remaining at Fredericksburg. General R. H. Anderson was also told to leave his position on James River and to follow Longstreet. Only the divisions of D. H. Hill and McLaws were left to watch McClellan.

On August 15th General Lee left Richmond in person to take command of the army assembling at Gordonsville, and the next day that army began to advance to the Rapidan on the north side of which, extending along the Orange and Alexandria Railroad in the direction of Culpeper Court House, the Federal Army under Pope lay. General Lee and General Jackson with their staffs ascended Clark's Mountain, a high hill near Pisgah church overlooking the valley of the Rapidan, and there had a full view of General Pope's men resting on the north side of the river and apparently entirely ignorant that the main body of the Confederate army was concentrated behind Clark's Mountain, on the south side of the Rapidan. General Lee, knowing that he had on the spot a superior force to that General Pope had ready for battle, at once determined to cross the river and attack the Federal Army between the Rapidan and the Rappahannock.

The plan of attack was that the troops under Jackson and Longstreet should cross the Rapidan at Somerville and Raccoon Fords respectively on August 18th, Jack-

D. H. HILL

son moving against the enemy's front while Longstreet assailed him in flank. The cavalry under General Stuart was ordered to cross the Rapidan in advance of the infantry and make its way round General Pope's left to the bridge over the Rappahannock River where it is crossed by the Orange and Alexandria Railroad near Brandy Station. After destroying that bridge, which it was thought would seriously hamper Pope's retreat, as the river was swollen by recent rains, and at the same time prevent the arrival of reinforcements for Pope, the cavalry was to attack the rear of the enemy, while he was engaged with Longstreet on his flank, and Jackson on his front. General Lee confidently expected that these movements would enable him to inflict a disastrous defeat on the army of General Pope, for the Federal Army lay in fancied security, apparently entirely unconscious of the proximity of the Confederate troops. Unfortunately the cavalry failed to arrive to take its part on August 18th. That part was an essential feature of the plan of attack and so the movement had to be delayed until the cavalry came up.

As I have said, a portion of the cavalry, Fitzhugh Lee's brigade, had been left in the vicinity of Fredericksburg to watch the enemy on the Rappahannock near that place, and it was this cavalry that was expected. General Stuart had personally reported to General Lee and had informed him that the cavalry would arrive in time to take part in the movement on August 18th, and he anxiously expected its arrival on that day. When the unexpected delay took place Stuart proceeded down the plank road from Orange Court House towards Fredericksburg to look for the missing troops. While

waiting for their approach he was nearly made prisoner
at Verdiersville by some of the enemy's cavalry that
had made its way to that place. General Stuart says
in his report: —

"General [Fitzhugh] Lee's brigade did not arrive until
the night of the 18th, a day behind time. Not appreciating the necessity of punctuality in this instance, he
changed his course after leaving me and turned back
by Louisa Court House following his waggons which I
had directed him to send to that point for provisions,
etc. By this failure to comply with instructions, not
only the movement of the cavalry across the Rapidan
was postponed a day, but a fine opportunity lost to over-
haul a body of the enemy's cavalry on a predatory ex-
cursion far beyond their lines. By the great detour
made by this brigade it was not in a condition to move
on the 19th upon a forced march to the enemy's rear;
but in accordance with instruction from the commanding general, the 19th was devoted to rest and preparation, moving down for bivouac near Mitchell's Ford late
in the evening." [5]

From this it would appear that General Stuart was
not aware of the more serious consequence that resulted from the unfortunate delay of the cavalry on
August 17th; it not only failed to intercept the cavalry
expedition of the enemy to which he refers, but caused
the postponement of the movement of the whole army,
which there is good reason to believe would have resulted in a crushing defeat of the army of General Pope,
for General Lee soon afterwards defeated the Federal Army on the battlefield of the second Manassas,

[5] *O. R.*, vol. XII, part II, p. 726.

although in the interval General Pope had been largely reinforced from the forces under General McClellan. To have opened the campaign in Northern Virginia with such a victory might have led to great consequences. As far as we can see, the battle of the second Manassas and the subsequent campaign in Maryland would have been avoided, for General Pope's army, defeated on the Rapidan, would not have been able to retreat at once to the protection of their lines around Washington.

The cavalry, not reaching its position until the time mentioned by General Stuart, did not cross the Rapidan until the 20th, but in the meantime General Pope, becoming informed of the presence of General Lee's army south of the Rapidan, withdrew across the Rappahannock River. The facts of the escape of General Pope's army came to light some days later. When Jackson, who was sent to turn the position of the enemy on the Rappahannock and gain his rear, reached Catletts Station on the night of August 22nd, Colonel W. H. F. Lee commanding one of Stuart's regiments captured the camp in which General Pope's headquarters tent was found. Among other things that were captured was General Pope's letter-book containing a copy of two letters. In the first of these letters General Pope stated that his army was approaching Gordonsville and that he was confident that he would reach that place the next day. The second letter was of the same date from Pope to Halleck and in it he says substantially: "I have just learned that the whole Confederate Army under General Lee has arrived on the south side of the Rapidan River and is about to advance.

I shall lose no time in placing this army north of the Rappahannock." [6]

It will thus be seen that in the interval while General Lee was waiting for the arrival of the cavalry to take part in the movement across the Rapidan his purpose became known to General Pope, who availed himself of that knowledge at once to retire beyond the Rappahannock, and thus avoided the consequences which there is every reason to believe would have followed had not the delay of the cavalry occurred.

The cavalry being ready to advance on August 20th, Jackson crossed the Rapidan at Somerville Ford and Longstreet at Raccoon Ford on that day. They marched according to General Lee's orders for the 18th and found that the army of General Pope had retired beyond the Rappahannock, the north side of which was occupied in force from the vicinity of the bridge of the Orange and Alexandria Railroad up to and above Warrenton Springs, all the fords of the Rappahannock being strongly guarded.[7]

[6] Other documents captured gave Lee exact information as to the approach of reinforcements from McClellan's army for Pope.

[7] As Colonel Marshall says, a great opportunity was lost to Lee by muddle and accident. Stuart's actual order to Fitzhugh Lee to be at Raccoon Ford on the evening of the 17th is not available, but the latter says of it himself: "The brigade commander he [Stuart] had expected did not understand from any instructions he received that it was necessary to be at this point on this particular afternoon, and had marched a little out of his way in order to reach his waggons and get from them a full supply of rations and ammunition." (Fitzhugh Lee's *General Lee*, p. 183.) Fitzhugh Lee, in saying that he went "a little out of his way," is making a poor case for himself, as by going to Louisa Court House for supplies he more than doubled the length of his march; but Stuart seems to have been to blame for not making his orders more explicit. Then when Stuart rode off to Verdiersville to look for the missing brigade he sent his staff officer, Major Fitzhugh, off alone to continue the search. Fitzhugh

There followed some exchange of artillery fire, and on August 23rd Jackson began to cross the river at Warrenton Springs, but it was soon found that the Rappahannock was so swollen by heavy rains that an attempt to force a passage would be attended with great danger. Accordingly on August 24th General Lee determined to send General Jackson's corps up the river to cross it above General Pope's right flank so as to strike the Orange and Alexandria Railroad in his rear.   Longstreet in the meantime was ordered to divert Pope's attention from Jackson's movement by threatening him in front, and was to follow Jackson as soon as the latter should be sufficiently advanced.[8]   The information which General Lee had obtained from General Pope's captured papers showed him that the latter would very soon receive large reinforcements from General McClellan's army.   He did not wish to fight a battle and incur heavy losses which it would be difficult to replace, if

rode into a party of the enemy's cavalry and was captured with a copy of Lee's orders on him, which in such circumstances he should not have had about his person.   Stuart himself only barely escaped capture, and had to leave his famous plumed hat behind him.   So not only was the cavalry late, but Pope received warning of his danger.

Colonel Marshall does not overrate the influence which a defeat of Pope on the Rapidan might have had on the course of the war.   Historians are wont to ascribe much of Lee's success to luck and chance, but he had, in fact, as full an experience of the mischances of war as falls to the lot of most generals, and this is a striking instance.   It is characteristic of Lee that he dismisses in his dispatch the reasons and responsibilities for a failure which must have been very bitter to him, in the words: "The movement was appointed for August 18th, but the necessary preparations not having been completed, its execution was postponed to the 20th."

[8] Colonel Marshall is clearly of opinion that this plan was Lee's alone. Henderson (vol. II, p. 152) suggests that it might have been Jackson's, but Longstreet takes the same view as Marshall and says Lee did not previously consult with anyone.   *Battles and Leaders*, vol. II, p. 522.

General Pope's strength proved to be much greater than his own. His object was to cause General Pope to retreat by cutting the railroad behind him, and at the same time to delay the arrival of reinforcements. By placing his army on General Pope's right flank, he would be able to use the Shenandoah Valley to approach the Potomac and so cause apprehension in the Federal Government for the safety of their capital. This General Lee told me himself.[9]

[9] No manœuvre of Lee's has been more criticized than this, in which he divided his army in the presence of Pope's superior forces for the famous march to Manassas. Colonel Marshall's account of Lee's intentions explains the latter's letter to Davis of August 30th, when the battle of second Manassas was actually in progress: "My dispatches will have informed you of the march of this portion of the army [i.e., Longstreet's corps, which Lee accompanied]. Its progress has been necessarily slow, having a large and superior force on its flank, narrow and rough roads to travel, and the difficulties of obtaining forage and provisions to contend with. It has so far advanced in safety, and has succeeded in deceiving the enemy as to its object. The movement has, as far as I am able to judge, drawn the enemy from the Rappahannock and caused him to concentrate his troops between Manassas and Centreville. My desire has been to avoid a general engagement, being the weaker force, and by manœuvring to relieve the portion of the country referred to. I think that if not over-powered we shall be able to relieve other portions of the country, as it seems to be the purpose of the enemy to collect his strength here." (*Lee's Confidential Dispatches to Davis*, p. 56 *et seq.*)

This letter was published years after Marshall's death, but it sufficiently confirms his account of Lee's intentions. Indeed, it is quite probable that he knew of the letter, which is not such as a commander would write who was engaged in a battle which he had deliberately planned, particularly when that battle resulted in a great victory. As Colonel Marshall tells us in Chapter III, it was Lee's general policy to avoid the losses of pitched battles, except when he had the enemy at a great disadvantage of numbers or position. Having lost by mischance the opportunity he had created of striking Pope a deadly blow on the Rapidan, and knowing that Pope was being rapidly reinforced, Lee decided to endeavor to manœuvre Pope out of Northern Virginia, "to relieve the portion of the country referred to" by threatening the Federal flank and communications. There was some risk in dividing his army, as Lee admitted later in life: "The

General Jackson crossed the Rappahannock at Hinson's Mill about four miles above Waterloo very early on the 25th and encamped on the night of the 25th near Salem after a long march. The next morning continuing his route he passed the Bull Run Mountains at Thoroughfare Gap and proceeding by way of Gainesville, where he was joined by Stuart's cavalry, reached the Orange and Alexandria Railroad at Bristoe Station about sunset. General Jackson was now between the army of General Pope and the Federal capital. No great force had been encountered, and General Pope did not seem to be aware of his situation. At Bristoe the track was torn up, two trains of cars moving northward from the direction of Warrenton were captured, and a number of prisoners were taken. As the interruption of the railroad must give the enemy warning of his presence, General Jackson determined, notwithstanding the darkness of the night, and the long and arduous march of the day, to lose no time in capturing the

disparity of force between the contending forces rendered the risks unavoidable" (Allan's *Army of Northern Virginia in 1862*, p. 200). But if his prime intention was, as Colonel Marshall says, not to risk a battle but to unite Longstreet and Jackson in the Valley after he had caused Pope to retreat, the risks are much reduced.

The facts then seem to be that neither the second battle of Manassas nor any battle at all formed part of Lee's original plan. That battle was brought on by Jackson's action on the evening of August 28th, in attacking King's division as it was marching across his front all unconscious of his presence. Lee, finding that the junction of Longstreet and Jackson was assured and Pope's forces scattered, allowed the battle to proceed, but he could, had he wished to do so, have avoided the battle and withdrawn Jackson by Aldie, through Snickers Gap into the Valley. Then, by holding the gaps in the Valley with part of his force and marching on Harper's Ferry with the remainder, he could have caused the withdrawal of the Federal army for the defense of Washington, and so achieved what he declared to be his purpose.

enemy's depot at Manassas Junction about seven miles distant on the road to Alexandria. So a detachment under General Stuart was sent forward for that purpose and about midnight Manassas Junction was captured; eight pieces of artillery with their horses, ammunition and equipment were taken; about 300 prisoners; 200 new tents and immense quantities of quartermaster's and commissary stores fell into our hands.

On receiving the news of this capture Jackson left Ewell's division with the 5th Virginia cavalry at Bristoe Station, and with the rest of his command proceeded to Manassas Junction where he arrived early in the morning. Soon afterwards a considerable force of the enemy under Brigadier General Taylor approached from Alexandria and pushed forward to recapture the stores which had been lost. After a sharp engagement the enemy was routed and driven back, leaving his dead and wounded on the field, General Taylor himself being mortally wounded during the retreat.[10] Jackson's troops remained at Manassas Junction during the rest of the day supplying themselves with everything they needed from the masses of captured stores. In the afternoon General Ewell was attacked at Bristoe Station by a force coming from the direction of Warrenton Junction; the attacking party was repulsed and broken, but their places were soon supplied with fresh troops, and it was apparent that the Federal commander had now become aware of the situation of affairs.[11] So Ewell upon per-

[10] The Federal troops consisted of a brigade of infantry and a battery of artillery, and were sent forward from Alexandria by Halleck under the impression that Jackson's force was no more than a raiding party.

[11] The troops that attacked Ewell belonged to Hooker's division of Heinzelman's corps.

ceiving the strength of the enemy withdrew his command, and rejoined General Jackson at Manassas Junction, having first destroyed the railroad bridge over Broad Run. The enemy being in greatly superior numbers, General Jackson determined to withdraw from Manassas Junction and take a position near Groveton, west of the turnpike road from Warrenton to Alexandria, where he could more readily unite with the column of Longstreet then known to be approaching.[12]

Having fully supplied the wants of his troops, Jackson was compelled from lack of transport to destroy the rest of the captured property, consisting of an immense amount of salt pork, corn beef, and flour, which were burned. General Taliaferro moved during the night by the road to Sudley's Ford and, crossing the turnpike, halted on the west side near the battlefield of July 21st, 1861, where he was joined on the 28th by the divisions of A. P. Hill and Ewell. Perceiving during the afternoon that the enemy, approaching from the direction of Warrenton, was moving down the Warrenton turnpike towards Alexandria, thus exposing his left flank, General Jackson advanced to attack.[13] After a fierce and sanguinary conflict which continued until about 9 P.M., the enemy slowly fell back leaving us in possession of the field; the loss on both sides was heavy, and among our wounded were Major General Ewell and Brigadier General Taliaferro, the former severely.

[12] From this position Jackson could communicate with Lee and Longstreet by way of Hopewell Gap and if need be retire through Aldie or Snickers Gap into the Valley.

[13] This was King's division, which marched down the road in front of Jackson, unaware of the Confederate position. Jackson's attack informed Pope where his enemy was and started the battle.

On the morning of the 29th the enemy had taken a position to interpose his army between General Jackson and Alexandria, and about 10 A.M. opened with artillery upon the right of Jackson's line. The troops of the latter were disposed in rear of Groveton along the unfinished branch of the Manassas Gap Railroad and extended from a point a short distance west of the turnpike towards Sudley Mills. The Federal Army was evidently concentrating upon General Jackson with the design of overwhelming him before the arrival of General Longstreet.

Meanwhile General Longstreet had after the departure of General Jackson been engaged in making demonstrations along the Rappahannock, but on the morning of the 26th it became evident that the enemy was beginning to move away from the river, so General Lee decided that Longstreet should follow Jackson at once. General R. H. Anderson's division was left at Waterloo to continue to attract the attention of the enemy,[14] and General Longstreet moved up to Hinson's Mill, and crossing the river reached Orleans that night. The Federal cavalry patrols were active, and early on the next morning when riding ahead of the column, General Lee narrowly escaped capture at Salem by a body of the enemy's cavalry which were beaten off by his staff and couriers.[15] Near that place General Lee received the first report bringing the welcome news of Jackson's success at Bristoe and Manassas.

[14] This appears to have had the desired effect, for Pope writes of the next day, August 27: "Heavy forces of the enemy still confronted us at Waterloo Bridge." Anderson's division numbered about 6000 men.

[15] It was Buford's cavalry brigade which harassed Longstreet on his march, and a patrol from this brigade that nearly captured General Lee and his staff.

On the 27th the column halted for the night between Salem and Whiteplains. Most of the cavalry was with Jackson, and Longstreet's movements were delayed by the want of sufficient cavalry to enable him to ascertain the meaning of certain movements of the enemy from the direction of Warrenton, which appeared to threaten his right flank.[16]

The following day General Longstreet reached Thoroughfare Gap, a narrow and difficult pass through the Bull Run Mountains. The mountains rise for several hundred feet on either side of the pass, through which flows a stream over a rough and stony bottom. The enemy was found to be holding the eastern extremity of the pass in large force and directed heavy artillery fire upon the road leading through it and upon the sides of the mountain. General G. R. Jones' division attempted to force its way through the gap and dislodge the enemy's sharpshooters from the trees and rocks on either side. But the ground afforded no opportunity for the employment of artillery in support of General Jones, so General Lee decided to send General Hood with two brigades and General Wilcox with three to turn the enemy's right. The former moved by a narrow path over the mountain on the north side of the gorge, and the latter further to the north to Hopewell Gap. Before these troops reached their destination the enemy advanced and attacked Jones' left, but being vigorously repulsed he withdrew to his position at the eastern end

---

[16] In comparing the progress of Jackson and Longstreet over the same ground, it must be remembered that when Longstreet marched the Federal Commander was aware of the movement round his right and took steps to investigate it.

of the pass, from which he kept up a heavy artillery fire until dark, when the progress of Good and Wilcox on his flank caused him to retire. That night Generals Jones and Wilcox bivouacked east of the mountain.[17]

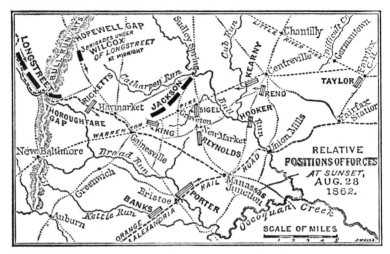

On the morning of the 29th Longstreet's whole command resumed its march. The sound of cannon was soon heard from the direction of Groveton, announcing that Jackson was already engaged. Longstreet's troops began to enter Warrenton turnpike near Gainesville about 9 A.M. and moving towards Groveton, the head of his column came upon the field in rear of the enemy's left, which had already opened with artillery upon Jackson's right. Longstreet immediately placed some of his batteries in position, but before he could complete his preparations for attack the enemy withdrew, not without suffering some loss from our artil-

[17] The force which opposed Longstreet at Thoroughfare Gap on the 28th consisted of Rickett's division.

lery. Longstreet then took position on the right of Jackson, Hood's two brigades supported by Evans being deployed across the turnpike and at right angles to the road. The line was continued to the right by a force under General Kemper, which was supported by Wilcox's three brigades. D. R. Jones' division formed the extreme right of the infantry, resting on the Manassas Gap Railroad. The cavalry guarded our right and left flanks, that on the right being under General Stuart in person. General Lee established his headquarters on a small hill just south of the Warrenton Pike behind Hood's troops. After the arrival of Longstreet the enemy changed his position and began to concentrate opposite Jackson's left, opening a brisk artillery fire which was responded to with effect by some of A. P. Hill's batteries. Colonel Walton, who commanded the Washington artillery of Longstreet's corps, placed a part of his artillery in a commanding position between the lines of Jackson and Longstreet by order of the latter, and engaged the enemy vigorously for several hours.

Soon after this artillery came into action Stuart reported the approach of a large force from the direction of Bristoe threatening Longstreet's right under D. R. Jones.[18] The brigades under General Wilcox were therefore sent to reinforce Jones, but no serious attack was made, and after firing a few shots the enemy withdrew. While this demonstration was being made on our right the enemy advanced to assail the left of Jackson's position occupied by the division of A. P. Hill; the attack

[18] This was the first arrival of Porter's corps. Pope maintained that Porter had come up before Longstreet was in position. But Porter was quite right in his opinion that he had a superior force in front of him.

was received by Hill's troops with their accustomed
steadiness, and the battle raged with great fury; the
enemy was repeatedly repulsed, but again pressed on
to the attack with fresh troops. Once he succeeded in
penetrating the interval between Gregg's brigade on
the left and that of Thomas, but was quickly driven
back with great slaughter by the 14th South Carolina
Regiment held in reserve, and the 49th Georgia of
Thomas's brigade. The contest was close and obstinate
the combatants sometimes delivering their fire at ten
paces. In the midst of the fierce struggle some of the
troops of General Starke, having exhausted their
ammunition, supplied the want of it by the use of stones,
taken from the railroad cut, which they hurled at the
enemy.

Gregg's brigade which was most exposed was reinforced by Hayes' brigade under Colonel Forno. All of
Forno's field officers except two being killed or wounded,
he was relieved after several hours of severe fighting by
Early's brigade and the 8th Louisiana Regiment.
Early drove the enemy back with heavy loss, and pursued about 200 yards beyond the line of battle when he
was recalled to the position on the unfinished railroad.
Here Thomas, Pender and Archer firmly held their
ground against every attack. While the battle was
raging on Jackson's left Longstreet ordered Hood and
Evans to advance, but before the order could be obeyed
Hood himself was attacked and his command became
at once warmly engaged.[19] Wilcox was recalled from

[19] This attack was made by Porter's corps, which had been moved by
Pope to the right to aid the attack on Jackson. Pope was apparently
still unaware that Longstreet's whole corps was in position on his left.

the right and ordered to advance on Hood's left, and one of Kemper's brigades under Colonel Hunton moved forward on his right. The enemy was repulsed by Hood after a severe contest and fell back closely followed by our troops. The battle continued until 9 P.M., the enemy retreating until he reached a strong position which he held with a large force. Darkness put an end to the engagement and our troops retained their advanced position until early next morning when they were withdrawn to their original line.[20]

On the morning of the 30th the enemy again advanced and skirmishing began along the line; the troops of Longstreet and Jackson maintained their positions of the previous day. During the forenoon General R. H. Anderson's division came up from Waterloo by the Warrenton turnpike and was held in reserve. The batteries of Colonel S. D. Lee took the position occupied the day before by Colonel Walton with the Washington artillery and engaged the enemy's artillery until noon, when firing ceased and all was quiet for several hours. About 3 P.M. the enemy, having massed his troops in front of General Jackson, advanced against his position with a strong force; his front line pushed forward until it was engaged at close quarters by Jackson's troops, when his progress was checked and a fierce and bloody struggle ensued. A second and a third line moved up to support the first, but in doing so the Federal troops came within easy range of a position a little in advance of Longstreet's left, whence they were exposed to enfilading fire. General Longstreet at once ordered up two batteries

---

[20] This withdrawal Pope took to be the beginning of a Confederate retreat.

and two others were thrown forward by Colonel S. D.
Lee.   Under their well directed and destructive fire the
supporting lines assailing Jackson's left were broken
and driven back in confusion.

Their repeated efforts to rally were unavailing, and
Jackson's troops being thus relieved from the pressure
of overwhelming numbers began to press steadily forward, driving the enemy before them.   He retreated
in confusion suffering severely from our artillery, which
advanced as he retired.   General Lee thereupon ordered a general advance and Longstreet, anticipating
this order, now threw his whole command against the
Federal centre and left.   Hood's two brigades, closely followed by Evans, led the attack; R. H. Anderson's division came up from reserve to the support of Hood, while
two of the three brigades under Wilcox moved forward
on Hood's left, and Kemper's troops on his right.   D. R.
Jones advanced on the extreme right and the whole line
swept steadily on driving the enemy with great carnage
from each successive position until 10 P.M., when darkness put an end to the pursuit.   During the latter part
of the engagement General Wilcox was ordered to take
his own brigade to the right, where the resistance
of the enemy was most obstinate, and he rendered
efficient assistance to the troops engaged in that part
of the line.   His other two brigades maintained their
positions in line and acted with General Jackson's
command.

The obscurity of the night rendered it necessary to
suspend operations until morning, when the cavalry
being pushed forward discovered that the enemy had
escaped to the strong position of Centreville about

JAMES LONGSTREET

four miles beyond Bull Run. A heavy rain which fell
during the night threatened to make Bull Run impassable and impeded our movements. Longstreet remained on the battlefield to engage the attention of the
enemy and cover the burial of the dead and the removal
of the wounded, while Jackson on the 31st proceeded
by way of Sudley Ford to the Little River Turnpike to
turn the enemy's right and intercept his retreat to
Washington. Jackson's progress was retarded by the
inclemency of the weather and the fatigue of his
troops who besides their arduous marching had fought
three severe engagements in as many days. He reached
Little River Turnpike in the evening, and the next
day, September 1st, advanced by that road towards
Fairfax Court House. The enemy in the meantime
was falling back rapidly towards Washington and had
thrown out a strong force towards Germantown on the
Little River Turnpike to cover his line of retreat from
Centreville.

Jackson's column encountered the enemy at Ox Hill
near Germantown about 5 P.M. when a line of battle
was at once formed and two brigades of A. P. Hill's
division, those of Branch and Field under Colonel
Brockenbrough, were thrown forward to ascertain the
strength and position of the enemy. A cold and drench-
ing rainstorm drove in the faces of our troops as they
advanced and gallantly engaged the enemy ; they were
subsequently supported by the brigades of Gregg,
Thomas, and Pender also of Hill's division which with
part of Ewell's became engaged. The conflict was ob-
stinately maintained by the enemy until dark, when he
retreated having lost two general officers, one of whom,

Major General Kearny, was left dead on the field.[21] Longstreet's command arrived after the battle was over, and the next day it was found that the enemy had conducted his retreat so rapidly that the attempt to intercept him was abandoned. . The proximity of the fortifications around Alexandria and Washington rendered further pursuit useless, and our army rested during September 2nd near Chantilly, the enemy being followed only by the cavalry, who continued to harass him until he reached the shelter of his Washington entrenchments south of the Potomac.

[21] General Kearny rode into the Confederate ranks in the dark. Lee sent his body back the next day with a note to General Pope, saying: "The body of General Philip Kearny was brought from the field last night, and he was reported dead. I send it forward under flag of truce, thinking the possession of his remains may be a consolation to his family."

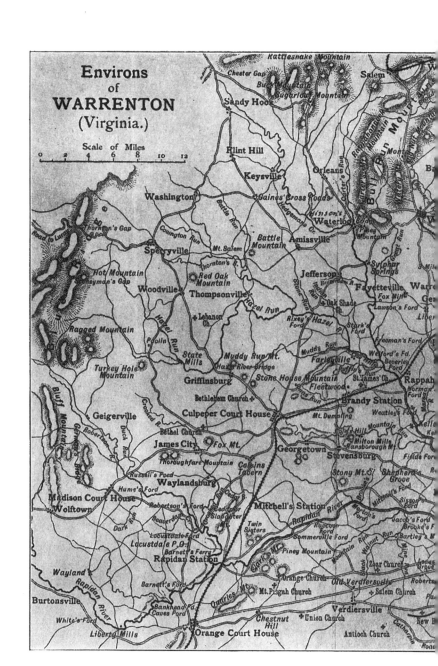

Environs
of
WARRENTON
(Virginia.)

Scale of Miles

0   2   4   6   8   10   12

Rattlesnake Mountain

Chester Gap

Buck Mountain

Sugarloaf Mountain

Salem

Sandy Hook

Flint Hill

Keysville

Orleans

Washington

Battle Run

Gaines Cross Roads

Waterloo

Covington Run

Sperryville

Mt. Salem

Battle Mountain

Amissville

Thornton's R.

Sulphur Springs

Jefferson

Fayetteville

Fox Mills

Warre

Thornton's Gap

Red Oak Mountain

Hot Mountain

Honeyman's Gap

Woodville

Thompsonville

Hazel Run

Oak Shade

Lawson's Ford

Lebanon Ch.

Rixey's Ford

Hazel

Stark's Ford

Freeman's Ford

Ragged Mountain

Pcoln

Hazel Run

Muddy Run

Welford's Fd.

Beverley Ford

Turkey Hole Mountain

State Mills

Muddy Run/Mt.

Hazel River Bridge

Farleyville

Stone House Mountain

Fleetwood

Ruffin

St. James' Ch.

Rappah

Griffinsburg

Bethlehem Church

Bull Run

Brandy Station

Weatley's F.

Bluff Mountain

Geigerville

Robertson

Duck Run

Culpeper Court House

Mt. Dumpling

Fields Mt.

Mountain

Kelle

Ke

Robertson

Bethel Church

James City

Fox Mt.

Milton Mills

Ransborough Mt.

Thoroughfare Mountain

Colvins Tavern

Georgetown

Stevensburg

Shepherd's Grove

Stony Mt.

Russell's Ford

Waylandsburg

Hums's Ford

Robertson's Ford

Beauer

Madison Court House

Wolftown

Dark Run

Locustdale Ford

Stoddor

Slaughter

Mitchell's Station

Rapidan

River

Morton's

Ruscue Ford

Sommerville Ford

Jacob's Ford

Brooke's F

Bartley's M

Twin Sisters

Locustdale P.O.

Barnett's Ferry

Rapidan Station

Piney Mountain

Zoar Church

Roberts

Wayland

Rapidan River

Barnett's Ford

Quarles

Mt. Pisgah Church

Orange Church

Old Verdiersville

Salem Church

Burtonsville

White's Ford

Bankhead Fd.

Caves Ford

Chestnut Hill

Union Church

Verdiersville

New R

Liberty Mills

Orange Court House

Antioch Church

Road

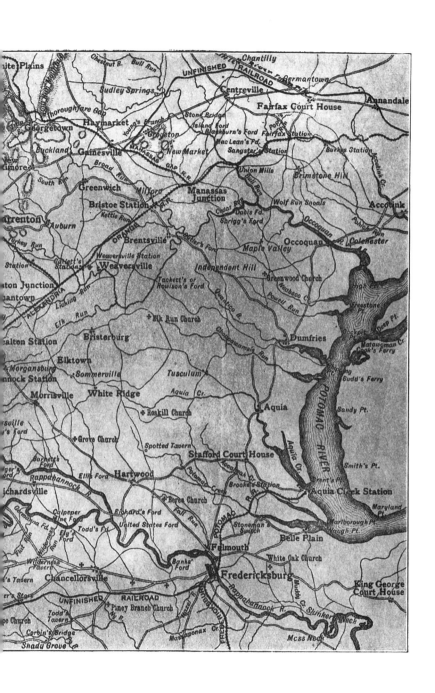

VII

THE MARYLAND CAMPAIGN

The editor must now reappear for a moment to play the part of Chorus. With the last chapter, the papers which Colonel Marshall had put together for his projected Life of Lee come to an end. He had begun them, as is the practice of biographers, with an account of the Lee family. This adds nothing to what has since been told, and I have put it aside. He continued with a statement of the Southern case in the controversies which provoked the war, but since he wrote many other pens have been busy with the same subject, and the controversies either are happily dead or have taken in the politics of the day an entirely new turn. He went on to describe, in the papers which I have put together to form the first chapters, the events of the war from the point of view of his chief. When he wrote, little, if any, intelligent criticism of Lee's conduct of the war had appeared, and therefore, while the information which he gives us of Lee's ideas and intentions does answer very effectually many of the critics, there is in his story of the events up to the second battle of Manassas no conscious reply to attack or comment.

When, however, Colonel Marshall had put aside his beginnings of a biography and was awaiting the opportunity and the means to check his statements, one of the most important of the contemporary accounts of the war appeared. From September 1861 two of the Orléans Princes, the Duc de Chartres and the Comte de Paris, were attached to McClellan's staff as aides-de-camp. Their uncle, the Prince de Joinville, accompanied them as mentor, but held no military position. After the war the Comte de Paris began work upon a "History of the Civil War in America." And in order to obtain information from the Confederate side he entered into a correspondence with Marshall, in the course of which he questioned the wisdom of Lee's first invasion of Maryland. In his answer, written in 1877, Marshall then appears for the first time as the defender of his chief against a definite criticism. Here is his reply:

"After the battle of the second Manassas, when the Federal Army had been driven into the entrenchments round Washington, the Confederate Army near Fairfax Court House was nearly 150 miles from its base,[1] and much further than that from the actual source of its supplies. The country around it within a compass of fifty miles had been stripped by both sides, and was wholly incapable of supporting an army. What was General Lee to do? His army could not be maintained where it was, and even if it could have remained there, as it was not possible to make a direct attack upon Washington, there was nothing to prevent the enemy as soon as he should recover from the recent disasters from repeating General McClellan's plan and sending such a force by water to Richmond as must have taken General Lee back immediately to the place from which he set out on his Northern campaign.

[1] Lee's line of communication at this time ran via Gordonsville to Richmond.

"If he had returned to the line of the Rapidan after the second battle of Manassas, so as to place himself within reach of his base at Richmond, or if he had taken up the position that he assumed later in the season at Fredericksburg, his only real alternative to an advance, what would have been the immediate result? Such action on his part would have been taken as an admission that he was really unable to put Washington in any serious danger, or to cross the Potomac river, and had no policy but to await such attacks as the Federals might make. This would have relieved the Government of Mr. Lincoln of its fears for the safety of Washington, and would have dispelled the belief that it was necessary to draw troops from all parts of the country for its defence, as completely as if General Lee had notified Mr. Lincoln that he need give himself no concern about the safety of his capital, or the security of the Federal frontier States.

"Mr. Lincoln could not have avoided one of two inferences, either that General Lee had been too much weakened to follow up his advantages, or that he considered any attempt against Washington as impracticable; and in either case it would have been too plain to escape the attention of the least observant that to cause General Lee to retreat it was only necessary to follow General McClellan's example when General Johnston retreated from before Washington in the spring, and transport their army by water to the vicinity of Richmond, as they had transported that army as soon as the retreat of General Johnston relieved them from all anxiety as to the safety of the city.

"I must again say that General Lee's policy was not

to capture any portion of Federal territory, but to protract the war by breaking up the enemy's campaigns
and so bringing about the pecuniary exhaustion of the
North.   At the same time he desired to increase the
power of resistance of the South by keeping the enemy
out of the Confederate territory.   If he had retired
after the second Manassas, none of these results would
have been obtained from the campaign of 1862.   That
campaign would have opened with the Federal Army
around Richmond ; bloody and successful battles would
have been fought; the Confederates by putting forth
their whole strength would have succeeded in raising
the siege of Richmond for a time, and in forcing the
enemy back to the Potomac River.   Then, had General
Lee been unable for any reason to follow up the advantage of the victory he had gained, the campaign would
have ended with the Federal Army once more besieging Richmond and the Confederate Army once more
defending it.

"There can be no doubt as to which side would have
appeared to have the substantial advantages of a campaign ending in the way supposed.   The great fact
would have remained that all the efforts of the Confederates had failed to loosen the hold the enemy had
upon Richmond, the key to the possession of the great
State of Virginia.   What effect would such a result
have had on the credit of the North?   The credit of
the Federal Government did not depend upon its actual
resources more than it depended upon moral causes,
that is, upon the prospect of ultimate success and
especially upon the prospect of speedy success.

"It can scarcely be doubted that had the second

battle of Manassas been followed by the retirement of General Lee's army to the line of the Rapidan, or that of the lower Rappahannock, the Northern people would have seen in such a result solid reasons for expecting ultimate and not very remote success, and so far as the pecuniary conditions of Mr. Lincoln's government depended upon popular belief that the war would end soon and successfully, that belief must have received substantial encouragement.

"It may be argued firstly: that General Lee could have remained near enough to Washington and the Potomac to have kept up the apprehension of the Lincoln government; or secondly: that the enemy would not, after General McClellan's failure, have gone again to Richmond by water, if General Lee had fallen back after the second battle of Manassas, but would have followed and given him an opportunity to fight at a distance from Richmond; or thirdly: that even had the enemy gone to Richmond it would have been better for General Lee to have thrown his army around the Confederate capital and to have engaged the enemy there.

"The first argument was answered at the time by the actual want of supplies on the spot and by the difficulty of drawing further supplies from Richmond, which made it actually necessary for the Confederate Army to leave the battle field and to move into Loudoun County two days after the second battle of Manassas was over, and even there it could not have remained for more than a short time.

"As to the second argument, it would have been rash in the extreme to have assumed that the enemy would forego so great and obvious an advantage as he possessed in his easy access to Richmond by water. I may say that after we returned to Virginia one of General Lee's first actions was to send General Stuart with the cavalry across the Potomac expressly to ascertain if any preparations were being made to move General McClellan's army again by sea to Richmond,[2] and later in the year when we were on the Rappahannock General Lee was constantly watching for any indication of such a movement.

"Thirdly: if there was to be a battle in Virginia Richmond was the last place General Lee would have selected for that battle, as the absolute necessity of guarding the communications by which the city was supplied would have left the army of the Confederacy engaged in its defence with the minimum force for active operations against the enemy.

"It follows therefore that as General Lee could not remain in Virginia near enough to Washington to detain the enemy's army there, and could not retire without the loss of the moral effect of a successful campaign, and without encouraging the enemy to return to his former position near Richmond, or at least without affording him such an opportunity to return as it cannot be supposed that the enemy would have neglected, General Lee had nothing left to do after the battle except to enter Maryland.

"It is also just, in deciding upon the merits of General Lee's plan, which led to the invasion of Maryland, to distinguish between those consequences that may be

[2] The reference is to Stuart's famous raid round McClellan's army, which began on October 8, 1862.

fairly traced to the nature of the campaign itself, and those consequences that are attributable to the manner of its execution in detail. This involves a brief examination of the facts.

"About September 2nd the last of the available troops from Richmond, the divisions of McLaws and D. H. Hill, joined the army, and on September 4th it began to march towards the Potomac, which was crossed between the 4th and 7th at the fords near Leesburg, and on September 8th assembled near Frederick. While the Confederate army was concentrated at that place, the Federal army, to the command of which General McClellan had been restored after the second battle of Manassas, advanced cautiously from Washington. Harper's Ferry with its strong Federal garrison was so situated as to endanger the road by which supplies and reinforcements could be drawn from Virginia, and to contribute a serious danger to our safety in case of disaster in Maryland, or even if we should retreat across the Potomac without a battle.

"It became necessary therefore to reduce Harper's Ferry, and as that would require a large force, if the place was to be taken without delay, which was absolutely necessary, General Lee detached at Frederick the greater part of his army under General Jackson for that purpose.

"The rest of his army was too small to remain at Frederick in the presence of the larger force under General McClellan, so General Lee withdrew to the west side of the Blue Ridge to await the results of General Jackson's movement against Harper's Ferry. Leaving part of his army under D. H. Hill at the head of Pleasant Valley to intercept any part of the garrison of Harper's Ferry that might attempt to escape by that route, General Lee with the rest of his force under General Longstreet proceeded to Hagerstown in order to stop the removal of supplies from Maryland. The whole army was to reunite at Sharpsburg or Hagerstown as soon as General Jackson should have reduced Harper's Ferry. General Stuart with the cavalry was left east of the mountains of the Blue Ridge to observe the movements of General McClellan, who for a few days after the army left Frederick was reported as stationary or advancing very slowly.

"Thus it will be seen that General Lee's plan of operations did not contemplate a general engagement unless General McClellan should cross the Blue Ridge west of Frederick and attack us."

The editor must again break in here in support of Colonel Marshall's arguments. Their value of course depends upon how far they were in Lee's mind at the time when he made the decision to cross the Potomac. Fortunately we have very satisfactory evidence as to this; for on September 3, 1862, Lee wrote this letter to Davis:

His Excellency President Davis
MR. PRESIDENT,

The present seems to be the most propitious time since the commencement of the war for the Confederate army to enter Maryland. The two grand armies of the United States that have been operating in Virginia, though now united, are much weakened and demoralized. Their new levies, of which I understand 60,000 men have been posted in Wash-

ington, are not yet organized, and will take some time to
prepare for the field. If it is ever desired to give material
aid to Maryland and afford her an opportunity of throwing
off the oppression to which she is now subject, this would
seem the most favourable.

After the enemy had disappeared from the vicinity of
Fairfax Court House and taken the road to Alexandria and
Washington, I did not think it would be advantageous to
follow him further. I had no intentions of attacking him
in his fortifications, and am not prepared to invest them.
If I possessed the necessary munitions I should be unable
to provide provisions for the troops. I therefore determined, while threatening the approaches to Washington, to
draw the troops into Loudoun, where forage and some provisions can be obtained, menace their possession of the
Shenandoah Valley, and, if found practicable, to cross into
Maryland. The purpose, if discovered, will have the effect
of carrying the enemy north of the Potomac, and if prevented will not result in much evil.

The army is not properly equipped for an invasion of an
enemy's territory. It lacks much of the material of war,
is feeble in transportation, the animals being much reduced,
and the men are poorly provided with clothes, and in thousands of instances are destitute of shoes. Still, we cannot
afford to be idle, and, though weaker than our opponents in
men and military equipments, must endeavour to harass
them if we cannot destroy them. I am aware that the
movement is attended with much risk, yet I do not consider
success impossible, and shall endeavour to guard it from
loss. As long as the army of the enemy are employed on
this frontier I have no fears for the safety of Richmond, yet
I earnestly recommend that advantage be taken of this
period of comparative safety to place its defence, both by
land and water, in the most perfect condition. A respect-

able force can be collected to defend its approaches by land, and the steamer Richmond, I hope, is now ready to clear the river of hostile vessels.[3]

The main points that Lee makes in this letter are that the object of the manœuvre is first to carry "the enemy north of the Potomac," and secondly to defend Richmond by keeping him there. His anxieties are for the supplies of his army and that every effort should be made to improve the defense of Richmond. Clearly, — as Marshall suggests, — General Lee was apprehensive of another expedition by sea against the Confederate capital. The next day, September 4, he wrote again to the President:

Since my last communication to you, with reference to the movements which I propose to make with this army, I am more fully persuaded of the benefit that will result from an expedition into Maryland, and I shall proceed to make the movement at once unless you signify your disapprobation. The only two subjects that give me any uneasiness are my supplies of ammunition and subsistence. Of the former I have enough for present use, and must await results before deciding to what point I will have additional supplies sent. Of subsistence, I am taking measures to obtain all that this region can afford; but to be able to obtain supplies to advantage in Maryland I think it important to have the services of some one known to and acquainted with the resources of the country. I wish, therefore, that if ex-Governor Lowe can make it convenient he will come to me at once, as I have already requested by telegram. As I contemplate entering a part of the state with which Governor Lowe is well acquainted, I think he could be of much service to me in many ways. Should the results of the expedition justify it, I propose to enter Pennsylvania, unless you should deem it inadvisable upon political or other grounds.

As to the movements of the enemy, my latest intelligence shows that the army of Pope is concentrating around Alexandria and Washington in their fortifications. Citizens of this country report that Winchester has been evacuated, which is confirmed by the Baltimore *Sun* of this morning, containing extracts from the Washington *Star* of yesterday. This will still further relieve our country and, I think, leaves the Valley entirely free. They will concentrate behind the Potomac.[4]

Here again we see that Lee's predominating anxiety was for the supplies of his army, and these two letters show that Colonel Marshall is quite right in insisting that the supply problem was the decisive factor in Lee's mind, for even Loudoun County could only furnish forage and provisions for a short period. The army could not remain where it was; it must either go forward or go back. If it went back it must go back a long way, for during the advance to the second Manassas the bridges over the Rapidan and the Rappahannock had been burned,[5] and until those bridges were restored Lee could not bring supplies forward in sufficient quantities for his army. Therefore, if he went back he would, as Colonel Marshall says, have to go behind the Rapidan, and sacrifice all the results of his victory. The critics, of whom the Comte de Paris

[4] *O. R.*, vol. XIX, part II, p. 591.
[5] How much this weighed with Lee is shown by his letter of September 5 to Davis: "I deem it important as soon as the bridge over the Rapidan shall be completed that over the Rappahannock should be constructed as soon as possible." — *O. R.*, vol. XIX, part II, p. 593.

was one of the first but by no means the last, have most of them overlooked this question of supplies. Lee's dispatch dated March 6, 1863, — which Marshall, as usual, drafted, — says:

"The armies of General McClellan and Pope had now been brought back to the point from which they set out on the campaigns of the spring and summer. The objects of those campaigns had been frustrated, and the designs of the enemy on the coast of North Carolina and in western Virginia thwarted by the withdrawal of the main body of his forces from those regions. Northeastern Virginia was freed from the presence of Federal soldiers up to the entrenchments of Washington, and soon after the arrival of the army at Leesburg information was received that the troops which had occupied Winchester had retired to Harper's Ferry and Martinsburg. The war was thus transferred from the interior to the frontier, and the supplies of rich and productive districts made accessible to our army.

"To prolong a state of affairs in every way desirable, and not to permit the season for active operations to pass without endeavouring to inflict further injury upon the enemy, the best course appeared to be the transfer of the army to Maryland. Although not properly equipped for invasion, lacking much of the material of war, and feeble in transportation, the troops poorly provided with clothing, and thousands of them destitute of shoes, it was believed to be strong enough to detain the enemy from the northern frontier until the approach of winter should render his advance into Virginia difficult, if not impossible. The conditions of Maryland encouraged the belief that the presence of our army, however inferior to that of the enemy, would induce the Washington Government to retain all its available force to provide against contingencies which its course towards the people of that state gave it reason to apprehend. At the same time it was hoped that military success might afford us an opportunity to aid the citizens of Maryland in any efforts they might be disposed to make to recover their liberties. The difficulties that surrounded them were fully appreciated, and we expected to derive more assistance in the attainment of our object from the just fears of the Washington Government, than from active demonstration on the part of the people, unless success should enable us to give them assurance of continued protection.

"Influenced by these considerations, the army was put in motion, D. H. Hill's division, which had joined us on the 2nd, being in advance, and between September 4th and 7th crossed the Potomac at the fords near Leesburg, and encamped in the vicinity of Fredericktown.

"It was decided to cross the Potomac east of the Blue Ridge in order, by threatening Washington and Baltimore, to cause the enemy to withdraw from the south bank, where his presence endangered our communications and the safety of those engaged in removing our wounded and the captured·property from the late battle fields. Having accomplished this result, it was proposed to move the army into western Maryland, establish our communications with Richmond through the Shenandoah Valley, and by threatening Pennsylvania induce the enemy to follow, and thus draw him from his base of supplies."

On this dispatch Palfrey makes this comment:

It may be remarked, in relation to this allegation of incomplete equipment, that it seems like an excuse for failure, made after the failure had occurred, and antedated, for Lee asserts in the same report that in the series of engagements on the plains of Manassas, which had taken place just before, there had been captured more than 9000 prisoners, wounded and unwounded, thirty pieces of artillery, upwards of twenty thousand stand of small arms, and a large amount of stores, besides those taken by General Jackson at Manassas Junction.   Jackson says that he captured there eight guns, with seventy-two horses, equipments and ammunition complete, "immense supplies" of commissary and quarter-master stores, etc.   With these additions to his supplies, it would seem as if the little army with which Lee says he fought the battles of the Maryland campaign might have been fairly well equipped, especially when we remember how far from scrupulous the Confederates were in exchanging their shoes and clothing for the better shoes and clothing of their prisoners.[6]

Lee's letter of September 3, written the day before his army began to march, is a sufficient answer to the suggestion that the supply difficulty was "an excuse for failure after the failure had occurred." Another critic, Longstreet, who should have known the facts, says: "The great mistake of the campaign was the division of Lee's army" (for the attack on Harper's Ferry).   "If General Lee had kept his forces together, he would not have suffered defeat. . . . The next year when on our way to Gettysburg, there was the

[6] Palfrey: *The Antietam and Fredericksburg*, p. 16.

same situation of affairs at Harper's Ferry, but we let it alone." [7]

It is true that in June 1863, when Lee made his second invasion of Northern territory, there was a Federal garrison at Harper's Ferry, as there was in September 1862, but in that respect only was the situation of affairs the same.   In 1863 Lee was able to plan deliberately his march into Pennsylvania, the railway bridges over the Rapidan and the Rappahannock were intact, and he could and did arrange for the due forwarding of supplies.   He was therefore able to ignore the garrison of Harper's Ferry, for the détour necessary, if that place was to be avoided, would not have unduly lengthened the march of his wagons from the railway.   But in 1862 his army was living from day to day on what the country could produce, a mischance might mean starvation, owing to the broken railway bridges his wagons had, by the shortest route, a dangerously long march, and he could not take risks.   He had, as he told Davis in his letter of September 4, expected that the evacuation of Winchester would be followed by that of Harper's Ferry, which would "leave the valley entirely free." When this did not happen, he had no choice but to reduce Harper's Ferry as quickly as possible.

I have dwelt on these points at some length to show that Colonel Marshall has honestly and fairly set down the reasons which prevailed with Lee at the time when he made his decisions, and has been remarkably successful in avoiding the wisdom of after knowledge.   It is this which gives his papers their peculiar value.   If I have here set down proof of this characteristic, I may

[7] *Battles and Leaders*, vol. II, p. 673.

say that I have throughout been at pains to test the
actuality of his statements, and have never found him
at fault.

He shall now return to his story.

General Jackson marched for Harper's Ferry on September 10th and it was confidently expected that the
place would be captured on the 13th. Unfortunately,
there was some delay owing to the difficulty of getting
the troops in position on the mountains overlooking
Harper's Ferry, and still more unfortunately by an
accident, as yet unexplained, a copy of the general
order directing the movement of the whole army and
showing the exact distribution of every part of it fell
into the hands of General McClellan soon after General
Lee left Frederick, and before General Jackson had
succeeded in the reduction of Harper's Ferry.[8]

To the surprise of General Lee and contrary to the
previous reports of General McClellan's movements
from Washington, the Federal army began to advance
rapidly and threatened the passes of the Blue Ridge at
Boonsboro' and at Crampton's Gap.

[8] Since Colonel Marshall wrote this, the story of the "Lost Order"
No. 191, of September 9, has become as fully known as it is ever likely
to be. The order prescribed the movements of the army for the capture
of Harper's Ferry. Lee's staff wrote out three copies of this order: one
for Longstreet, who after he had read it chewed it up; one for Jackson,
who pinned it to the inside of his coat; and the third for D. H. Hill, who,
having recently come up from Richmond, was not definitely attached
either to Longstreet or to Jackson. Jackson assumed that Hill was under
his command, and wrote out for him a copy of the order, which Hill duly
received and produced after the war. The copy sent for Hill from Headquarters was never delivered to him, and was presumably dropped by an
orderly. It was found in Frederick about noon on September 13, wrapped
round three cigars, and was in McClellan's hands that evening.

The movements of these troops endangered that part of General Jackson's army engaged in the capture of Harper's Ferry which had been ordered to ascend Maryland Heights, overlooking Harper's Ferry from the north side of the Potomac River and commanding that place, and would have tended to separate the troops under General Jackson's command from those under D. H. Hill and Longstreet.

General D. H. Hill was accordingly ordered to hold the passes of the mountain, aided by General Stuart, who had fallen back before the advance of General McClellan; and Longstreet hastened from Hagerstown to the assistance of General Hill. The consequence was that the command of Longstreet, reduced by the detachment of a large force, that of A. P. Hill, to the assistance of Jackson in the attack on Harper's Ferry, was forced to sustain the attack of General McClellan's army at South Mountain and Crampton's Gap, and outnumbered as they were, they only succeeded in detaining the enemy until night, when they retreated to Sharpsburg, so as to effect more easily a junction with the force under Jackson.

The time gained by the resistance at Boonsboro' Gap, generally known as South Mountain, enabled General Jackson to accomplish his object in the capture of Harper's Ferry, which surrendered to him on September 15th, but the losses of D. H. Hill and Longstreet were severe, and Jackson's command was obliged to make a forced march to reach the appointed rendezvous at Sharpsburg, a large part of his command, the troops of McLaws and A. P. Hill, not arriving on the field until the battle of September 17th had been raging for some hours. It was under these conditions that General Lee's army fought at Sharpsburg. Instead of being united and fresh as it would have been had General McClellan continued his slow rate of advance for twenty-four hours longer, as there is reason to believe he would have done but for the loss of the order above mentioned, it had to engage the enemy at great disadvantage. The troops of Longstreet and D. H. Hill went into the battle under the disheartening effects of the disaster at Boonsboro', and considerably reduced in number by that engagement, while those of General Jackson had to make a long march in intensely warm weather and go into battle without opportunity for necessary repose and refreshment.

In considering the Maryland campaign, it is proper to take into account the effect of the accident of the lost order upon the result — a misfortune that was not incident to the plan of campaign, although it had a most important influence upon the result.

General Lee did not become aware of the cause that led to the sudden advance of the Federal army after he had left Frederick until the official report of General McClellan was published some months later, when he learned for the first time that the movement of General McClellan had been caused by the loss of the order.[9]

[9] This very definite statement by Colonel Marshall, that Lee did not know of the loss of the order until the publication of McClellan's dispatch, throws considerable doubt on a story which has obtained very general currency. Allan, in his *Army of Northern Virginia in 1862*, p. 345, says that a citizen of Frederick whose sympathies were with the Confederate cause was accidentally present at McClellan's headquarters during the afternoon of the 13th. He heard expressions of gratification at the find-

The effect of the loss of that order does not show any want of wisdom or prudence in the policy of the invasion of Maryland in 1862. But for that, no battle need have been fought at Sharpsburg, or at South Mountain, or anywhere except at a time and upon terms of General Lee's own selection.

The effect of the Sharpsburg campaign in attaining the great ends for which it was undertaken, that is, the employment of the enemy's army north of the Potomac River, the relief of the people of Virginia of the presence of that army, and the reduction of the enemy's resources by which he was enabled to carry on the war, was greater than could have been accomplished by any other campaign which General Lee might have undertaken without crossing the Potomac River.

The loss of the campaign, so far as the Confederate army was concerned, was not due to any defect in the conception of it, but to an unforeseen accident which

ing of the document, and learned that orders were being given for a vigorous pursuit. Appreciating the importance of this information, he made his way through the Federal lines and brought the information after dark to Stuart, who at once sent it on to Lee. The story is quoted and accepted by Ropes (*The Story of the Civil War*, part II, p. 343), by General Alexander (*The American Civil War*, p. 230), by Rhodes (*History of the Civil War*, p. 169), and many others, including myself (*Robert E. Lee, the Soldier*, p. 149). But it seems incredible that so important a fact should not have been known to Lee's staff. Neither of Colonel Marshall's colleagues, General Long and Colonel Taylor, mentions it; and Longstreet, who gives an account of an interview with Lee on the night of the 13–14th, says nothing about it. Stuart makes no mention of it in his dispatch. If Lee knew nothing of the loss of the order, the promptness with which he met the emergency is the more creditable to him; and some further confirmation of Allan's story is now required before it can be accepted.

might have happened in the conduct of a campaign in
the state of Virginia, or anywhere else.[10]

[10] The one criticism of Lee's conduct of this campaign which Marshall
did not foresee and therefore did not meet, was that Lee might have
recrossed the Potomac on September 16, and so returned to Virginia with
the prestige of the capture of Harper's Ferry, and have avoided the bloody,
and for his purpose useless, battle of Sharpsburg. Had he done this,
he might well have been able to attack the heads of McClellan's columns
to advantage as they were crossing the Potomac, as he did on September
20, when he drove back Porter's advance guard at Boteler's Ford.

It is generally said, in explanation of Lee's action, that having invaded
Maryland he did not want to retreat without a fight, because to do so
would affect the morale of his troops. But as Colonel Marshall says and
as his own statements show, he did not enter Maryland with the object of
fighting a pitched battle, and that explanation does not therefore seem
adequate. It is more probable that he wanted to gain time for the repair
of the railway bridges over the Rapidan and the Rappahannock, as he
feared that if he reëntered Virginia before those bridges were restored he
would have to fall back a long way to obtain supplies. The supply situation of the Confederate army is the key to the whole campaign.

VIII

CHANCELLORSVILLE

As among Colonel Marshall's papers there is nothing dealing specifically with the campaigns of Fredericksburg or Chancellorsville except the drafts of Lee's dispatches, the editor must again intervene. But about Chancellorsville Marshall made a statement which is of peculiar interest, and adds the final piece of evidence which should settle a question long discussed. Among soldiers generally there has been very little doubt as to whom the credit for Chancellorsville is due. Lee was in command and on the spot, the responsibility was his, the blame for failure would have fallen on him, and therefore his must be the reward of victory. But the public is always curious to trace the origin of a great idea. Browning's "Who fished the murex up?" is a question it is eager to have answered; and till to-day there has been some doubt as to whether Lee or Jackson first devised the bold scheme for turning Hooker's right. The doubt arose in Lee's lifetime, and was given some currency by Dabney, the author of the *Life of Stonewall Jackson*. Mrs. Jackson wrote to Lee on the subject, and he replied : —

LEXINGTON, VA. 25th January, 1866

MY DEAR MRS. JACKSON,

Dr. Brown handed me your note of the 9th, when in Richmond on business connected with Washington College. I have delayed replying since my return, hoping to have sufficient time to comply with your request. Last night I received a note from Mrs. Brown, enclosing one from Dr. Dabney, stating that the immediate return of his manuscript was necessary. I have not been able to open it, and when I read it when you were here it was for the pleasure of the narrative, with no view of remark or correction and I took no memoranda of what seemed to be errors. I have not thought of them since, and do not know that I can now recall them; and certainly have no desire that my opinions should be adopted in preference to Dr. Dabney's. . . .

I am misrepresented at the battle of Chancellorsville in proposing an attack in front, the first evening of our arrival. On the contrary I decided against it and stated to General Jackson, we must attack on our left as soon as practicable; and the necessary movements of the troops began immediately. In consequence of a report received about that time from General Fitz Lee describing the position of the Federal army and the roads which he held with his cavalry leading to its rear, General Jackson after some enquiry concerning the roads leading to the Furnace, undertook to throw his command entirely on Hooker's rear, which he accomplished with equal skill and boldness; the rest of the army being moved to the left flank to connect with him as he advanced.

Lee's statement that he told Jackson "We must attack on our left," would appear conclusive, while his "I decided against it" suggests that Jackson or someone else had proposed an attack in front; but to the minds of critics some doubt still remained as to the originator of the enterprise, because of Lee's further statement: "General Jackson after some enquiry concerning the roads leading to the Furnace undertook to throw his command entirely on Hooker's rear."

This would seem to imply that Lee's proposal was no more than a suggestion and that the responsibility for making the decision rested with Jackson.

Accordingly, General Long, in his *Memoirs of R. E. Lee*, reopened the question and produced a reply from Lee to the direct question asked by Dr. Blesdoe, whether the flank movement at Chancellorsville originated with Jackson or with himself. Lee's answer was : — [1]

DR. A. T. BLESDOE, Office *Southern Review*, Baltimore, Maryland,

MY DEAR SIR:

In reply to your enquiry, I must acknowledge that I have not read the article on Chancellorsville in the last number of the *Southern Review*, nor have I read any of the books published on either side since the termination of hostilities. I have as yet felt no desire to revive any recollections of those events, and have been satisfied with the knowledge I possessed of what transpired. I have, however, learned from others that the various authors of the life of Jackson award to him the credit of the success gained by the army of Northern Virginia when he was present, and describe the movements of his corps or command as independent of the general plan of operations and undertaken at his own suggestion and on his own responsibility.

I have the greatest reluctance to do anything that might be considered detracting from his well-deserved fame, for I believe no one was more convinced of his worth or more highly appreciated him than myself; yet your knowledge of military affairs, if you have none of the events themselves, will teach you that this could not have been so. Every movement of an army must be well considered and properly

---

[1] A. L. Long, *Memoirs of R. E. Lee*, p. 253.

ordered, and everyone who knew General Jackson must know that he was too good a soldier to violate this fundamental principle. In the operations round Chancellorsville I overtook General Jackson, who had been placed in command of the advance, as the skirmishers of the approaching armies met, advanced with the troops to the Federal line of defences, and was on the field until their whole army recrossed the Rappahannock. There is no question as to who was responsible for the operations of the Confederates, or to whom any failure would have been charged.

What I have said is for your information. With my best wishes for the success of the *Southern Review* and for your own welfare, in both of which I take a lively interest,

I am with great respect, your friend and servant,

R. E. LEE

This letter throws no light on the origin of the plan, though it makes it clear that Lee took full responsibility for it — a matter on which there was little or no doubt. This letter from Lee then does not help us to a conclusion.

Next comes the evidence that Henderson gives in his *Stonewall Jackson*, and this appears to tilt the balance in favor of the conclusion that Jackson conceived the plan and Lee approved of it. Henderson quotes a letter written to himself by Major Hotchkiss of Jackson's staff : —[2]

About daylight on May 2 [says Major Hotchkiss], General Jackson awakened me, and requested that I would at once go down to Catherine Furnace, which is quite near, and where a Colonel Welford lived, and ascertain if there was any road by which we could secretly pass round Chancellorsville to the

[2] Henderson, *Stonewall Jackson*, vol. II, p. 531.

vicinity of Old Wilderness Tavern. I had a map which our engineers had prepared from actual surveys of the surrounding country, showing all the public roads, but with few details of the intermediate topography. Reaching Mr. Welford's, I aroused him from his bed, and soon learned that he himself had recently opened a road through the woods in that direction for the purpose of hauling cordwood and iron ore to his furnace. This I located on the map, and having asked Mr. Welford if he would act as a guide if it became necessary to march over the road, I returned to headquarters. When I reached those I found Generals Lee and Jackson in conference, each seated on a cracker box, from a pile that had been left there by the Federals the day before.

In response to General Jackson's request for my report, I put another cracker box between the two generals, on which I spread the map, showed them the road I had ascertained, and indicated, as far as I knew it, the position of the Federal army. General Lee then said, "General Jackson, what do you propose to do?" He replied, "Go round here," moving his finger over the road I had located on the map. General Lee said, "What do you propose to make this movement with?" "With my whole corps," was the answer. General Lee then asked, "What will you leave me?" "The divisions of Anderson and McLaws," said Jackson. General Lee after a moment's reflection remarked, "Well, go on," and then, pencil in hand, gave his last instructions. Jackson with an eager smile on his face, from time to time nodded assent, and when the Commander-in-Chief ended with the words, "General Stuart will cover your movements with his cavalry," he rose and saluted, saying, "My troops will move at once, sir."

Lee's question, "General Jackson, what do you propose to do?" and Jackson's answer, "Go round here," appear to indicate that the idea was Jackson's; but there really is nothing in the reported conversation of the two generals incompatible with the supposition that Lee had given Jackson orders for the march round Hooker's flank and that Jackson was awaiting the result of the reconnaissance of his staff to decide on the exact route which he would take.

Major T. M. R. Talcott of Lee's staff was also directed by his general to make a reconnaissance and appears to have returned about the same time as Major Hotchkiss, for he gives a very different account of what is clearly the same conversation. He says: —[3]

My recollections of the night before the battle of Chancellorsville are briefly as follows:

About sunset General Jackson sent word to General Lee (by me) that his advance was checked and that the enemy was in force at Chancellorsville. This brought General Lee to the front, and Jackson met him in the south-east angle of the Chancellorsville and Catherine Forge roads.

General Lee asked General Jackson whether he had ascertained the position and strength of the enemy on our left, to which General Jackson replied by stating the result of an attack made by Stuart's cavalry near Catherine Forge about dusk. The position of the enemy immediately in front was then discussed, and Captain Boswell and myself were sent to make a moonlight reconnaissance, the result of which was reported about 10 P.M., and was not favourable to an attack in front.

At this time Generals Lee and Jackson were together, and Lee, who had a map before him, asked Jackson, "How can we get at these people?" To which Jackson replied, in effect, "You know best. Show me what to do and we will

[3] A. L. Long, *Memoirs of R. E. Lee*, p. 254.

LEE AND JACKSON IN CONFERENCE ON THE NIGHT BEFORE
CHANCELLORSVILLE

try to do it." General Lee looked thoughtfully at the map; then indicated on it and explained the movement he desired General Jackson to make, and closed by saying, "General Stuart will cover your movement with his cavalry." General Jackson listened attentively, and his face lighted up with a smile while General Lee was speaking. Then rising and touching his cap, he said, "My troops will move at four o'clock."

Still it is not possible to form a final conclusion from the varying recollections of two officers of a conversation overheard in circumstances of great stress and anxiety. Each quite naturally and quite honestly gives to his own chief the credit for the plan which brought victory. Mr. Gamaliel Bradford is therefore justified in saying, on the evidence so far produced, that it is "impossible to say where Lee's conception ended and Jackson's began."[4]

Next we come to the evidence of Jackson himself. In his last moments he said: "Our movement was a great success. I think the most successful military movement of my life. But I expect to receive far more credit for it than I deserve. Most men will think that I planned it all from the first, but it was not so. I simply took advantage of circumstances that were presented to me in the providence of God. I feel that His hand led me — let us give Him the glory."[5]

When Jackson said, "Most men will think I planned it all from the first, but it was not so," did he mean that the plan was Lee's, or was this an ascription, by a man of exceptional piety, of all his achievements to his Maker?

[4] Bradford, *Lee the American*, p. 149.
[5] Henderson, *Stonewall Jackson*, vol. II, p. 573.

This is the question which, it seems to me, Colonel Marshall settles conclusively. He says not only that the plan was Lee's, but that Jackson at first demurred to it as being too hazardous. However, on learning that Lee had decided that a frontal attack on Hooker's entrenchments in the Wilderness was out of the question, and that a way had been found round Hooker's flank, Jackson at once accepted Lee's plan and threw himself with enthusiasm into the task of carrying it through. Marshall adds to this statement an interesting comparison between Jackson and Longstreet. He says that whenever Jackson disagreed with a plan of Lee's, he said so; but having stated his objection, he always deferred to Lee's decision and executed his orders with as much zeal and energy as if he had designed the plan himself. Longstreet, on the other hand, when he disagreed with Lee, always maintained that his own plan was best, and to the last moment of action endeavored to get his plan adopted.

We now have Lee's statement to Mrs. Jackson that he had told her husband that he was opposed to a frontal attack and that the attack must be made by the Confederate left; Talcott's statement that Jackson said to Lee, "Show me what to do and I will try to do it"; Jackson's statement: "Most men will think I planned it all from the first but it was not so"; and finally Marshall's statement that "Jackson was at first opposed to the flank movement." This accumulation of evidence is decisive, and should settle forever a matter which has been debated for sixty years.

I cannot leave Chancellorsville without giving in full a speech delivered by Marshall in Baltimore on an anniversary of Lee's death, from which one passage, that describing Lee in the hour of victory, has been freely quoted, but the whole is worthy of preservation : —

"In presenting the Resolutions of the Committee, I cannot refrain from expressing the feelings inspired by the memories that crowd upon my mind, when I reflect that these resolutions are intended to express what General Lee's soldiers feel towards General Lee. The Committee are fully aware of their inability to do justice to the sentiments that inspire the hearts of those for whom they speak. How can we portray in words the gratitude, the pride, the veneration, the anguish, that now fill the hearts of those who shared his victories and his reverses, his triumphs and his defeats? How can we tell the world what we can only feel ourselves? How can we give expression to the crowding memories called forth by the sad event we are met to deplore?

"We recall him as he appeared in the hour of victory — grand, imposing, awe-inspiring, yet self-forgetful and humble. We recall the great scenes of his triumph when we hailed him victor of many a bloody field, and when, above the pæans of victory, we listened with reverence to his voice as he ascribed "all glory to the Lord of Hosts, from whom all glories are." We remember that grand magnanimity that never stooped to pluck from the tree of victory those meaner things that grow nearest the earth, but which, with eyes turned to the stars and hands raised towards heaven, gathered the golden fruits of mercy, pity, and holy charity, that ripen on its topmost boughs, beneath the approving smile of the great God of Battles.

"We remember the sublime self-abnegation of Chancellorsville, when in the midst of his victorious legions, who, with the light of battle still in their faces, hailed him conqueror, he thought only of his great lieutenant lying wounded on the field, and transferred to him all the honour of that illustrious day. I will be pardoned, I am sure, for referring to an incident which affords to my mind a most striking illustration of one of the grandest features of his character.

"On the morning of May 3, 1863, as many of you will remember, the final assault was made upon the Federal lines at Chancellorsville. General Lee accompanied the troops in person, and as they emerged from the fierce combat they had waged in the depths of that tangled wilderness, driving the superior forces of the enemy before them across the open ground, he rode into their midst. The scene is one that can never be effaced from the minds of those who witnessed it. The troops were pressing forward with all the ardour and enthusiasm of combat. The white smoke of musketry fringed the front of the line of battle, while the artillery on the hills in the rear of the infantry shook the earth with its thunder, and filled the air with the wild shrieks of the shells that plunged into the masses of the retreating foe. To add greater horror and sublimity to the scene, Chancellor House and the woods surrounding it were wrapped in flames. In the midst of this awful scene, General Lee, mounted upon that horse which we all remember so well, rode to the front of his advancing battalions. His presence was the signal for one of those outbursts of enthusiasm which none can appreciate who have not witnessed them.

"The fierce soldiers with their faces blackened with the smoke of battle, the wounded crawling with feeble limbs from the fury of the devouring flames, all seemed possessed with a common impulse. One long, unbroken cheer, in which the feeble cry of those who lay helpless on the earth blended with the strong voices of those who still fought, rose high above the roar of battle, and hailed the presence of the victorious chief. He sat in the full realization of all that soldiers dream of — triumph; and as I looked upon him in the complete fruition of the success which his genius, courage, and confidence in his army had won, I thought that it must have been from such a scene that men in ancient days rose to the dignity of gods.

"His first care was for the wounded of both armies, and he was among the foremost at the burning mansion where some of them lay. But at that moment, when the transports of his victorious troops were drowning the roar of battle with acclamations, a note was brought to him from General Jackson. It was brought to General Lee as he sat on his horse, near the Chancellor House, and, unable to open it with his gauntleted hands, he passed it to me with directions to read it to him. The note made no mention of the wound General Jackson had received, but congratulated General Lee upon the great victory.

"I shall never forget the look of pain and anguish that passed over his face as he listened. With a voice broken with emotion, he bade me say to General Jackson that the victory was his, and that the congratulations were due to him. I know not how others may regard this incident, but to myself, as I gave expres-

sion to the thoughts of his exalted mind, I forgot the
genius that won the day in my reverence for the generosity that refused its glory.

"There is one other incident to which I beg permis-
sion to refer, that I may perfect the picture. On the
3rd day of July, 1863, the last assault of the Confederate
troops on the heights of Gettysburg failed, and again
General Lee was among the baffled and shattered battalions as they sullenly retired from their brave attempt.
The history of that battle is still to be written, and the
responsibility for the result is yet to be fixed.

"But there, with the painful consciousness that his
plans had been frustrated by others, and that defeat
and humiliation had overtaken his army, in the presence of his troops he openly assumed the entire responsibility of the campaign and of the last battle. One
word from him would have relieved him of the responsibility, but that word he refused to utter until it could
be spoken without fear of doing the least injustice.

"Thus, my fellow soldiers, I have presented to you
our great commander in the supreme moments of
triumph and defeat. I cannot more strongly illus-
trate his character. Has it been surpassed in history?
Is there another instance of such self-abnegation among
men? The man rose high above victory in the one
instance, and, harder still, the man rose superior to
disaster in the other. It was such incidents as these
that gave General Lee the absolute and undoubting
confidence and affection of his soldiers.

"Need I speak of the many exhibitions of that confidence? You all remember them, my comrades. Have
you not seen a wavering line restored by the magic of

his presence? Have you not seen the few forget that they were fighting against the many, because he was among the few?

"But I pass from the contemplation of his greatness in war to look to his example under the oppressive circumstances of final failure — to look to that example which is most useful for us now to refer to for our guidance and instruction. When the attempt to establish the Southern Confederacy had failed, and the event of the war seemed to have established the indivisibility of the Federal Union, General Lee gave his adhesion to the new order of affairs.

"His was no hollow truce; but with that pure faith and honor that marked every act of his illustrious career, he immediately devoted himself to the restoration of peace, harmony, and concord. He entered zealously into the subject of education, believing, as he often declared, that popular education is the only sure foundation of free government. He gave his earnest support to all plans of international improvement designed to bind more firmly together the social and commercial interests of the country; and among the last acts of his life was the effort to secure the construction of a line of railway communication of incalculable importance as a connecting link between the North and the South. He devoted all his great energies to the advancement of the welfare of his countrymen, while shrinking from public notice, and sought to lay deep and strong the foundations of the new fabric of government which it was supposed would arise from the ruins of the old. But I need not repeat to you, my comrades, the history of his life since the war. You have watched it to its close, and you know how faithfully and truly he performed every duty of his position.

"Let us take to heart the lesson of his bright example. Disregarding all that malice may impute to us, with an eye single to the faithful performance of our duties as American citizens, and with the honest and sincere resolution to support with heart and hand the honor, the safety, and the true liberties of our country, let us invoke our fellow-citizens to forget the animosities of the past by the side of this honored grave, and joining hands around this royal corpse, friends now, enemies no more, proclaim perpetual truce to battle."

IX

THE GETTYSBURG CAMPAIGN

(a) THE OBJECT OF THE CAMPAIGN

AT this point Colonel Marshall resumes his story.

I propose to write the history of the campaign of the Army of Northern Virginia which resulted in the Battle of Gettysburg.

My object in undertaking this work is to preserve for the historian facts not generally known, and which by lapse of time will become more and more obscure; to do justice to the Army, as far as it is in my power to do so; and to correct many erroneous impressions which I find to prevail with respect to the object, conduct, and failure of this memorable campaign.

It will be necessary for me to speak of the acts of some who have passed by a soldier's death beyond the reach of praise or blame. I feel the delicacy and responsibility of saying aught that may seem to imply a censure of men who deserved and enjoyed the confidence, admiration, and gratitude of their countrymen, and for whom I feel the warmest personal friendship. These feelings become oppressive when I reflect that I may be misunderstood as casting censure upon some whose memory I cherish as sacred, whose friendship I enjoyed, and whose services I hold in most grateful remembrance. But it is due to the noble Army of Northern Virginia, to its illustrious chief, and to the cause of truth, that the facts of this great event should be faithfully recorded.   So far as those facts are known to me I shall narrate them with the most cautious observance of accuracy, always distinguishing between what actually occurred and my own speculation, or reports for the accuracy of which I cannot vouch.

It is proper that I should state the means of information that I possess, in order that the value of what I say may be fully appreciated.

I was a member of the staff of General R. E. Lee and wrote most of his letters to the President and War Department.   Besides this it was my duty to compile his official reports of operations.   Sometimes in the course of my work it seemed to me necessary to speak strongly of events that were calculated to call forth words of praise or blame.   He often struck out observations of mine on subjects that aroused my liveliest interest and excited my feelings, saying in a playful way, "Colonel, if you speak so strongly of this you will have nothing left to say of something better."   The world knows in part his moderation, but none can know it fully but those who have seen him as it was my privilege to do.   Directing affairs that concentrated the attention of the civilized world, accomplishing results that compelled the admiration of his bitterest enemies, he brought to the narration of his achievements a devotion to truth, and an utter forgetfulness of self, that made me lose my admiration of the great soldier in my reverence for the excellence of the man.

I have now in my possession a copy of the official report of the Pennsylvania Campaign, forwarded by General Lee to the Secretary of War.   That report was prepared by myself with every facility to make it accurate which General Lee could give me. I had the official reports of the Corps, Division, and Brigade Commanders, those of the Artillery and Cavalry Commanders, and of the Medical staff. I had opportunities of conversing with the authors of these reports, and of getting explanations of what was doubtful, and declining that which was conflicting or contradictory. I had General Lee's private correspondence with the officers of his army, with the President and Departments, his orders, general and special, public and confidential, and more than all, I had the advantage of full and frank explanations of his own plans and purposes from General Lee himself.

When from the various sources I have mentioned I had compiled a continuous narrative it was submitted to him for examination. He would peruse it carefully, make such alterations as his personal knowledge suggested, and when there was a material difference in the statements contained in the reports, he required it to be brought particularly to his notice, read the conflicting reports himself, sought every opportunity by conversation or correspondence of reconciling the discrepancies, and in some instances changed his own report to such a statement of the general outlines of the facts as to omit entirely those things which his efforts could not render altogether free from doubt. He weighed every sentence I wrote, frequently making minute verbal alterations, and questioned me closely as to the evidence on which I based all statements which he did not know to be correct. In short, he spared no pains to make his official reports as truthful as possible, and for whatever errors they contain I can safely say that he is wholly free from responsibility.

Since the end of the war I have had frequent opportunities of comparing the official reports thus made up with those of Federal officers, and of correcting errors by discussing with them the events in which they participated.   I have availed myself of this valuable source of information on all possible occasions, and have found those officers of the United States Army, who had borne an active part in the events, very fair and just in their views of our operations and candid in their statements of their own.   I believe that this feeling pervades almost universally that class of Federal officers who took the most distinguished part in military operations and were least dependent for their reputations upon the praises of newspaper correspondents.   I have observed that in proportion as men rendered real service are they brief and truthful in narrating them.   To the above sources of information I may add my own personal observations.   I have thought it proper to state whence my information is derived, to enable the reader to estimate its value and credibility, my chief desire being to arrive at the truth.

It is proper that I should say one thing more by way of introduction.   The official report of General Lee is I believe substantially true, as far as it goes.   But it is not complete in many particulars which should be known to understand the campaign fully.   He struck from the original draft many statements which he thought might affect others injuriously, his sense of justice frequently leading him to what many considered too great a degree of lenience.   It is well known that he assumed the entire responsibility of the issue of the battle of Gettysburg, and thus covered the errors and omissions of all his officers. He declined to embody in his report anything that might seem to cast the blame of the result upon others, and in answer to my appeal to allow some statements which I deemed material to remain in the report, he said he disliked in such a communication to say aught to the prejudice of others, unless the truth of such statements had been established by an investigation in which those affected by them had been afforded an opportunity to defend or justify their actions. But there are material facts resting upon official statements which in my opinion are necessary to a correct understanding of the campaign, and the statement of which can do injustice to no man. I feel impelled to give these facts, so far as they are known to me, a place in the following narrative. As I have said, it is my purpose to give as full and truthful an account of this campaign as possible, and no account can be of that character which omits the facts to which I have alluded.

Before proceeding to narrate the particular events of the campaign of the Army of Northern Virginia in Pennsylvania, some general observations are necessary to render the operations of General Lee more intelligible. Great diversity of opinion exists as to the expediency of his offensive campaigns as well as to the manner in which they were conducted. Without attempting to argue these questions I shall content myself with the statement of the motives and objects of his movements.

The operations of the United States Army, based upon political as well as military reasons, had given great prominence in the struggle to the possession of the Confederate capital. This view of its importance had been accepted by the Confederate authorities, and their operations had been so conducted as to render the possession of Richmond a test of Confederate success, not only in the estimation of our own people and of the world, but also in point of fact. The Confederate Government, assuming that Richmond must be held, if we were to succeed, dealt with the town in such wise that to retain it in fact became essential. Its loss would not only have been disastrous in the moral effect which it would have produced both upon the people of the United States and of the Confederate States, but the material loss would have been very difficult to bear. The fall of Richmond and the suppression of the "rebellion" were regarded in the North as almost synonymous, and had become so in a great measure among the people of the South. Until the summer of 1864 Richmond was an indispensable base for General Lee's army if it was to operate in Northern Virginia, but after that time, when the siege had been formed and when it had become apparent that we were too weak to make a diversion by again crossing the Potomac, the continuance of the attempt to hold Richmond was contrary to the advice of the Confederate Commander and was due to political rather than military considerations.

The great object then of the Confederate operations in Virginia was to defend Richmond, and that was the principal end that General Lee proposed to himself. Of course the incidental advantages of preserving that part of Virginia north of the James and of keeping it free from the presence of the enemy were not disregarded, but the defence of Richmond controlled all other considerations.

Now from the time that General Lee was first placed on duty in Richmond in March 1862 by the order of President Davis, and even before that time, as I have heard, he was convinced that the only way of defending the city successfully was by occupying the Federal Army at a distance from the capital and preventing the formation of a siege.

He frequently spoke and often wrote to the effect that if the siege of Richmond were once undertaken by an army too strong to be beaten off, the fall of the place would be inevitable, no matter how successfully it might be defended against a direct attack. His reasons for this opinion are obvious now, though they were not fully appreciated at first by many beside himself. Richmond was chiefly dependent for its supplies upon the James River Canal, and upon three long lines of railway : the road through Petersburg and Wilmington to the south, that through Danville with its connecting road to Lynchburg and southwest Virginia, and the Virginia Central to Gordonsville and thence to the Shenandoah. The canal connected the city with the rich counties of the upper James.

There were two other roads, that to Fredericksburg, and the York River Railroad, but they were of less importance as sources of supply. General Lee was of opinion that should the enemy succeed in establishing himself near Richmond in too great force to be dislodged, it would be easy for him to cut any or all of these lines of communication with his cavalry, and render them practically useless for the purpose of supplying the city. An active cavalry commander could readily accomplish this, as it was impossible with the limited resources of the Confederacy to do more than provide guards for the principal bridges of the roads, while the rest of the lines would have to be defended by the cavalry of the army, and it was always possible for that of the enemy to get so far advanced before its movements became known, that the railroads could be seriously interrupted before our cavalry could arrive for their protection. By continuing these operations and by extending the lines of the besiegers so as to cover the railroads, the city would be finally entirely isolated.

This truth was very clearly demonstrated in the campaigns of 1864 and 1865, when General Grant established his army on both sides of the James River, threatening Richmond and Petersburg at the same time. Such was the facility with which he could transfer his troops from one side of the James to the other, massing them now before the defences of Richmond and now before those of Petersburg, that the two lines could only be held safely by a force on each side of the river sufficient to repel any attack. By threatening the Richmond lines Grant compelled Lee to withdraw troops from those of Petersburg, and availing himself of their absence he succeeded in extending his lines around Petersburg and established his troops in works from which the small available force that we could collect from the defence of our extended lines was unable to dislodge them. In this manner he first entirely closed Weldon Road, and then by his cavalry interrupted the South Side and Danville Roads, until the further extension of his lines enabled him to cover the South Side Road completely, which compelled the evacuation of Petersburg and Richmond.

Foreseeing the possibility of such results, General Lee adopted as the only practicable way of defending Richmond the plan of retaining the main body of the Federal Army near its own capital, and thereby preventing the formation of a close siege of our own. He acted upon this plan as long as his means allowed him to do so.

As in the campaign of 1862, so again in the campaign of 1863 the desire to keep the enemy employed at a distance from Richmond, and the impossibility of maintaining his army near enough to Washington to accomplish this object without moving north of the Potomac, led to the invasion of Maryland and Pennsylvania. So, also, in 1864, when sorely reduced in strength after the Wilderness campaign, General Lee made a final effort to force General Grant to withdraw from Richmond by detaching all the troops he could spare under General Early to threaten Washington. The campaigns of 1862 and 1863 were unsuccessful as far as the issues of the battles which closed them were concerned. But they effected one of their great objects in preventing the siege of Richmond in those years.

Of course, while seeking to obtain these ends, General Lee was not unmindful of the valuable results that might follow a decided success in the field. In comparing the relative merits of a plan for manœuvering in Virginia and of one for entering the enemy's country, the relative value of success in the one or in the other must be considered. I will not attempt to describe in detail the possible consequences of the defeat of McClellan in 1862, or of Meade in 1863, but it is safe to say that the defeat of either north of the Potomac would have been of vastly greater importance than an equal or greater success won in Virginia. A victory won in Maryland or in Pennsylvania, in 1863, might reasonably have been expected to have caused the withdrawal of the Federal troops from the South West to defend the more important Federal interests which would in that event have been exposed. Indeed it was in the hope and expectation that his movement northwards, if attended by any considerable military success, would relieve the pressure of the enemy in the South West, that General Lee began his campaign. He hoped that if any such withdrawal of Federals took place reinforcements from that quarter would enable him to confirm and extend the successes of his own army, but he knew that if his army were weakened in order to assist the defenders of Vicksburg against General Grant, then his army would be unable to undertake any offensive operations and even to defend Richmond. If the safety of Richmond were endangered then it would be necessary to withdraw troops from the Mississippi for the defence of the capital. So if General Lee remained inactive, both Vicksburg and Richmond would be imperilled, whereas if he were successful north of the Potomac, both would be saved.

Yet another important consideration was the moral effect of a victory north of the Potomac upon the people of the North. A victory over the Federal Army in Virginia would have tended to strengthen the peace party in the North, only in so far as it would have tended to

assure the Northern people that they could not succeed. They would not have been impressed by our consideration for their peace or comfort in keeping the
war from their homes and firesides. The "copperheads" were never weaker than when the Federal
armies were successful, and the arguments for peace
in the North would have been much more convincing
if victory had placed Washington, Baltimore or Philadelphia within our reach than if gained in Virginia.[1]
Those of us who have studied Confederate policy during the war know too well the baleful influence upon
the energy and efforts of the South, which was exercised by the delusion that the Confederacy could rely
upon anything but her deeds for success.

There were some additional considerations operative
in 1863 that deserve mention. The Confederate Army
in Virginia was better disciplined and far more efficient
than when it marched from Richmond into Maryland in 1862, for then a large part of that army consisted of men who had been brought into service for the
first time after the beginning of that year. But in
1863 it was numerically considerably weaker.[2]

After the battle of Fredericksburg, in which our loss
was less than 4500 men, and when the sick and wounded
in the campaign of 1862 had pretty well returned to
duty, as far as we had reason to suppose that they ever

[1] Lee wrote to Davis on June 10, that is, just after he had begun his
movement towards Pennsylvania: "We should neglect no honourable
means of weakening and dividing our enemies. We should give all the
encouragement we can, consistently with truth, to the rising peace party
in the North."

[2] Marshall here refers to the Confederate forces in Virginia generally.
Actually the army which passed the Potomac in 1863 was stronger than
that which had passed the previous year.

would return, and after the recruiting agencies under the Conscription Law of April 1862 had been actively at work for nearly a year and a fair opportunity had been afforded to test the ability of the South to keep up the strength of its army, it was found that the general aggregate of the army was steadily and sensibly decreasing. In other words, General Lee was conscious that if the war were to continue much longer on a scale of such magnitude, the South must fail from the exhaustion of her manhood capable of bearing arms. Recruiting was becoming more and more slow, owing chiefly to the decrease in the number of men subject to military service, but also in a considerable degree from the danger and weariness of war, and distrust as to the issue of the struggle.

The causes that brought about the decrease in the army in 1863 as compared with the previous year were likely to become more and more potent in their influence, and the decline in the strength of the Confederate army was likely not only to continue but to progress more rapidly as the war was protracted. Unlike the North, the South could easily see the limit in her resources in men nor was that limit very remote.

It therefore became important to consider how to accomplish quickly the greatest possible results with the smallest loss, and how to make a limited number of men most effective in attaining both the chief end of bringing a satisfactory peace, and the immediate object of thwarting and frustrating the designs of the enemy.

The campaign of Chancellorsville had demonstrated to the enemy what it must be confessed he appears to have been slow to learn, that the peculiar situation of Richmond would enable him with a comparatively small force to compel a large detachment from General Lee's army. The report of a movement of Federal troops to the south side of James River in the early part of 1863 had led to the detachment of the greater part of Longstreet's corps to Petersburg, and the authorities at Richmond deemed that the danger to that city which this movement caused was sufficient to detain those troops from General Lee's army when he called for them to aid in the unequal struggle in which he was about to engage at Chancellorsville.[3] Jackson's corps and the divisions of Anderson and McLaws of Longstreet's corps were barely strong enough to repulse the army of General Hooker, while the fine divisions of Hood and Pickett lay inactive below the James, watching what might have proved a real danger to Richmond. Had the force that was supposed to threaten Richmond from the south side of the James at that time been large enough to require the detachment of more of General Lee's army than the two divisions of Longstreet's corps, it is extremely questionable whether the battle of Chancellorsville would have been fought at all. A larger detachment from the army of General Lee would have made that army too weak to oppose General Hooker.

After the battle of Chancellorsville, it was in the

[3] In January 1863 a Federal force of about 15,000 had occupied Suffolk, south of the James River. Partly to oppose this threat and partly because of the difficulty of feeding a large force at Fredericksburg, Lee agreed that Longstreet with Hood's and Pickett's divisions should go south of the James. Longstreet became involved in a siege of Suffolk, and was too late to take part in the battle of Chancellorsville.

power of the enemy, if not prevented, not only to detain
Hood and Pickett below Richmond, but to compel
General Lee to reinforce them, in which event he must
have withdrawn from Fredericksburg and fallen back
on Richmond, or he must have assumed the risk of
fighting a greatly superior force with smaller numbers
than had been found barely sufficient to win at Chancellorsville.

As Hooker's army lay near the Potomac, he could
embark any part of it at Acquia Creek with little difficulty and land on the James in dangerous proximity
to Richmond, almost before General Lee could learn
that they had left his front.   Such was the position of
affairs after the battle of Chancellorsville, and the questions presented to General Lee were not only how to
avert the manifest danger to which his army was always
exposed but also how to use his army so as to bring the
enemy's plans to naught.

Let us then consider the possible plans from which
he had to make his choice.   First; suppose he had
remained where he was, and awaited the movements
of the enemy.   It is safe to assume that the enemy
would not renew the attempt of General Burnside in
1862 or that of General Hooker in April 1863, unless
indeed the latter effort had been repeated with a greatly
increased force.

But General Lee was bound to assume, unless he was
prepared to act on the assumption of absolute incapac-
ity on the part of his adversary, that if he remained
inactive the enemy would abandon his effort to dislodge him from his position at Fredericksburg, and
would move his army to Richmond by water, as he

could easily and safely do. Such a movement must have led to the abandonment of all Northern Virginia by the Confederates and the concentration of their available force to defend Richmond, with all the disadvantages already mentioned as incident to the defence of the city against a siege, or against a direct assault.

During the retreat on Richmond accident might bring on an engagement on ground unfavourable to the Confederates, without the fault of their leader, but even if that eventually were avoided nothing could justify the deliberate adoption of a policy the immediate and unavoidable result of which would be to impose upon the Confederate army the burden of such a defence. Better far to risk the battlefield which chance might bring us during a movement northwards than deliberately to accept what we knew to be altogether favourable to the enemy, and altogether unfavourable to us.

Next, suppose General Lee had attacked Hooker in his position opposite Fredericksburg. This position was one of great strength and security, so far as any attempt on our part to dislodge the enemy by direct attack was concerned. A short line of railway connected the Federal encampment with the Potomac River, which offered a secure and easy line of communication with Washington and the North. The railway was only twelve miles long and lay immediately in [the] rear of the Federal lines, which completely protected it. The river was in their undisputed possession, so that nothing could be effected by operating on their line of communication.

The Rappahannock River which separated the two armies is deep and impassable except by bridges, from Fredericksburg to its mouth. At that place, where tide water begins, the course of the river changes. The part that lies below the town turns sharply to the south east, while above its course is more nearly easterly. On the north side the hills approach very near the river, so that the guns placed on the heights behind Falmouth commanded the course of the stream below Fredericksburg, and made the construction of a bridge from the south to the north side on that portion of the river almost impracticable. In like manner the guns on the heights a little below and opposite Fredericksburg command the course of the stream above the town, making the crossing at that part, if otherwise feasible, a matter of great risk and danger.

Besides this, the hills on the south side of the Rappahannock are at a considerable distance from the river, and are separated from it by a wide open plain, entirely commanded by the guns on the opposite heights. Troops moving from the heights occupied by the Confederate army to the river would be exposed to the artillery on the opposite side from these directions. To attempt to force a passage immediately in front of the Federal Army would therefore have been madness.

The only way that we could have attacked that army in its position would have been by crossing the river above, and moving down upon its right flank. But this would have been attended by great loss and difficulty, besides being of very doubtful utility. Had the attempt been made, we must have ascended the river some distance, and as all the fords and practicable crossings were closely guarded, our movement would undoubtedly have been discovered as soon as it began. Before we could force the passage, the enemy could have changed front and met our attack on ground altogether favourable to him, or he could have withdrawn to the Potomac and placed his army under the guns of his shipping, in a country nearly or quite impracticable for military operations. At the same time it was desirable for many reasons to force General Hooker to leave the vicinity of Fredericksburg. We were so far from Washington as to make the authorities there feel so secure that they would not hesitate to detach troops to operate against either Richmond or Vicksburg while our army remained confronting that of General Hooker, and the resources of the North in men were such that they could have sent off a sufficient force for either purpose without materially weakening the army at Fredericksburg.

But it is an error to compare the possible results of any other plan of operations with the result which actually followed the movement into Pennsylvania.

The true standard is to compare the Pennsylvania campaign as it might have been, and as General Lee had reason to believe it would be, with any other plan that he could have adopted in 1863.

If it shall be found that such a campaign was wisely adapted to attain the end proposed, and that it was reasonable to expect that it could be so conducted as to accomplish the end proposed in the way intended, there only remains the enquiry, why was it not conducted in the way in which it was intended to be conducted ? Why did it result in a great battle with the advantage of position on the side of the enemy, when it had not been intended to fight a great battle, or if at all, only on such grounds as General Lee might select?

How these things occurred I will now proceed to explain.

X

THE GETTYSBURG CAMPAIGN

(b) THE INVASION OF PENNSYLVANIA

GENERAL LEE began his advance by moving the commands of Longstreet and Ewell to Culpeper Court House, where both were assembled by June 7th [1863]. The corps of A. P. Hill was left at Fredericksburg in observation of the enemy, who threw quite a large force across the Rappahannock, but made no attempt to attack.[1]

On June 10th General Lee started a manœuvre which was in a measure independent of the general purposes of his campaign. He sent Ewell into the Valley to Winchester, where he was ordered to attack the enemy and pursue him to the Potomac, believing that this movement would cause General Hooker to withdraw from Fredericksburg. In the meantime he remained with General Longstreet's corps at Culpeper Court House, where he was near enough to support Hill in case Ewell's action failed to cause the withdrawal of the troops on his front.

As soon as Ewell's appearance in the Valley began to be felt, the enemy in Hill's front did recross the Rappahannock, and indications that General Hooker would leave his former position were reported. So on June 15th General Lee advanced with Longstreet's

---

[1] This was a portion of Sedgwick's corps which Hooker threw across the river in an endeavor to discover what Lee was doing.

corps from Culpeper Court House towards the Potomac River, ordering Hill to follow him as soon as the
enemy should disappear from his front altogether.

Hill's march was up the south side of the Rappahannock, and there was danger that the Federal army might
intercept him. To prevent this General Lee moved
Longstreet's corps northwards along the east side of
the Blue Ridge as if he would cross the Potomac
east of the mountains, and between them and Washington, intending by this movement to cause General
Hooker to throw his army between him and the lower
fords of the Potomac, thus leaving Hill to continue
his march to the Rappahannock unmolested.

The result was as General Lee intended, and, as
soon as he heard that Hill was well on his way to cross
the Shenandoah at Front Royal, he moved Longstreet
through Ashby's Gap to the west side of the Blue
Ridge into the Valley, but to make sure that General
Hooker would be drawn well away from the Rappahannock he directed Ewell, who had driven the Federal troops from Winchester on the 15th, to cross the
Potomac on June 17th and advance into Pennsylvania, being satisfied that this would assure a counter
movement on the part of the enemy, and not only save
Hill from molestation, but at the same time remove all
apprehension of General Hooker's availing himself of
the opportunities afforded by the withdrawal of our
whole army from between him and Richmond.

It will thus be seen that the first movement of Ewell
into Pennsylvania was merely for the purpose of compelling the recall of Hooker from the Rappahannock
and enabling the parts of General Lee's army to reunite

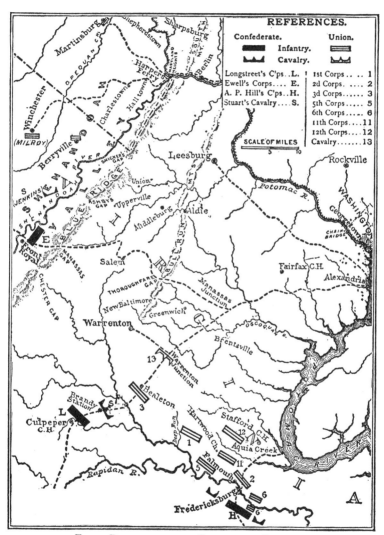

EARLY POSITIONS IN THE GETTYSBURG CAMPAIGN

without hindrance. Ewell's movement therefore was a good one, and if the sole object of General Lee had been to withdraw the Confederate army safely from Fredericksburg and concentrate it on the northern frontier of Virginia, thereby causing in the meantime the abandonment of any plan the enemy might have formed while his army lay opposite to Fredericksburg, the plan was effectual.

Let us now look at the details of the subsequent movements. The events above referred to resulted in transferring the army of General Hooker from the vicinity of Fredericksburg to the Potomac River near Leesburg. The Federal army was then between that of General Lee and Washington, but was still in Virginia.

General Hill had entered the Valley on June 19th, and as soon as his approach was known Longstreet crossed the Shenandoah and also entered the Valley thus reuniting the two corps. General Lee then resolved to cross the Potomac, with the object of compelling General Hooker to do the same so as to cover Washington, and it is at this point that circumstances occurred that gave character eventually to the whole movement and brought about its actual result.

General Lee left Paris in Fauquier County in the afternoon of June 21st and proceeded to a place a short distance beyond Milwood in Clark County, where we encamped that night. There was a very severe storm, I remember, and our tents were pitched in a stubble field near a large white house, which General Lee said was built by British prisoners of war sent from Winchester by General Morgan during the Revolutionary War. I forget the name of the owners.

The next morning we proceeded to Berryville and encamped about noon in a field about a mile beyond that place on the road to Charlestown. The infantry had left Ashby's Gap and crossed the Shenandoah at Berry's and Snicker's Ferries on the 21st, but a part of them was ordered back on a report that Stuart, who had remained between Paris and Middleburg, was being pressed by the enemy's infantry.

General Lee designed to wait near Berryville until A. P. Hill should come up. Hill had left Fredericksburg when the enemy in his front moved off, and had marched through Culpeper Court House, by way of Gaines' Woods and Chester Gap to Front Royal.

While we were in camp near Berryville on the 22nd General Lee directed me to write a letter to General Stuart, and as this letter is of great importance I will state the particulars. It was soon after we went into camp on the 22nd, when we had heard that Hill was crossing at Front Royal, and his advance was expected to reach Berryville the same day, which actually occurred. General Lee had therefore determined to move on the 23rd and cross the Potomac at Shepherdstown and Williamsport, so as to be within supporting distance of Ewell who was directed to move into Pennsylvania.

At General Lee's request, I wrote the following letter to General Ewell, who had arrived at Shepherdstown : —

June 22nd., 1863

Lieut. General R. S. Ewell

GENERAL,

Your letter of 6 P.M. yesterday has been received.   If you are ready to move you can do so.   I think your best course will be towards the Susquehanna, taking the routes by Emmittsburg, Chambersburg, and McConnellsburg.   Your trains had better be as far as possible kept on the centre route.   You must get command of your cavalry [2] and use it in gathering supplies, obtaining information and protecting your flank.   If necessary send a staff officer to remain with General Jenkins; it will depend upon the quantity of supplies obtained in that country whether the rest of the army can follow; there may be enough for your command, but none for the others.   Every exertion should therefore be made to locate and secure them.   Beef we can drive with us, but bread we cannot carry and must secure it in the country.   I send the copies of a general order on this subject, which I think is based on rectitude and sound policy, and the spirit of which I want to see enforced in your command.[3] I am much gratified with the success that has attended your movements, and feel assured that if they are conducted with the same energy and circumspection it will continue.   Your progress and direction will of course depend upon the development of circumstances.   If Harrisburg comes within your means, capture it.   General A. P. Hill arrived yesterday in the vicinity of Berryville.   I shall move him on to-day if possible.   Saturday Longstreet withdrew from the Blue Ridge; yesterday the enemy pressed our cavalry with infantry on the Upperville Road, so that McLaws had to be sent back to hold Ashby's Gap.   I have not yet heard from there

[2] Jenkins's cavalry brigade had been ordered to join Ewell.
[3] This was an order directing that all supplies should be purchased by duly authorized persons, and forbidding looting.

RICHARD S. EWELL

this morning. General Stuart could not ascertain whether it was intended as a real advance towards the Valley or to ascertain our position.

I am with great respect,

Your obedient servant,

R. E. LEE, General

After this letter was sent off General Lee explained to me that he had had a conversation with General Stuart when he left him near Paris, and that his own view was to leave some cavalry in Snicker's and Ashby's Gaps to watch the army of General Hooker, and to take the main body of the cavalry with General Stuart to accompany the army into Pennsylvania. It is much to be regretted that this course was not pursued. General Lee added that Stuart suggested that he could move down with his cavalry near Hooker, and annoy him if he attempted to cross the river, and when he found that he was crossing he could rejoin the army in good time.

General Lee said that General Longstreet thought well of the suggestion and had assented, but he added that he had told General Stuart that, as soon as he found that General Hooker was crossing the Potomac, he must immediately cross himself and take his place on our right flank as we moved north. General Lee then told me that he was anxious that there should be no misunderstanding on General Stuart's part, and that there should be no delay in his joining us as soon as General Hooker had crossed. He said that in reflecting on the subject, while it had occurred to him that it might be possible for General Stuart, when the time came for him to cross the river, to cross east of the

Blue Ridge and above General Hooker, thus avoiding
the delay of returning through Snicker's or Ashby's
Gap and crossing above Harpers Ferry, yet he added
that circumstances might prevent Stuart from crossing
east of the Blue Ridge. He said that he desired to
impress upon General Stuart the importance of his
rejoining the army with the least possible delay as soon
as General Hooker had crossed, and he then directed
me to write to General Stuart expressing these views.

I wrote a letter to General Stuart to the effect following, and showed it to General Lee before dispatching : —

HEADQUARTERS, 22nd *June*, 1863

Major General J. E. B. Stuart, Commanding Cavalry

GENERAL :

I have just received your note of 7 : 45 this morning to
General Longstreet. I judge the efforts of the enemy yesterday were to arrest our progress and ascertain our whereabouts. Perhaps he is satisfied. Do you know where he
is and what he is doing ? I fear he will steal a march on us
and get across the Potomac before we are aware. If you
find that he is moving northward, and that two brigades can
guard the Blue Ridge and take care of your rear, you can
move with the other three into Maryland and take position
on General Ewell's right, place yourself in communication
with him, guard his flank and keep him informed of the
enemy's movements, and collect all the supplies you can for
the use of the army. One column of General Ewell's army
will probably move towards the Susquehanna by the
Emmittsburg route, another by Chambersburg. Accounts
from him last night state that there was no enemy west of
Fredericktown. A cavalry force (about one hundred strong)
guarded the Monocacy Bridge, which was barricaded.

You will of course take charge of Jenkins's brigade and give him necessary instructions. All supplies taken in Maryland must be by authorized staff officers for their respective departments, by no one else. They will be paid for or receipts will be sent to the owners. I will send you a general order on this subject, which I wish you to see is strictly complied with.

I am, very respectfully, your obedient servant

R. E. LEE, General

Later on the same day, General Lee wrote the following letter to General Ewell to inform him of the instructions which had been sent to Stuart.

HEADQUARTERS, June 22nd, 1863, 3 : 30 P.M.

GENERAL : —

I have just received your letter of this morning from opposite Shepherdstown; mine of to-day authorizing you to move towards Susquehanna has reached you ere this. After dispatching my letter, learning that the enemy had not renewed his attempt of yesterday to break through the Blue Ridge, I directed R. H. I. Anderson's division to commence its march towards Shepherdstown; it will reach there to-morrow. I also directed General Stuart, should the enemy so far have retired from his front as to permit of the departure of a portion of the cavalry, to march with three brigades across the Potomac and place himself on your right and in communication with you, keep you advised of the movements of the enemy and assist in collecting supplies for the army. I have not heard from him since; I also directed Imboden if the opportunity occurred to cross the Potomac and perform the same offices on your left.

I am

Yours most respectfully,

R. E. LEE, General

General Lee's letter to General Stuart of the 22nd,
giving him specific directions as to his movements, was
sent by General Lee through General Longstreet, who
was with his troops on the east side of the Blue Ridge,[4]
and under whose immediate command General Stuart
was.

I have not a copy of the letter from General Lee to
General Longstreet enclosing the letter to General
Stuart, but I have a copy of General Longstreet's
letter to General Lee.   It is as follows: —

HEADQUARTERS, *June* 22, 1863, 7 : 30 P.M.
General R. E. Lee, Commanding etc.

GENERAL : Yours of 4 o'clock this afternoon was received.
I have forwarded your letter to General Stuart, with the
suggestion that he was to pass to the enemy's rear, if he
thinks he may get through.   We have seen nothing of the
enemy to-day.
              Most respectfully
                        JAMES LONGSTREET
                  Lieutenant General Commanding

General Lee's letter to General Stuart, which I have
quoted, and which General Stuart received through
General Longstreet, contained an order to the former,
in case he found that the enemy was moving northward and that he could protect his rear with two
brigades of his force, to move the other three into
Maryland and take position on General Ewell's right,
place himself in communication with him, guard his
flank, and keep him informed of the enemy's movements.

[4] The portion of Longstreet's corps which had turned back to help
Stuart at Ashby's Gap.

This order was sent through General Longstreet, that he might decide whether cavalry could be spared to execute the order, and also that he might direct how the cavalry should best move to carry it out, in view of the state of things existing when the order was delivered to General Stuart.

General Lee's letter, however, shows that when it was written he expected that General Stuart would pass, with all his cavalry except two brigades, to the west of the Blue Ridge, and cross the Potomac on that side of the mountains, leaving two brigades in the gaps to guard his rear as long as the enemy threatened to attempt to penetrate through the gaps into the Valley.

The letter which General Lee sent to General Ewell informing that officer of the order to be given to Stuart, if General Longstreet decided that Stuart could be spared, makes it very clear that General Lee assumed that Stuart would cross into Maryland and put himself on Ewell's right.

General Longstreet's reply to General Lee, acknowledging the receipt of the letter to General Stuart, states that he had forwarded that letter with the suggestion that Stuart should pass to the enemy's rear "if he thinks he can get through."

His letter to General Stuart was as follows: —

MILLWOOD, *June* 22, 1863, 7 P.M.
Major General J. E. B. Stuart, Commanding Cavalry
GENERAL,

General Lee has enclosed to me this letter to you, to be forwarded to you, provided you can be spared from my front, and provided I think you can move across the Potomac without disclosing our plans. He speaks of your leaving via Hopewell Gap,[5] and passing by the rear of the enemy. If you can get through by that route, I think you will be less likely to indicate what our plans are than if you should cross by passing to our rear.   I forward the letter of instruction with these suggestions.   Please advise me of the conditions of affairs before you leave, and order General Hampton, whom I suppose you will leave here in command, to report to me at Millwood either by letter or in person, as may be most agreeable to him.

Most respectfully

JAMES LONGSTREET
Lieutenant General

N. B.   I think your passage of the Potomac by our rear at the present moment will, in a measure, disclose our plans. You had better therefore not leave us unless you can take the proposed route in rear of the enemy.

This letter of General Longstreet's appears to have been entirely controlled by the idea that General Stuart was to cross the Potomac in such a way as would best conceal the movements of the Confederate army, but it does not notice the positive instruction contained in General Lee's letter to General Stuart, that should the latter cross the Potomac he was to place himself as speedily as possible, after the enemy began to move northwards, upon General Ewell's right.

General Longstreet's suggestion that he should proceed by way of the enemy's rear to reach the Potomac and cross into Maryland contemplated the possibility of the entire detachment of the cavalry from the rest

---

[5] This must have been in the missing letter from Lee to Longstreet. There is no mention of Hopewell Gap or of passing by the rear of the enemy in Lee's letter to Stuart.

of the army. To obey the order, Stuart had to pass through the Bull Run mountains across the enemy's line of march from the Rappahannock to the Potomac river, if the way was open. That line of march was east of the Bull Run mountains. The cavalry under Stuart was on the east side of the Blue Ridge, and the enemy was already known to be assembling on the Potomac in Loudoun, so that Stuart's march as proposed by General Longstreet would take the cavalry east of the Bull Run mountains and bring it to the Potomac river, below where the enemy's army was concentrated. This might readily prove to be inconsistent with the chief aim of the movement ordered by General Lee, which was that General Stuart should place himself on the right of General Ewell after crossing the river, for there was evident danger that if General Stuart acted under the order of General Longstreet and the enemy should cross the Potomac before General Stuart, the latter would be separated from General Ewell, who was moving west of the Blue Ridge.

After this letter of the 22nd was sent General Lee directed me to repeat it. I remember saying to the General that it could hardly be necessary to repeat the order, as General Stuart had had the matter fully explained to himself verbally and my letter had been very full and explicit. I had retained a copy of my letter in General Lee's confidential letter book. General Lee said that he felt anxious about the matter and desired to guard against the possibility of error, and desired me to repeat it, which I did, and dispatched the second letter, which ran : —

June 23, 1863, 5 P.M.

Major General J. E. B. Stuart, Commanding Cavalry

GENERAL,

Your notes of 9 and 10:30 A.M. today have just been received. As regards the purchase of tobacco for your men, supposing that Confederate money will not be taken, I am willing for commissaries or quarter masters to purchase this tobacco, and let the men get it from them, but I can have nothing seized by the men. If General Hooker's army remains inactive you can leave two brigades to watch him, and withdraw the three others, but should he not appear to be moving northward I think you had better withdraw this side of the mountains to-morrow night, cross at Shepherdstown next day, and move over to Fredericktown. You will, however, be able to judge whether you can pass around their army without hindrance, doing them all the damage you can, and cross the river east of the mountains.[6] In either case, after crossing the river you must move on and feel the right of Ewell's troops collecting information, provisions, etc. Give instructions to the commander of the brigades left behind to watch the flank and rear of the army, and, in the event of the enemy leaving their front, to retire from the mountains west of the Shenandoah, leaving sufficient pickets to guard the passes, and to bring in everything clean along the valley, closing upon the rear of the army. As regards the movements of the two brigades of the enemy moving towards Warrenton, the commander of the brigades to be left in the mountains must do what he can to counteract them, but I think the sooner you cross into Maryland after to-morrow the better. The movements of

---

[6] These were the fatal words. Lee certainly meant that Stuart was to cross *immediately* east of the mountains, so as to be close to the right flank of the army. Stuart interpreted the words to mean that he might cross anywhere east of the mountains.

Ewell's corps are, as stated in my former letter. Hill's First Division will reach the Potomac to-day and Longstreet will follow to-morrow. Be watchful and circumspect in your movements.

I am very respectfully and truly yours,

R. E. LEE, General

This letter was written and received before General Stuart started on his march "around the rear of the enemy," and was General Lee's last direction to him before the army left Virginia. It covers the case of the Federal commander remaining inactive, and also that of his not moving northward.[7] In the former event Stuart was to leave two brigades to watch him and with the other three to withdraw, and in the latter event Stuart's whole command was to be withdrawn "this side of the mountains to-morrow" across the Potomac at Shepherdstown and move toward Fredericktown the next day.

The order leaves Stuart to decide whether he can move around the Federal Army in either eventuality, without hindrance, doing it all the damage he can, and cross east of the mountains. In either case, after crossing the river, Stuart is directed to move on and feel the right of Ewell's troops, collecting information, etc.

Whether Stuart should cross the Potomac at Shepherdstown, or in the exercise of the discretion given him, pass round the rear of the enemy and cross the Potomac east of the mountains, he was ordered unconditionally "after crossing the river" to move on and "feel the right of Ewell's troops." This explicit order precluded

[7] The letter of the 22nd had covered the case of the enemy moving northward.

any movement by Stuart that would prevent him from "feeling the right of Ewell's troops" after crossing the Potomac. So that under these restrictions he was practically instructed not to cross the Potomac east of the Federal Army, and thus interpose that army between himself and the right of General Ewell. There were places where the Potomac could be crossed between the enemy's army, at or near Edward's Ferry, and the Blue Ridge, and General Stuart had discretion to use the fords east of the Blue Ridge, but he had no discretion to use any ford that would place the enemy's army between him and the troops of General Ewell.

The report of General Stuart of his operations in this campaign states that he had submitted to General Lee a plan of leaving a brigade or two, to use his own language, "in my present front and passing through Hopewell or some other gap in Bull Run Mountains, attain the enemy's rear, pass between his main body and Washington, and cross into Maryland, joining our army north of the Potomac.

"The commanding general wrote me, authorizing this move, if I deemed it practicable, and also what instructions should be given the officer in command of the two brigades left in front of the army. He also notified me that one column would move via Gettysburg, the other by Carlisle towards the Susquehanna, and directed me, after crossing, to proceed with all dispatch to join the right (Early) [8] in Pennsylvania."

There is no such letter as is mentioned by General Stuart contained in the book in which are found copies of all the other letters of General Lee to him, which

[8] Early commanded Ewell's right division.

letters I have cited, and it is inconsistent with those letters. General Stuart's report evidently refers to the letter of General Lee of June 23rd. That letter contains the instructions to be given to "the officer in command of the two brigades to be left in front of the enemy"; it also contains the information as to Ewell's movements referred to in the report. General Stuart constructed that letter to mean what he, in his report, states. That construction, however, is not justified by the letter itself.

General Stuart's report proceeds as follows: —

"Accordingly three days' rations were prepared, and on the night of the 24th the following brigades, Hampton's, Fitz Lee's, and W. H. F. Lee's, rendezvoused secretly near Salem Depot. We had no waggons or vehicles, except six pieces of artillery, caissons and ambulances. Robertson's and Jones's brigades under the command of the former were left in observation of the enemy on the usual front, with full instructions as to following up the enemy, in case of withdrawal, and rejoining our main army. Brigadier-General Fitz Lee's brigade had to march from north of Snicker's Gap to the place of rendezvous. At one o'clock at night the brigades, with noiseless march, moved out. This precaution was necessary on account of the enemy's having possession of the Bull Run mountains, which in the day time commanded a view of every movement of consequence in that location. Hancock's corps occupied Thoroughfare Gap. Moving to the right we passed through Glasscock's Gap without serious difficulty, and marched for Haymarket. I had previously sent Major Mosby, with some picked men, through to gain the vicinity of Dranesville, and bring intelligence to me near Gum Spring to-day."

Haymarket is in Prince William County east of the Bull Run mountains, and that was the first point to which General Stuart directed his march, using Glasscock's Gap in the mountains, Glasscock's Gap being further to the south than Thoroughfare Gap.

"As we neared Haymarket [continued General Stuart's report], we found Hancock's Corps was en route for Gum Springs through Haymarket, his infantry well distributed through his trains.

"As Hancock had the right of way on my road, I sent Fitz Lee's brigades to Gainesville to reconnoitre, and devoted the remainder of the day to grazing our horses, the only forage procurable in the country. The best of information represented the enemy still at Centreville, Union Mills and Wolf Run Shoals. I sent a dispatch to General Lee concerning General Hancock's movements, and moved back to Buckland to deceive the enemy. It rained heavily that night. To carry out my original design of passing west of Centreville would have involved so much detention on account of the presence of the enemy that I determined to cross Bull Run further down and pass through Fairfax for the Potomac the next day. The sequel shows this to have been the only practicable course.

"We marched through Brentsville to the vicinity of Wolf Run Shoals, and had to halt again to graze our horses, which hard marching without grain was fast breaking down. We met the enemy to-day, the 26th. On the following morning, 27th, having ascertained that on the night previous the enemy had disappeared entirely from Wolf Run Shoals, a strongly fortified position on the Occoquan, I marched to that point, and thence directly for Fairfax Station, sending General Fitz Lee to the right to cross by Burke Station and effect a junction at Fairfax Court House, or further on according to circumstances.

"Reaching Fairfax Court House a communication was received from General Fitz Lee from Annandale. At these two points there were evidences of very recent occupation, but the evidence was conclusive that the enemy had left this point entirely, the mobilized army having the day previous moved over towards Leesburg, while the locals had retired to the fortifications near Washington. I had not yet heard from Major Mosby, but the indications favoured my successful passage in the rear of the enemy's army. After a halt of a few hours to rest and refresh the command, which regaled itself on stores left by the enemy in the place, march was resumed at Dranesville late in the afternoon. The campfires of Sedgwick's sixth corps just west of the town were still burning, it having left that morning. General Hampton's brigade was still in advance, and was ordered to move directly for Rowser's Ford on the Potomac, Chambliss's brigade being held at Dranesville until Brigadier General Fitz Lee could close up.

"As General Hampton approached the river he fortunately met a citizen who had just crossed the river, who informed us that there were no pickets on the other side of the river, and that the river, though fordable, was two feet higher than usual. Hampton's brigade crossed early in the night, but reported to me that it would be utterly impossible to cross the artillery at that ford. In this the residents were also very positive that vehicles could not cross. A ford lower down was examined, and found quite as impracticable, from quicksands, rocks and rugged banks. I, however, determined not to give it up without a trial, and before twelve o'clock that night, in spite of the difficulties, to all appearances insuperable, indomitable energy and resolute determination triumphed. Every piece was brought safely over, and the entire command bivouacked on Maryland soil."

I shall not quote further from General Stuart's report. That portion which I have cited shows that he crossed the Potomac east of the army of General Hooker, so as to render it extremely difficult if not impossible, for him to comply with the repeated injunctions he had received from General Lee to place himself on Ewell's right as soon as he entered Maryland.

I must here break my story to refer to what took place long afterwards.

During the winter of 1863–4 while we lay on the Rapidan I was engaged in preparing the report on the Gettysburg campaign. I had received all the reports of the infantry and artillery commanders, and I was only waiting for General Stuart's, to complete General Lee's official report. Some delay took place, and General Stuart was applied to more than once. He said he was busy preparing it, and promised me several times to send it in. General Lee was urging me to prepare his report before active operations should be resumed, and I think that when I told him the cause of the delay, he either wrote or spoke to General Stuart on the subject himself. I know that I was unable to complete and forward General Lee's report until some time in January or February, 1864.[9] At last General Stuart brought his report and asked me to read it carefully, and to tell him what I thought of his conduct.

In speaking of his having crossed the Potomac east of General Hooker on June 27th, instead of between Hooker and Harper's Ferry, General Stuart stated that he had at one time contemplated a dash on Washington, but did not undertake it because his orders were to join the infantry as soon as possible. He further stated that his orders had been to place his command on the right of our line of ranks, but argued that had he done so, he would have attracted the enemy's cavalry, which was more numerous than his, to that quarter. He said they could have broken through the mountains at some pass, as he was not strong enough to hold all, and thus endangered our trains which were moving north on the west side of the Catoctin. General Stuart asked me if I did not consider his excuse for not putting himself on our right satisfactory, alleging that his movement had drawn the enemy's cavalry away from the Catoctin to watch him, and thus secured our trains.

I told him that I thought it would have been far better for him to have obeyed his orders; that General Lee had not ordered him to protect our trains, but had disposed his infantry so as to do that, most of the trains having crossed at Williamsport, while Hill's corps or most of it crossed at Shepherdstown, and moved through Sharpsburg, to Hagerstown, thus keeping

[9] Lee's Gettysburg dispatch is dated January, 1864.

between the trains and the enemy, while the trains were so distributed that infantry support was near all parts of the line.

I called his attention to the fact that the great object of having his cavalry on our right was to keep us informed of the enemy's movements. I pointed out the disastrous consequence of our being without cavalry to get information for us, and the fact that, owing to our not hearing from him, General Lee had been led to believe that General Hooker had not crossed the Potomac for several days after that event had occurred. I told him how General Lee, being confident that he would give him immediate information of Hooker's crossing, had assumed from not receiving the information that Hooker had not crossed and acted on that belief.

Stuart said that when he crossed at Rowser's Ferry, and found that Hooker had crossed the day before above him, he had sent a dispatch to General Lee back by way of Ashby's Gap. We never got that dispatch, and, as I showed him, if we had, still we had no cavalry to get information for us.

General Stuart admitted that he had made the movement at his own discretion, and that he had General Lee's letter written by me. He said that he was confident that he could get around Hooker and join us in Pennsylvania before the two armies could meet.

I mention these facts to show that General Stuart felt it necessary to defend his course, which he would not have done had he been justified by his orders.

I must now return to the movements of the main body of the army. On June 22nd Ewell had marched into

Pennsylvania, with Rodes' and Johnson's divisions, preceded by Jenkins' cavalry, taking the road from Hagerstown through Chambersburg to Carlisle, where he arrived on the 27th. Early's division moved by a parallel road to Greenwood, and, in pursuance of instructions previously given to General Ewell, marched towards York. On the 24th Longstreet and Hill were put into motion to follow Ewell, and on the 27th encamped near Chambersburg. General Imboden's command, which had been directed to cross the Potomac and take position on General Ewell's left, as he moved northward, reached Hancock, while Longstreet and Hill were at Chambersburg, and was directed to proceed to the latter place.

General Lee had most implicit confidence in the vigilance and enterprise of General Stuart. He had not heard from him since the army left Virginia, and was confident from that fact, in view of the positive orders that Stuart had received, that General Hooker's army had not yet crossed the Potomac. He remained at Chambersburg from the 27th to the 29th and repeatedly observed while there that the enemy's army must still be in Virginia, as he had heard nothing from Stuart.

Assuming that such was the fact and that the movements of the Confederate Army into Pennsylvania had, contrary to his confident expectation, failed to withdraw that of General Hooker from Virginia, General Lee began to become uneasy as to the purpose of the Federal commander, and to fear that he contemplated a strong movement against Richmond. He remarked that such a proceeding on the part of the enemy would compel the immediate return of his own army to Virginia, if it could indeed reach Richmond in time to defend the city. I heard General Lee express this apprehension more than once while we lay at Chambersburg, and the apprehension was due entirely to his hearing nothing from General Stuart.

In these circumstances he determined to take such action as would compel the enemy to leave Virginia, and deter him from any attempt upon Richmond. General Longstreet's corps was at Chambersburg with the commanding general. General A. P. Hill's corps was about four miles east of Chambersburg on the road to Gettysburg. General Ewell was then at Carlisle. On the night of the 28th June I was directed by General Lee to order General Ewell to move directly upon Harrisburg, and to inform him that General Longstreet would move next morning, the 29th, to his support.

General A. P. Hill was directed to move eastward to the Susquehanna, and cross the river below Harrisburg, seize the railroad between Harrisburg and Philadelphia, it being supposed that all reinforcements that might be coming from the north would be diverted to the defence of that city and that there would be such alarm created by these movements that the Federal Government would be obliged to withdraw its army from Virginia and abandon any plan that it might have for an attack on Richmond.

I sent the orders about 10 o'clock at night to General Ewell and General Hill, and had just returned to my tent, when I was sent for by the commanding general. I found him sitting in his tent with a man in citizen's dress, whom I did not know to be a soldier, but who,

General Lee informed me, was a scout of General Longstreet's, who had just been brought to him.[10]

He told me that this scout had left the neighbourhood of Frederickstown that morning, and had brought information that the Federal army had crossed the Potomac,[11] and that its advance had reached Frederickstown, and was moving thence westward towards the mountains. The scout informed General Lee that General Meade was then in command of the army, and gave him the first information that he had received since he left Virginia of the movements of the enemy. He inferred from the fact that the enemy had turned westward from Frederickstown that his purpose was to enter the Cumberland Valley south of our army, and obstruct our communications through Hagerstown with Virginia. General Lee said that, while he did not consider that he had complete communication with Virginia, he had all the communication that he needed, as long as the enemy had no considerable force in the Cumberland Valley. His principal need for communication with Virginia was to procure ammunition, and he thought that he could always do that with an escort, if the valley were free from a Federal force, but should the enemy have a considerable force in the valley this would be impossible. He considered it of great importance that the enemy's army should be kept east of the mountains, and consequently he determined to move his own army to the east side of the Blue Ridge so as

[10] This scout's name was Harrison. Longstreet had sent him off to Washington before the army left Fredericksburg, with a good supply of money, to gather information. *Battles and Leaders*, vol. II, p. 249.

[11] Four corps of Hooker's army had crossed the Potomac on June 25th.

to threaten Washington and Baltimore, and detain the Federal force on that side of the mountains to protect those cities. He directed me to countermand the orders to General Ewell and General Hill, and to order the latter to move eastward on the road through Cashtown or Gettysburg as circumstances might direct. He ordered General Longstreet to prepare to move the next morning, following Hill.

The army moved very slowly and there would have been no difficulty whatever in having the whole of it at Gettysburg by the morning of July 1st had we been aware of the movements of the enemy on the other side of the mountains.

Thus the movement towards Gettysburg was the result of the want of information which the cavalry alone could obtain for us, and General Lee was compelled to march through the mountains from Chambersburg eastward without the slightest knowledge of the enemy's movements, except that brought by the scout. While making this march the only information he possessed led him to believe that the army of the enemy was moving westward from Frederick to throw itself upon his line of communication with Virginia, and the object of the movement was simply to arrest the execution of this supposed plan of the enemy, and keep his army on the east side of the Blue Ridge.

It would have been entirely within the power of General Lee to have met the army of the enemy while it was moving on the road between Frederick and Gettysburg, or to have remained west of the mountains. It had not been his intention to deliver battle north of the Potomac if it could be avoided, except upon his

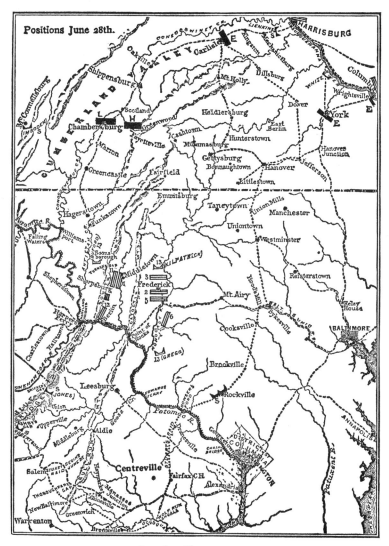

Stuart's raid --------------

own terms, and yet, by reason of the absence of the cavalry, his own army marching slowly from Chambersburg eastward and southward from Carlisle came unexpectedly upon the Federal advance on July 1st, a considerable part of the Confederate army not having then reached the field of battle.

It has been my object to correct the impression that has prevailed that the movement of the cavalry was made by General Lee's orders, and that at a critical moment of the campaign he crossed the Potomac river and moved into Pennsylvania, sending the entire cavalry force of his army upon a useless raid. That this is not true I think the evidence I have produced abundantly establishes. The suggestion of General Longstreet in communicating the order of General Lee to General Stuart of June 22nd, that the latter should pass by the enemy's rear, need not have led to the results which I have described.

General Longstreet's suggestion was qualified, as was General Lee's letter to General Stuart of June 22nd, by saying that the latter should go by the enemy's rear, "if he thinks he can get through." The first movement of General Stuart after leaving Salem depot early in the morning of the 25th brought him in conflict with General Hancock's corps, near Haymarket, and finding that he could not pass round the rear of the enemy,[12] the discretion so given him by General Longstreet was at an end, and there was yet time for General Stuart to retrace his steps and obey the order he had

[12] Marshall evidently means by this, "finding that he could not pass round the rear of the enemy and rejoin the right of Lee's army quickly." Stuart did in fact pass round Hooker's rear, but could not get into touch with Lee until July 1st.

received from General Lee in the letter of June 23rd, to cross the Potomac west of the Blue Ridge and move on until he felt the right of Ewell's column. But, instead of pursuing this course, General Stuart, as I have already pointed out, moved to Buckland, east of Bull Run mountains, and proceeded from that place to Brentsville, down to Wolf Run Shoals, and thence across the country by way of Fairfax Station to the Potomac river.

This latter movement was not sanctioned either by the suggestion of General Longstreet or by the positive orders of General Lee, and from the tenour of General Stuart's report it would seem that he entirely mistook the part that he was expected to take in the movement of the army. He placed himself east of the Federal Army, with that army between himself and the Confederate force. He left General Lee without any information as to the movements of the enemy from the time he crossed the Potomac river until July 2nd. By his silence, as I have described, he caused General Lee to move his army to Gettysburg, not with the expectation or purpose of meeting the enemy, but simply to prevent a movement which he supposed the enemy was making to obstruct his line of communication with Virginia, and caused him to fight the battle of Gettysburg without having his whole force present except on the third day, when it was equally possible, had General Lee been informed of what the enemy was doing, for him to have fought that battle with his entire force while the enemy's forces were still approaching Gettysburg, or to have remained west of the mountains and have met the Federal army on some other field.

The result of General Stuart's action was that two armies invaded Pennsylvania in 1863, instead of one. One of those armies had little cavalry, the other had nothing but cavalry. One was commanded by General Lee, the other by General Stuart.[13]

[13] I agree entirely with Colonel Marshall that the wanderings of Stuart's cavalry were, from the Confederate point of view, the decisive factor in the Gettysburg campaign. I agree also that it was Lee's intention to have had Stuart on his right during his march through Pennsylvania, and that Stuart should have appreciated both that such was Lee's intention and the vital importance of giving effect to it. Still, it is not possible for the impartial critic to absolve either Lee or his staff entirely from blame in the matter. It is evident that Lee in his conversation with Stuart and Longstreet had given a conditional assent to the proposed movement round Hooker's rear. On thinking the matter over, he came to the conclusion that such a movement might prevent Stuart from taking his place in the right flank of the army. He therefore directed the letters of the 22nd and 23rd to Stuart to be written and sent. The letter of the 23rd provided for Stuart's action, (1) if Hooker remained inactive; (2) if Hooker did not move northwards. Neither of these cases arose, as Hooker did cross the Potomac promptly.

The letter of the 22nd provided for the case which arose of Hooker's moving northwards. But this letter was sent through Longstreet, who added to it suggestions which, following on Stuart's conversation with Lee, evidently confused the mind of the cavalry commander and let him suppose that if Hooker moved north he was free to ride round the Federal rear if he could. Longstreet could not know all that was in Lee's mind, and it would have been better, since Lee proposed to use Stuart for the purpose of protecting and getting information for his whole army, to have first ascertained from Longstreet whether the three brigades of Stuart's cavalry could have been spared from Ashby's Gap, and, on receiving Longstreet's reply in the affirmative, to have given Stuart his orders direct, and thus have avoided the intervention of an intermediary, which is always liable to cause confusion and misunderstanding.

Finally, in view of the great importance which Lee attached to having Stuart on his flank, it would have been better to have told Stuart specifically that if he crossed the Potomac east of the Blue Ridge at all it must be by the fords near the mountains, so that he could rejoin the army quickly.

Colonel Marshall gives us here much the fullest account which has yet appeared of the most vital incident in the Gettysburg campaign, and the general conclusion to be drawn from his story is that military orders cannot be too simple, clear, and definite.

XI

THE GETTYSBURG CAMPAIGN

(c) THE BATTLE [1]

In accordance with the order issued by General Lee late on the night of the 28th, after he had received information of the enemy's movements from General Longstreet's scout, Heth's division of Hill's corps arrived at Cashtown on the 29th. The weather being inclement, the marches were conducted with a view to the comfort of the men and not with the object of a rapid concentration of the army. On the following morning Pettigrew's brigade was sent by General Heth to procure supplies [2] at Gettysburg, there being no information of an advance of the enemy to that place. Pettigrew found that Gettysburg was occupied by Federal troops, and being ignorant of their strength and unwilling to hazard an attack with his single brigade, he returned to Cashtown.

General Hill arrived at Cashtown with Pender's division on the evening of June 30th, and on the following morning, July 1st, he advanced with Heth's and Pender's divisions, accompanied by Pegram's and McIntosh's battalions of artillery towards Gettys-

---

[1] This account of the battle is based upon Marshall's draft of Lee's Gettysburg dispatch. I have marked with a black line the principal additions Marshall makes to the published dispatch. Many of these are significant.

[2] The supplies Pettigrew was seeking were boots for his men.

burg, in order to ascertain the strength of the enemy, whose force was supposed to consist chiefly of cavalry.[3] Heth's division, which was leading, found the enemy's vedettes about three miles west of Gettysburg, and proceeded to advance until within a mile of the town. Two brigades were then sent forward to reconnoitre.

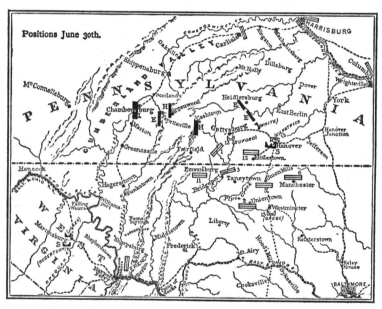

They drove in the advance of the enemy very gallantly, but subsequently encountered largely superior numbers, and were compelled to retire with loss.

General Heth then prepared for action, and as soon as Pender arrived to support him, was ordered by General Hill to advance. The artillery was placed in position, and the engagement opened with vigor. General Heth pressed the enemy steadily back, breaking his

[3] This was Buford's cavalry brigade.

first and second line and attacking his third with great resolution.[4] About 2 : 30 P.M. the advance of Ewell's corps, consisting of Rodes' division with Carter's battalion of artillery, arrived by Middleton Road, and forming on Heth's left nearly at right angles with his line, became warmly engaged with fresh numbers of the enemy.[5]

Heth's troops, having suffered severely in their protracted contest with a superior force, were relieved by Pender's, and Early, coming up by Heidlersburg Road, soon afterwards took position on the left of Rodes', when a general advance was made.

The enemy gave way on all sides and was driven through Gettysburg with great loss; Major-General Reynolds, who was in command, was killed. More than 5000 prisoners, exclusive of a large number of wounded, three pieces of artillery, and several colors were captured. Among the prisoners were two Brigadier-Generals, one of whom was badly wounded. Our own loss was heavy, including a number of officers, among whom were Major-General Heth slightly and Brigadier-General Scales of Pender's division severely wounded. The enemy retired to a range of hills south of Gettysburg,[6] where he displayed a strong force of infantry and artillery.

General Lee, on hearing the noise of Hill's battle, had ridden forward, and he arrived on the Seminary Ridge, about one mile west of Gettysburg. He established his headquarters near where the Chambersburg pike

[4] This attack was made upon the 1st Federal Corps under Reynolds, which had come up to support Buford.
[5] Howard's 11th corps.   [6] Cemetery Hill.

crosses the ridge soon after 2 P.M., and from that position he observed the retreat of the enemy through Gettysburg before General Ewell's advance. Owing to the absence of the cavalry, he was still without definite information as to the position of the enemy. It was ascertained from prisoners that we had been engaged with two corps and that the remainder of the army under General Meade was approaching Gettysburg. Until the position of the remaining corps of General Meade's army was ascertained with more certainty, General Lee decided that to make a general attack with the four divisions present would be dangerous. He therefore sent orders to General Ewell to carry the hill, to which the enemy had retired from Gettysburg, known as the Cemetery Hill, if practicable, but to avoid a general engagement until the arrival of the other divisions of the army, which were ordered to hasten forward.

General Ewell decided to await the arrival of Johnson's division, which had marched from Carlisle by the road west of the mountains, to guard the trains of his corps, and consequently did not reach Gettysburg until a late hour. In the meantime the enemy occupied the point which General Ewell designed to seize, but in what force he was could not be ascertained owing to the darkness. An intercepted dispatch showed that another Federal corps had halted that afternoon four miles from Gettysburg.

In these circumstances it was decided not to attack until the arrival of General Longstreet, two of whose divisions, those of Hood and McLaws, encamped about four miles in the rear during the night. Anderson's division of Hill's corps came up after the engagement of July 1st.

The movement of the Confederate army to Gettysburg was very deliberate. The whole of it could easily have been there by July 1st, or indeed, had the real position and movements of General Meade been known in time, General Lee if he had so desired could have been at Gettysburg on June 29th, instead of remaining at Chambersburg.

Whether, if he had had his cavalry to give information of the real movements of the enemy, he would have crossed the Blue Ridge earlier and struck the army of General Meade as it was hurrying up from the Potomac, stretched out as that army was, or whether he would have concentrated his own forces west of the mountains, and there have awaited the movements of his adversary, it is unnecessary to inquire.

It is plain, however, that with such an active and vigilant officer as Stuart, who had the largest cavalry force under his command that was ever assembled in Virginia at any time during the war, to inform him of the enemy's movements, either course would have been open to General Lee.

The result of the movement into Pennsylvania up to June 30th would have been to present a good opportunity to fight the Federal Army at a disadvantage, or to await its attack, our own army in the meantime living on the country, had General Lee possessed such information concerning the movements of the enemy as General Stuart would have been able to furnish, if the cavalry had moved upon the right of our army as it advanced from the Potomac River.

Had Stuart been where he was ordered to be, he could have informed General Lee before June 29th that the Federal army had crossed the Potomac and left Virginia, and certainly the cavalry would have been able, as it marched along our right, to ascertain that the reported movement of the enemy from Frederick westward, — which induced General Lee to place his army east of the mountains, — was incorrect. As it was, we were entirely ignorant until the afternoon of July 1st of the whereabouts of General Stuart; there was a small cavalry force with Ewell at Carlisle,[7] but none at all with the main body of the army.

We knew that Stuart was not west of the mountains, and if no misfortune had befallen him we knew that he would rejoin us east of the mountains; as it was, however, we moved slowly on towards Gettysburg, believing that the enemy was yet in Maryland, to the south of us, moving from Frederick across our line of communication through Cumberland Valley, and with no other knowledge of his place and movements.

That we came unexpectedly upon the Federal Army at Gettysburg may be inferred from the fact that, although our whole army could have been there on July 1st as easily as a part of it, only two of Ewell's and two of Hill's divisions were on the field during the engagement of that day, and the chief reason for not following up our first success was the absence of Longstreet's corps and of one division of each of the other two.

Four divisions were on the ground, and five others might have been there had the necessity of their pres-

[7] Jenkins's brigade.

ence been suspected. Had all the army been up, there is no reason to suppose that there would have been any fighting at Gettysburg after the first day, to say nothing of the other consequences to General Meade's army that might have followed the crushing defeat or destruction of its advanced corps.

It had not been intended to deliver a general battle so far from our base unless attacked, but coming unexpectedly upon the whole Federal army, to withdraw through the mountains with our extensive train would have been difficult and dangerous. At the same time we were not able to await an attack, as the country was unfavourable for collecting supplies in the presence of the enemy, who could restrain our foraging parties by holding the mountain passes with local and other troops.

A battle was therefore become in a measure unavoidable, and the success already gained gave hopes of a favourable issue.

In order to arrange for the plans of attack upon the enemy, General Lee, as soon as he saw that General Ewell's attack was not continued, rode to the Confederate left to see that General. An examination of the ground shewed the difficulty of attack in that quarter. The enemy occupied a strong position with his right upon two commanding elevations, adjacent to each other, one southeast,[8] and the other, known as Cemetery Hill, immediately south of the town, which lay at its base. His line extended thence upon the high ground along the Emmittsburg road with a steep ridge in rear, which was also occupied. This ridge was difficult of ascent, particularly the two hills above men-

[8] Culp's Hill.

tioned as forming its northern extremity, and a third at the other end on which the enemy's left rested.

Numerous stone and rail fences along the slope served to afford protection to the enemy's troops, and impede our advance. In his front the ground was undulating, and generally open for about three-quarters of a mile. General Ewell's corps constituted our left; Johnson's division being opposite the height adjoining Cemetery Hill, Early's in the centre in front of the north face of the latter, with Rodes' division upon his right.

Hill's corps faced the west side of Cemetery Hill, and extended nearly parallel to the Emmittsburg Road, making an angle with Ewell. Pender's division formed Hill's left; Anderson's his right; Heth's division under Brigadier General Pettigrew being in reserve. Hill's artillery under Colonel R. L. Walker was posted in eligible positions along his line.

After consultations with Generals Hill and Ewell, General Lee at one time contemplated a movement round the left flank of the enemy, but he abandoned this plan in view of the facts that he was uncertain of the position of General Meade's corps, that in the absence of the cavalry such a movement could not be concealed from the enemy, and that our line of march must have necessarily been so close to the enemy's position as to have exposed us to a very dangerous attack. It was therefore determined to attack the enemy's left.

After his consultation with Generals Hill and Ewell, General Lee returned to his position on Seminary Ridge where he met General Longstreet. The latter proposed to General Lee the plan, which he had already considered and rejected, of turning the enemy's left.

General Lee informed him that he had decided to attack the enemy the next day as early as practicable, and directed General Longstreet to place the divisions of McLaws and Hood on the right of Hill, partially enveloping the enemy's left, which he was to drive in. General Hill was ordered to threaten the enemy's centre to prevent reinforcements being drawn to either wing, and to co-operate with his right division in Longstreet's attack. General Ewell was instructed to make a simultaneous demonstration upon the enemy's right, to be converted into a real attack should opportunity offer.

General Lee slept that night in a small house east of the Seminary Ridge and just north of the Chambersburg pike, his staff bivouacking in an orchard near by. Early on the 2nd, General Longstreet came to see General Lee and renewed his proposal that a movement should be made to turn the enemy's left, and to this General Lee answered that he was determined to attack the enemy where he was. General Longstreet then rode off to meet his troops.

After waiting some time for the expected development of General Longstreet's attack and expressing his surprise that it had not begun, General Lee rode to the right to see General Ewell, and to ascertain whether a reconnaissance made of Cemetery Hill in daylight shewed that an attack on that position would be more promising. It was found that the enemy had strengthened his position greatly during the night, and that an attack upon the enemy's right would have little prospect of success unless it was combined with other attacks on his left and centre. General Lee thereupon returned to Seminary Ridge, and about 11 o'clock issued orders to General Longstreet to begin his attack upon the enemy's left as soon as possible.[9]

It was not however until 4 P.M. that Longstreet's batteries opened and soon afterwards Hood's division on his extreme right moved to the attack. McLaws followed somewhat later, four of Anderson's brigades, those of Wilcox, Perry, A. R. Wright, and Posey supporting him in the order named. The enemy was soon driven from his position on the Emmittsburg road to the cover of a ravine and of a line of stone fences at the foot of the ridge in his rear. He was dislodged from these after a severe struggle, and retired up the ridge leaving a number of his batteries in our possession.

Wilcox's and Wright's brigades advanced with great

[9] This account of Lee's dealings with Longstreet and the latter's attitude confirms other accounts from Southern sources. A Confederate attack delivered before the arrival of Sedgwick's 6th corps, which came on the field early in the afternoon of July 2nd, had every prospect of success. Both the 1st and 11th Federal corps had been severely handled on the 1st, and a concerted attack delivered by Ewell, A. P. Hill, and the two divisions of Longstreet's corps, which were up, would almost certainly have carried the Gettysburg Ridge. The evidence that Lee intended such an attack to be made early on the 2nd is overwhelming. Generals Long and Pendleton, and now Colonel Marshall of Lee's staff, assert that that was so, and they are confirmed by A. P. Hill and Ewell. Longstreet asserts no less positively that he received no orders to attack before 11 A.M. on July 2nd.

From what Colonel Marshall here says, it would appear that Lee in his conversation with Longstreet on the night of July 1st and the early morning of July 2nd expressed his intention of attacking as early as possible. Longstreet, who, as usual, considered his own plan the best, did not take this to be a definite order, and appears to have delayed in the hope of changing Lee's mind. The mistake made was in not committing the instructions to Longstreet to writing, and in not giving those orders in a precise form. This mistake proved fatal; for after about 3 P.M. on July 2nd the Confederates had little or no chance of being able to carry the Federal position.

gallantry, breaking successive lines of the enemy's infantry and compelling him to abandon much of his artillery. Wilcox reached the foot and Wright gained the crest of the ridge itself, driving the enemy down the opposite side, but having become separated from Mc-Laws and gone beyond the other two brigades of the division, they were attacked in front and on both flanks, and compelled to retire, being unable to bring off any of the captured artillery.

McLaws' left also fell back, and it being now nearly dark General Longstreet determined to await the arrival of Pickett's division. He disposed his command to hold the ground gained on the right, withdrawing his left to the first position from which the enemy had been driven. Four pieces of artillery, several hundreds of prisoners, and two regimental flags were taken.

As soon as the engagement began on our right, General Johnson opened with his artillery, and about two hours later advanced up the hill [10] next to the Cemetery Hill with three brigades, the fourth being detained by a demonstration on his left. Soon afterwards General Early attacked Cemetery Hill with two brigades supported by a third, the fourth having been previously detached. The enemy had greatly increased the strength of his position assailed by Johnson and Early. The troops of the former moved steadily up the steep and rugged ascent under a heavy fire, driving the enemy into his entrenchments, part of which was carried by Stuart's brigade and a number of prisoners taken.

[10] Culp's Hill.

On Cemetery Hill the attack by Early's leading brigades, those of Hayes and Hoke, under Colonel I. E.
Avery was made with vigor; two lines of the enemy's
infantry were dislodged from the cover of some stone
and board fences on the side of the ascent, and driven
back into the woods on the crest, into which our troops
forced their way and seized several pieces of artillery.
A heavy force then advanced against their right, which
was unsupported, and they were compelled to retire,
bringing with them 100 prisoners and four stands of
colors.

General Ewell had directed General Rodes to attack
in concert with Early, whose right he was told to cover,
and had requested Brigadier-General Lane, then commanding Pender's division, to co-operate on the right
of Rodes. When the time to attack arrived, General
Rodes, not having his troops in position, was unpre-
pared to co-operate with General Early, and before he
could get in readiness the latter had been obliged to
retire for want of the expected support on his right.
General Lane was prepared to give the assistance required of him, and so informed General Rodes but the
latter deemed it useless to advance after the failure of
Early's attack.

General Rodes in his report gives his reasons for this
momentous and fatal want of co-operation. He says:
"Orders given during the afternoon and after the
engagement had opened on the right required me to
co-operate with the attacking force as soon as any opportunity to do so with good effect was offered. Seeing
the stir alluded to, I thought the opportunity had come
and immediately sought General Early with a view of

J. A. EARLY

making an attack in concert with him; he agreed with me as to the propriety of attacking, and made preparations accordingly. I hastened to inform the officer commanding the troops on my right, part of Pender's division, I would attack just at dark, and proceeded to make my arrangements; but having to draw my troops out of town by the flank, change the direction of the line of battle, and then traverse a distance of 1200 or 1400 yards, while General Early had to move only half that distance without change of front, the result was that before I drove the enemy's skirmishers in, General Early had attacked and been compelled to retire."

If General Rodes had prepared his troops to advance on the right of General Early the latter would not have been compelled to withdraw from a successful attack, and the position on Cemetery Hill would have been held. The capture of that hill would have enabled General Early to have enfiladed the Federal troops opposed to those of General Longstreet, and the effect of such fire at that time might have changed the result of the day. At one time on July 2nd victory was within our certain reach. It was lost by delay and by the failure of co-operation on the part of the troops engaged.

The result of this day's operations induced the belief that with proper concerted action, and with the increased support that the positions gained on our right would enable the artillery to give to the assaulting columns, we should ultimately succeed, and it was accordingly determined to continue the attack. The general plan was unchanged. Longstreet, reinforced by Pickett's three brigades, which arrived near the battle field on the afternoon of the 2nd, was ordered to attack next morning, and General Ewell was directed to assail the enemy's right at the same time. The latter during the night reinforced General Johnson with two brigades from Rodes' and one from Early's divisions. At an early hour on July 3rd General Lee met General Longstreet, who again proposed that a movement should be made round the enemy's left. General Lee however decided that the attack should be made as ordered. General Longstreet's dispositions were not completed as early as was expected, but before notice of this could be sent to General Ewell, General Johnson had already become engaged and it was too late to recall him. The enemy attempted to recover the works taken the previous evening, but was repulsed and General Johnson attacked in turn.

After a gallant and prolonged struggle, in which the enemy was forced to abandon part of his entrenchments, General Johnson found himself unable to carry the strongly fortified crest of the hill. The projected attack on the enemy's left by General Longstreet not having been made, he was enabled to hold his right with a force largely superior to that of General Johnson, and finally to threaten his flank and rear, rendering it necessary for him to retire to his original position about 1 P.M.

General Longstreet was delayed by a force occupying the high rocky hills[11] on the enemy's left, from which his troops could be attacked in reverse as they advanced. His operations had been embarrassed a day previous

[11] The Round Tops

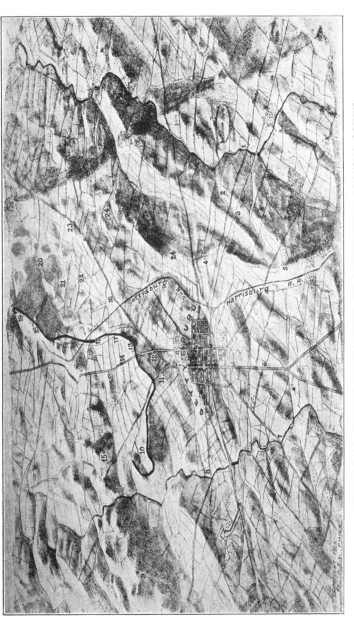

RELIEF MAP OF THE BATTLEFIELD OF GETTYSBURG, LOOKING SOUTH

Federal Main Position ⌒

1. Chambersburg pike bridge over Willoughby Creek — beginning of the battle of the first day. 2. McPherson's farm and woods — Lee's quarters at night. 3. Railway cuts. 4. Seminary. 5. Oak Hill. 6. Carlisle Road. 7. Harrisburg Road Bridge over Rock Creek. 8. Hanover Road. 9. Wolf Hill. 10. Culp's Hill. 11. East Cemetery Hill. 12. Cemetery Hill. 13. Ziegler's Grove. 14. Meade's headquarters on the Taneytown Road. 15. Slocum's headquarters on Power's Hill. 16. Codori's. 17. Cemetery Ridge. 18. Little Round Top. 19. Round Top. 20. Devil's Den. 21. Wheat field. 22. Trostle's farm. 23. Emmitsburg Road. 24. Seminary Ridge — Lee's day headquarters. 19 to 25. About extreme right of Longstreet's line.

and he now deemed it necessary to defend his flank and rear with the divisions of McLaws and Hood. He was therefore reinforced by Heth's division, and two brigades of Pender's to the command of which Major General Trimble was assigned. General Hill was directed to hold his line with the rest of his command, giving General Longstreet further assistance if called for, and to avail himself of any success that might be gained. A careful examination of the ground secured by Longstreet during the engagement of the 2nd was made, and his batteries placed in position, which [it] was believed would enable him to silence those of the enemy.

A. P. Hill's artillery and part of Ewell's was ordered to open simultaneously, the assaulting column to advance under cover of the combined fire of the three. The batteries were directed to push forward as the infantry progressed, protect their flanks and support their attacks closely. About 1 P.M., at a given signal a heavy cannonade was opened and continued for about two hours with marked effect on the enemy.

His batteries replied vigorously at first, but towards the close their fires slackened perceptibly, and General Longstreet ordered forward the column of attack, consisting of Pickett's and Heth's divisions in two lines, Pickett on the right. Wilcox's brigade marched in rear of Pickett's right to guard that flank and Heth supported by Lane's and Scales' brigades under General Trimble.

The troops moved steadily on under a heavy fire of musketry and artillery, the main attack being directed against the enemy's left centre; his batteries reopened as soon as they appeared; our own having nearly exhausted their ammunition in the protracted cannonade that preceded the advance of the infantry were unable to reply, or render the necessary support to the attacking party.

The fact that the artillery ammunition had been so far reduced was known to General Longstreet, but was not reported to General Lee. No order issued by General Lee justified the omission of notice of this important fact by General Longstreet.

Owing to this fact, the enemy was enabled to throw a strong force of infantry against our left, already wavering under a concentrated fire of artillery from the ridge in front, and from Cemetery Hill on the left. It finally gave way, and the right after penetrating the enemy's lines, entering his advance work, and capturing some of his artillery, was attacked simultaneously in front and on both flanks, and driven back with heavy loss. The troops were rallied and reformed, but the enemy did not pursue.

A large number of brave officers and men fell or were captured on this occasion. Pickett's three brigade commanders, General Armistead, and R. B. Garnet were killed and General Kemper dangerously wounded. Major General Trimble and Brigadier General Pettigrew were also wounded, the former severely.

The movements of the army preceding the battle of Gettysburg had been greatly embarrassed by the absence of the cavalry. As soon as it was known that the enemy had crossed into Maryland orders were sent back to the brigades of B. H. Robinson and William

GEORGE E. PICKETT

E. Jones, which had been left to guard the passes of the
Blue Ridge, to rejoin the army without delay, and it
was expected that General Stuart with the remainder
of his command would soon arrive. In the exercise of
the discretion given him, General Stuart determined
to pass round the rear of the Federal army then lying
on the Potomac River. He thus disregarded repeated
instructions given to him that as soon as he had ascertained that the Federal army had crossed the Potomac
River and had left Virginia, one of the results that was
confidently expected to take place from the movements
of our army northward from the river, he should lose
no time in reporting the fact and place himself on the
right of our troops, giving them information of the
enemy's movements and guarding their flank.

General Stuart, marching from Salem on the night of
June 24th, found the enemy's forces so distributed as to
render that route impracticable; he nevertheless
adhered to his original plan and was forced to make a
wide detour through Buckland and Brentsville, and
crossed the Occoquan at Wolf Run Shoals, on the morning of the 27th. Continuing his march through Fairfax Court House and Dranesville, he arrived at the
Potomac below the mouth of Seneca Creek in the evening. He found the river much swollen by the recent
rains, but after great exertions gained the Maryland
shore before midnight with his whole command. General Stuart now ascertained that the Federal army,
which he had discovered to be drawing towards the
Potomac, had crossed the river on the 26th, and was
moving towards Frederick, thus interposing itself
between him and our forces.

General Stuart accordingly marched northward through Rockville and Westminster to Hanover, Pennsylvania, where he arrived on the 30th, but the enemy advancing with equal rapidity on his left continued to obstruct communication with our main body.

Supposing from such information as he could obtain that part of the army was at Carlisle, he left Hanover that night and proceeded to Carlisle by way of Dover. He reached Carlisle on July 1st, where he received orders to proceed to Gettysburg; he arrived at Gettysburg in the afternoon of the following day, and took position on General Ewell's left. His leading brigade, under General Hampton, encountered and repulsed a body of the enemy's cavalry at Hunterstown endeavouring to reach our rear.

General Stuart had several skirmishes during his march, and at Hanover quite a severe engagement took place with a strong force of cavalry which was finally compelled to withdraw from the town.

The prisoners taken by the cavalry and paroled at various places amounted to about 800, and at Rockville a large train of wagons coming from Washington was intercepted and captured. Many of them were destroyed, but 125 with all animals of the train were secured. The ranks of the cavalry were much reduced by its long and arduous march, repeated conflicts, and insufficient food and forage, but the day after its arrival at Gettysburg it engaged the enemy's cavalry with unabated spirit and effectually protected our left. In this action General Hampton was seriously wounded while acting with his accustomed gallantry. Robertson's and Jones' brigades arrived on July 3rd and were stationed upon our right flank.

The severe loss sustained by the army and the reduction of its ammunition rendered another attempt to dislodge the enemy unadvisable, and it was therefore determined to withdraw. The trains with such of the wounded as could bear removal were ordered to Williamsport on July 4th, part moving through Cashtown and Greencastle, escorted by General Imboden, and the remainder by the Fairfield road. The army retained its position until dark, when it was put in motion for the Potomac by the last named route. A heavy rain continued throughout the night and so much impeded its progress that Ewell's corps, which brought up the rear, did not leave Gettysburg until late in the forenoon of the following day.

The enemy offered no serious interruption and after an arduous march we arrived at Hagerstown, in the afternoon of the 6th and morning of July 7th. The great length of our trains made it difficult to guard them effectually in passing through the mountains and a number of wagons and ambulances were captured.

The trains succeeded in reaching Williamstown on the 6th, but were unable to cross the Potomac on account of the high state of water. Here they were attacked by a strong force of cavalry and artillery, which was gallantly repulsed by General Imboden, whose command had been strengthened by several batteries and two regiments of infantry, which had been detached at Winchester to guard prisoners and were returning to the army.

While the enemy was being held in check, General Stuart arrived with the cavalry, which had performed valuable service in guarding the flanks of the army during the retrograde movement, and after a short engagement drove the enemy from the field. The rains that had prevailed almost without intermission since our entrance into Maryland and greatly interfered with our movements had made the Potomac unfordable, and the pontoon bridge left at Falling Waters during the advance of the army had been partially destroyed by the enemy. The wounded and prisoners were sent over the river as rapidly as possible in a few ferry boats, while the trains awaited the subsidence of the water and the construction of a new pontoon bridge.

On July 8th the enemy advanced towards Hagerstown, but was repulsed by General Stuart and pursued as far as Boonesborough; with this exception nothing occurred but occasional skirmishings until July 12th when the main body of the enemy arrived. The army then took up a position previously selected covering the Potomac from Williamsport to Falling Water, where it remained for two days with the enemy immediately in front, manifesting no disposition to attack, but throwing up entrenchments all along his line.

By the 13th the river at Williamsport though still deep was fordable, and a good bridge was completed at Falling Waters; new boats having been constructed and some of the old recovered. As further delay would enable the enemy to obtain reinforcements and as it was difficult to procure a sufficient supply of flour for the troops, the working of the mills being interrupted by high water, it was determined to await an attack no longer. Orders were accordingly given to cross the Potomac that night; Ewell's corps by the ford at Williamsport, and the corps of Longstreet and Hill by the bridge. The cavalry was directed to relieve the infantry skirmishers and bring up the rear; the movement was much retarded by a severe rainstorm and the darkness of the night.

Ewell's corps having the advantage of a turnpike road marched with less difficulty, and crossed the river by 8 o'clock the following morning. The condition of the road to the pontoon bridge and the time consumed in the passage of the artillery, ammunition wagons, and ambulances, which could not ford the river, so much delayed the progress of Longstreet and Hill that it was daylight before their troops began to cross. Heth's division was halted about a mile and a half from the bridge to protect the passage of the column. No interruption was offered by the enemy until about 11 A.M. when his cavalry supported by artillery appeared in front of General Heth.

A small number in advance of the main body were mistaken by our men for our own cavalry retiring, no notice having been given of the withdrawal of the latter, and was suffered to approach our lines. The party was immediately captured or destroyed with the exception of two or three, but General Pettigrew, an officer of great merit and promise, was mortally wounded in the encounter, and survived his removal to Virginia only a few days.

The bridge being clear, General Heth began to withdraw. The enemy advanced but his efforts to break our line were repulsed and the passage of the river was completed by 1 P.M. Owing to the extent of General Heth's line some of his men most remote from the bridge were cut off before they could reach it, but the greater part of those taken by the enemy, supposed to amount in all to about 500, consisted of men from various commands who lingered behind, overcome by previous labors and hardships, and the fatigue of a most trying march.

There was no loss of material, except a few broken wagons, and two pieces of artillery which the horses were unable to draw through the deep mud. Other horses were sent back for them, but the rear of our column had passed before they arrived; the army proceeded to the vicinity of Bunker Hill and Darkesville where it halted to obtain the necessary repose.

The enemy made no effort to follow except with his cavalry, which crossed the Potomac at Harper's Ferry and advanced towards Martinsburg on July 16th; they were attacked by General Fitz Lee with his own and Chambliss' brigades, and driven back with loss. When the army returned to Virginia it was intended to move into Loudoun, but the Shenandoah was found to be impassable. While waiting for it to subside the enemy crossed the Potomac River east of the Blue Ridge and seized the passes we had designed to use. As he continued to advance along the eastern slope, apparently with the purpose of cutting us off from the railroad to Richmond, General Longstreet was ordered on July 19th to proceed to Culpeper Court House by way of Front Royal. He succeeded in passing part of his command over the Shenandoah in time to prevent the occupation of Manassas and Chester Gaps by the enemy, and marched through Chester Gap to Culpeper Court House, where he arrived on the 24th. He was followed without serious opposition by General A. P. Hill.

General Ewell having been detained in the Valley by an effort to capture a force of the enemy guarding the Baltimore and Ohio Railroad west of Martinsburg, Wright's brigade [12] was left to hold Manassas Gap until his arrival. He reached Front Royal on the 23rd, with Johnson's and Rodes' divisions, Early's being near Winchester, and found General Wright skirmishing with the enemy's infantry, which had already appeared in Manassas Gap.

General Ewell supported Wright with Rodes' division and some artillery, and the enemy was held in check. Finding that the Federal force greatly exceeded his own, General Ewell marched through Slaughter's Gap and ordered Early to move up the Valley to Strasburg and New Market. He encamped near Madison Court House on July 29th. The enemy massed his army in the vicinity of Warrenton, and on the night of July 31st his cavalry with a large supporting force of infantry crossed the Rappahannock at Rappahannock Station and Kelly's Ford.

The next day they advanced towards Brandy Station, their progress being gallantly resisted by General Stuart with Hampton's brigade, commanded by Colonel L. S. Baker, who fell back gradually to our lines about two miles south of Brandy. Our infantry skirmishers advanced and drove the enemy beyond Brandy Station. It was now determined to place the army in a position to enable it more readily to oppose the enemy

[12] Of A. P. Hill's corps.

should he attempt to move southward, that near Culpeper Court House being one he could easily avoid. Longstreet and Hill were put in motion on August 3rd, leaving the cavalry at Culpeper. Ewell had previously been ordered from Madison, and by the 5th the army occupied the line of the Rapidan.

Among Colonel Marshall's papers is a memorandum dated April 15th, 1868, by Colonel William Allan, author of *The Army of Northern Virginia in 1862*, of a conversation which Allan had just held with Lee. This conversation was occasioned, Allan says, by a letter of inquiry addressed to him by W. M. Macdonald. Lee submitted his answer to Allan. Macdonald asked:

1. Why in 1862, Lee, at Frederick City, turned round to Harper's Ferry, and did not march at once on Baltimore?
2. Why Burnside was not attacked in the plain at Fredericksburg after his repulse?
3. Why Gettysburg was fought and lost?

Colonel Allan's memorandum of Lee's replies to these questions was: —

(1) "In regard to the first, General Lee said he had never invaded the North with an eye to holding permanently the hostile portions of it. He said that especially in 1862 his object was not primarily to take Baltimore, or to undertake any very decided offensive movement. It was, in the first place, to get the enemy away from the works in front of Washington, which he thought it folly to attack from the Manassas side; his next object was to subsist our own army. He could not

stay where he was at Manassas from want of supplies and adequate transportation. He could not go straight forward, for he thought it injudicious to attack the fortifications. To have returned into Loudoun was to give the enemy possession of Fairfax, *etc.*, and to invite him to flank him towards Richmond. By crossing the river and thus threatening Washington and Baltimore, he drew the enemy from their works, thus relieved Virginia from their presence, and got ample supplies from Maryland for his troops. Once there, in order to remain for any time, or to be in proper position for battle, when he chose or should be forced to deliver one, his communications had to be kept clear through the Valley, and to clear them and to capture the detached force at Harper's Ferry was the object of his movement then. He would have fought McClellan after Harper's Ferry if he had had his troops all in hand, and McClellan out where he could get at him. Sharpsburg was forced on him by McClellan finding out his plans and moving quickly in consequence.

(2) "In regard to Burnside, he stated, as he had said to me before, that it was folly to attack the enemy under the guns on the Stafford side; that the larger part of our losses at Fredericksburg resulted from pursuing the enemy too far into the plain, that he had carefully examined the whole river, and was convinced that a thing of that sort could not have been judiciously undertaken, unless he might when the enemy was retiring. This effort he would have made, but did not know of their retreat till morning. He did not expect them to retreat, and had hoped they would have tried his lines again.

(3) "As for Gettysburg — First, he did not intend to give battle in Pennsylvania if he could avoid it. The South was too weak to carry on a war of invasion, and his offensive movements against the North were never intended except as parts of a defensive system. He did not know the Federal Army was at Gettysburg, *could not believe it*, as Stuart had been specially ordered to cover his (Lee's) movements, and keep him informed of the enemy's position, and he (Stuart) had sent no word. He found himself engaged with the Federal Army, therefore, unexpectedly, and had to fight. This being decided on, victory would have been won if he could have gotten one decided simultaneous attack on the whole line. This he tried his uttermost to effect for three days and failed. Ewell he could not get to act with decision. Rodes, Early, Johnson, attacked, and were hurt in detail. Longstreet, Hill, etc. could not be gotten to act in concert. Thus the Federal troops were enabled to be opposed to each of our corps, or even divisions in succession. As it was, however, he inflicted more damage than he received, and broke up the Federal summer campaign. When he retired he would have crossed the Potomac at once if he could have done so. It was so swollen as to delay him, and hence his works at Hagerstown. He would not have been sorry if Meade had attacked him then, but he did not stop specially to invite it, but because the river was high. Meade's failure to attack showed how he had suffered.

"In regard to going into Pennsylvania at all: He thought it was far better than remaining at Fredericksburg. He had twice been attacked there, and had succeeded in repulsing the attacks, but he did not wish again to remain there to risk another attempt. The position was easily flanked, and the plan Grant afterwards pursued might have been tried at any time. He thought it best to improve the advantage gained by marching north, thus drawing the enemy away from the Rappahannock, exciting their fears for Washington, and by watching his opportunities baffle and break up their plans. To have lain at Fredericksburg would have allowed them time to collect force and initiate a new campaign on the old plan. In going into Pennsylvania he diverted their attention, kept them thinking of Washington instead of Richmond, and got ample supplies for his army. He did not want to fight unless he could get a good opportunity to hit them in detail. He expected, however, probably to find it necessary to give battle before his return in the fall, as it would have been difficult to retreat without. He had no idea of permanent occupation of Pennsylvania. He was troubled as it was to forage, so weak was the force he could spare for the purpose. He expected therefore to move about, manœuvre, and alarm the enemy, threaten their cities, hit any blows he might be able to deliver without risking a general battle, and then, towards fall, return and recover his base. Stuart's failure to carry out his intentions forced the battle of Gettysburg, and the imperfect, halting way in which his corps commanders, especially Ewell, fought the battle gave victory, which as he says trembled for three days in the balance, finally to the foe. He says that one day, I think the second, he consulted Ewell and told him that if he could not carry his part of the line he would move the second corps to the right of Longstreet and threaten their communications with Baltimore, but E. Johnson and Ewell said the line then held could be carried. Johnson, Rodes, and Early however attacked in succession, and were not able to hold any advantage.

"General Lee spoke feelingly of the criticism to which he had been subjected, said critics talked much of that they knew little about, said he had fought honestly and earnestly to the best of his knowledge and ability for the Cause, and had never allowed his own advantage or reputation to come into consideration. He cared nothing for these. Success was the great matter. He instanced General Joe Johnston's sensitiveness on this score, and how wrong and unwise it was.

"He referred to a reported conversation of Longstreet, in which the latter was reported to have said that General Lee was under a promise to the Lieutenant General not to fight a general battle in Pennsylvania. General Lee said he did not believe this was ever said by Longstreet. That the idea was absurd. He never made any such promise and never thought of doing any such thing."

This memorandum is evidence that if Lee was careful to avoid in his dispatches, often to Marshall's grief, any appearance of defending his own reputation by casting blame upon subordinates, he was yet in general agreement with the criticisms and strictures which Marshall makes. It is also evidence that the prime cause of the Confederate failure in the campaign was Stuart's absence, and of their failure in the battle the lack of clear written orders, specifying how and when the attacks should be delivered.

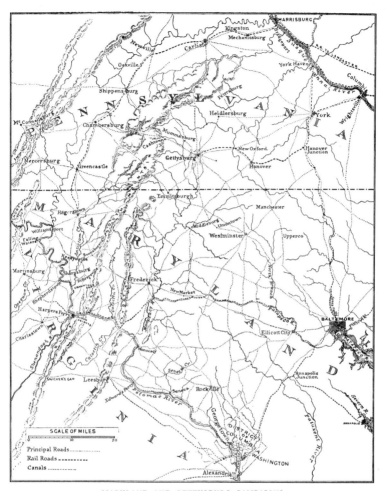

MARYLAND AND GETTYSBURG CAMPAIGNS

XII

APPOMATTOX

Colonel Marshall's Story of the Surrender

There have been great events in our history. York-town was a great event, Saratoga was a great event, and there have been great events in our history since the war of the Revolution; but the greatest was that which occurred on April 9th, 1865, at the little village of Appomattox, when General Lee met General Grant and the question of the indissoluble union of these States passed into history, never to be revived.

Perhaps the most impressive feature of that occasion was the fact that there American soldiers met together, who dealt with each other as American soldiers. If the officers of General Grant's army had been instructed how to act; if they had learned their parts; if they had been taught by the greatest actors how to play them, how to act at a time when one of the loftiest souls that God ever sent upon earth was humbled, how to act so as to show their respect and veneration, they could not have done better than they did. They could not have done better, because they were and behaved as American soldiers; they loved their enemies and they did good to those who hated them.

I shall begin my narrative of this stirring episode with the opening of the correspondence between General Lee and General Grant.

After the disaster of Sailor's Creek,[1] the Army of
Northern Virginia, reduced to two corps under the command of Generals Longstreet and Gordon, moved
through Farmville, where rations were issued to some
of the starving troops. A close pursuit by the overwhelming army of General Grant made it necessary to
remove the wagon trains before all the men could be
supplied, and the remnant of the great Army of Northern Virginia, exhausted by fight and starvation, moved
on the road to Appomattox Court House. On the
afternoon of the 7th of April, 1865, General Grant sent
to General Lee the first letter. It read : —

April 7th, 1865

General R. E. Lee, Commanding C. S. A.
GENERAL, —
   The result of the last week must convince you of the hopelessness of further resistance on the part of the Army of
Northern Virginia in this struggle. I feel that it is so, and
regard it as my duty to shift from myself the responsibility
of any further effusion of blood by asking of you the surrender of that portion of the Confederate States Army known
as the Army of Northern Virginia.
                    Very respectfully, your obedient servant
                         U. S. GRANT, Lieutenant General

There was some difference of opinion among the
general officers as to the nature of the reply to be made
to General Grant's letter, some thinking it was yet
possible to save the remnant of the army.[2] It was

[1] At Sailor's Creek, a small affluent of the Appomattox, Ewell's corps
was surrounded on April 6th and surrendered.
[2] Among these was Lee himself. General Long (*Memories of R. E.
Lee*, p. 416) describes what happened on April 7th before Grant's first
letter arrived : —

greatly reduced; it was starving; but it was as brave an army as ever carried a gun, and General Lee had such confidence in it as, I believe, would have made him risk anything, if there had been any chance of success. Finally, of course under General Lee's instructions, I wrote the following answer to General Grant's letter : —

April 7th, 1865

GENERAL, —

I have received your note of this date.   Though not entertaining the opinion you express of the hopelessness of further resistance on the part of the Army of Northern Virginia, I reciprocate your desire to avoid the useless effusion of blood, and therefore before considering your proposition, ask the terms you will offer on condition of its surrender.

Very respectfully, your obedient servant,

R. E. LEE, General

To Lieut.-Gen. U. S. Grant, Commanding Armies of the United States

---

"Perceiving the difficulties that surrounded the army and believing its extrication hopeless, a number of the principal officers from a feeling of affection and sympathy for the Commander-in-Chief and with a wish to lighten his responsibility and soften the pain of defeat, volunteered to inform him that in their opinion the struggle had reached a point when further resistance was hopeless, and that the contest should be terminated and negotiations opened for a surrender of the army.   The delivery of this opinion was confided to General Pendleton, who by his character and devotion to General Lee was well qualified for such an office.   The names of Longstreet and some others who did not coincide in opinion with their associates did not appear in the list presented by Pendleton.   The interview that succeeded is thus described by General Pendleton :

" 'General Lee was lying on the ground.   No others heard the conversation between him and myself.   He received my communication with the reply, "Oh! no! I trust it has not come to that," and added: "General, we have yet too many bold men to think of laying down our arms.   The enemy do not fight with spirit, while our boys still do.   Besides, if I were to say a word to the Federal Commander, he would regard it as such a confession of weakness as to make it the condition of demanding an unconditional surrender — a proposal to which I will never listen." ' "

The next day Grant replied as follows : —

April 8th, 1865

General R. E. Lee, Commanding C. S. A.
GENERAL, —

Your note of last evening in reply to mine of same date, asking the conditions on which I will accept the surrender of the Army of Northern Virginia, is just received. In reply, I would say, peace being my great desire, there is but one condition that I insist on, namely, that the men and officers surrendered shall be disqualified for taking up arms against the Government of the United States, until properly exchanged.

I will meet you, or will designate officers to meet any officers you name for the same purpose, at any point agreeable to you, for the purpose of arranging definitely the terms upon which the surrender of the Army of Northern Virginia will be received.

Very respectfully, your obedient servant

U. S. GRANT, Lieutenant General

It will be observed that General Grant, in this letter, manifested that delicate consideration for his great adversary which marked all his subsequent conduct towards him. He offered to have the terms of the capitulation arranged by officers to be appointed for the purpose by himself and General Lee, thus sparing the latter the pain and mortification of conducting personally the arrangements for the surrender of his army.

I have no doubt that this proposition proceeded from the sincere desire of General Grant to do all in his power to spare the feelings of General Lee, but it is not unworthy of remark that when Lord Cornwallis opened his correspondence with General Washington which

ended in the surrender at Yorktown, his lordship proposed in his letter of October 17, 1781, "a cessation of
hostilities for 24 hours, and that two officers may be
appointed by each side to meet at Mr. Moore's house
to settle terms of surrender of the posts of York and
Gloucester."

In view of this letter, and of the fact that Cornwallis
declined to attend the ceremony of the surrender of his
army, deputing General O'Hara to represent him on
that occasion, it is very plain that his lordship shrunk
from sharing with his army the humiliation of surrender.

General Grant's letter offered General Lee an opportunity to avoid the trial to which the British commander felt himself unequal. But General Lee was
made of different stuff. It is not without interest to
recall what General Lee's father, Light Horse Harry
Lee, says of the conduct of Cornwallis at Yorktown.

In Lee's (Light Horse Harry's) *Memoirs of the War*,
the author, who was a witness of what occurred,
says : —

"Every eye was turned searching for the British
Commander-in-Chief, anxious to look at that man,
heretofore so much the object of their dread. All were
disappointed. Cornwallis held himself back from the
humiliating scene, obeying emotions which his great
character ought to have stifled. He had been unfortunate; not from any false step or deficiency on his
part, but from the infatuated policy of his superior and
the united power of his enemy brought to bear upon
him alone. There was nothing with which he could
reproach himself; there was nothing with which he

could reproach his brave and faithful army; why not then, appear at its head in the day of its misfortune, as he had always done in the day of triumph? The British general in this instance deviated from his general line of conduct, dimming the splendour of his long and brilliant career."

Little did the father think when he wrote those words that he was marking the arduous path of duty along which his son was one day to be called upon to walk. That son was worthy of such a father and of such teaching.[3]

The march was continued during the 8th of April with little interruption from the enemy, and in the evening we halted near Appomattox Court House, General Lee intending to march by way of Campbell Court House, through Pittsylvania County, toward Danville, with a view of opening communication with the army of General Joseph E. Johnston, then retreating before General Sherman through North Carolina. General Lee's purpose was either to unite with General Johnston in order to attack Sherman or call Johnston to his aid in resisting Grant, whichever might be found best. The exhausted troops were halted for rest on the evening of April 8th near Appomattox Court House, and the march was ordered to be resumed at 1 o'clock A.M.

I can convey a good idea of the condition of affairs

---

[3] In fairness to Cornwallis it must be said that the circumstances in 1781 and 1865 were somewhat different. Historians are agreed that Cornwallis at Yorktown behaved with dignity and good feeling. He took an early opportunity of meeting Washington and at a dinner given by the French and American officers to the British officers proposed Washington's health in very happy terms.

by telling my own experience. When the army halted on the night of the 8th, General Lee and his staff turned out of the road into a dense wood to seek some rest. The General had a conference with some of the principal officers, at which it was determined to try to force our way the next morning with troops of Gordon, supported by the cavalry under General Fitz Lee, the command of Longstreet bringing up the rear. With my comrades of the staff, and staff officers of Generals Longstreet and Gordon, I then sought a little much needed repose.

We lay upon tne ground near the road, with our saddles for pillows, our horses, picketed near by, eating the bark of trees for want of better provender, our faces covered with the capes of our greatcoats to keep out the night air. Soon after 1 o'clock I was roused by the sound of a column of infantry marching along the road. We were so completely surrounded by the swarming forces of General Grant that at first when I woke I thought the passing column might be Federal soldiers.

I raised my head and listened intently. My doubts were quickly dispelled. I recalled the order to resume the march at that early hour and knew that the troops I heard were moving forward to endeavour to force our way through the lines of the enemy at Appomattox Court House. I soon knew that the command that was passing consisted, in part at least, of Hood's old Texas brigade.

It was called the Texas brigade, although it was at times composed in part of regiments from other states. Sometimes there was a Mississippi regiment, sometimes an Arkansas regiment, sometimes a Georgia regiment mingled with the Texans, but all the strangers called themselves Texans, and all fought like Texans.

On this occasion I recognised these troops as they passed along the road in the dead of night by hearing one of them repeat the Texan version of a passage of scripture with which I was familiar — I mean with the Texan version.

The Texan rendition of the text that fell upon my ear as I lay in the woods by the roadside that dark night was : —

> " The race is not to them that 's got
> The longest legs to run,
> Nor the battle to that people
> That shoots the biggest gun ! "

This simple confession of faith assured me that the immortal brigade of Hood's Texans was marching to battle in the darkness.

Soon after they passed we were all astir and our bivouac was at an end. We made our simple toilet, consisting mainly of putting on our caps and saddling our horses. We then proceeded to look for something to satisfy our now ravenous appetites.

Somebody had a little cornmeal, and somebody else had a tin can, such as is used to hold hot water for shaving. A fire was kindled, and each man in his turn, according to rank and seniority, made a can of cornmeal gruel and was allowed to keep the can until the gruel became cool enough to drink. General Lee, who reposed, as we had done, not far from us, did not, as far as I remember, have even such refreshment as I have described. This was our last meal in the Confederacy. Our next was taken in the United States.

As soon as we had all had our turn at the shaving can, we rode toward Appomattox Court House, when the sound of guns announced that Gordon had already begun the attempt to open the way.

He forced his way through the cavalry of the enemy only to encounter a force of infantry far superior to his own wearied and starving command. He informed General Lee that it was impossible to advance further, and it became evident that the end was at hand.

General Lee had replied to the letter of General Grant of the 8th of April: —

April 8th, 1865

To Lieutenant-General U. S. Grant, Commanding Armies of the United States

GENERAL, —

I received at a late hour your note of to-day. In mine of yesterday I did not intend to propose the surrender of the Army of Northern Virginia, but to ask the terms of your proposition. To be frank, I do not think the emergency has arisen to call for the surrender of this army; but as the restoration of peace should be the sole object of all, I desire to know whether your proposals will lead to that end. I cannot, therefore, meet you with a view to surrender the Army of Northern Virginia; but as far as your proposal may affect the Confederate States' forces under my command, and tend to the restoration of peace, I should be pleased to meet you at 10 A.M. to-morrow, on the old stage road to Richmond, between the picket lines of the two armies.

Very respectfully, your obedient servant,

R. E. LEE, General

No reply to this letter had been received when, early on the morning of April 9, General Lee, after receiving

Gordon's report, directed me to come with him and go down on the Lynchburg road to meet General Grant, expecting that he would meet him in accordance with the terms of his letter. An orderly by the name of Tucker, a soldier from Maryland and one of the bravest men that ever fought, — he was with A. P. Hill when he was killed and brought Hill's horse off the place where he sacrificed his life so unnecessarily, — [4] accompanied us. The flag of truce was a white handkerchief, and Tucker rode ahead of us carrying it. General Lee and myself rode side by side until we came to our rear line, which was composed of the remnants of Longstreet's corps.

The men in the last hours of the Confederacy cheered General Lee to the echo, as they had cheered him many a time before. He waved his hand to suppress the cheering, because he was afraid the sound might attract the fire of the enemy, and we rode on through the line. Longstreet's men had thrown up breastworks, and could have held their position against a strong force. We rode on down the Lynchburg road with Tucker ahead of us, until he was halted by the skirmish line of the Federal Army. Our own skirmish line had been thrown forward and there was some fighting going on between the two bodies of the skirmishers.

As soon as Tucker was halted, General Lee directed me to go forward and seek the Federal commanding officer. I took off my sword and disarmed myself, and walked forward with a handkerchief in my hand, and an officer met me. It was Lieutenant Colonel Whittier.

[4] A. P. Hill was killed on April 2, 1865, during the battle of Five Forks. He rode unexpectedly into a party of stragglers, who shot him down.

He was a staff officer of General Humphreys, whose division was immediately at our rear. We had a very agreeable correspondence with each other afterwards. He was an old officer of the engineer service in the United States Army, and one of the most accomplished officers in that service. I met with him and he gave me a letter from General Grant in reply to the letter that was written the day before on the subject of general pacification. General Grant said : —

April 9th, 1865

To General R. E. Lee, Commanding C. S. A.

GENERAL, —

Your note of yesterday is received. As I have no authority to treat on the subject of peace, the meeting proposed for 10 A.M. to-day could lead to no good. I will state however, General, that I am equally anxious for peace with yourself, and the whole of the North entertains the same feeling. The terms upon which peace can be had are well understood. By the South laying down their arms they will hasten that most desirable event, save thousands of human lives and hundreds of millions of property not yet destroyed.

Sincerely hoping that all our difficulties may be settled without the loss of another life, I subscribe myself,

Very respectfully, your obedient servant,

U. S. GRANT, Lieutenant-General

Colonel Whittier gave me this letter and I walked back, I suppose about one hundred yards, to where General Lee was, and read it to him. After a few moments' reflection he said, "Well, write a letter to General Grant and ask him to meet me to deal with the question of the surrender of my army, in reply to the letter he wrote me at Farmville." I sat down and wrote: —

HEADQUARTERS ARMY NORTHERN VIRGINIA
April 9, 1865

Lieut-Gen. U. S. Grant, Commanding United States Armies
GENERAL, —

I received your note this morning in the picket line, whither I had come to meet you and ascertain definitely what terms were embraced in your proposition of yesterday with reference to the surrender of this army.

I now request an interview in accordance with the offer contained in your letter of yesterday for that purpose.

Very respectfully, your obedient servant

R. E. LEE, General

I took the letter after General Lee had signed it, and walked up to the skirmish line, and Colonel Whittier met me. I said, "Colonel, here is a letter General Lee wants forwarded to General Grant, but it requires a suspension of hostilities."

"Well," Colonel Whittier said, "I do not think my commanding officer has any power to suspend hostilities."

Then I said to him, "Let him read this letter, and when he sees it he will probably find the contents of it of a nature to justify him in taking authority to suspend."

He went away with the letter and came back in about five minutes. His commanding officer must have been very near. We were in very thick woods into which I could not see plainly, but the skirmish line was all round.

He told me that he had reported my request that hostilities be suspended pending the correspondence, but that he had been directed to say that an attack had been ordered and that the officer in command of the force in our rear had no discretion. He added that General Grant had left General Meade some time before, and that General Lee's letter could not reach him in time to receive orders as to the intended attack.

I expressed my regret, and again asked him to request the officer commanding the troops then moving to the attack to read General Lee's letter to General Grant, saying that perhaps that officer would feel authorized under the circumstances to suspend the movement and avoid the useless sacrifice of life.

I have said that as General Lee passed through his rear guard on his way to the place where this conference took place the men cheered him as of old. They were the flower of the old Army of Northern Virginia, and I felt quite sure that if the officer commanding the advancing Federal troops should consider himself bound by his orders to refuse my request for a suspension of hostilities until General Lee's letter could reach General Grant, the rear guard of the Army of Northern Virginia would secure all the time necessary.

What occurred at that time I never heard till long after the war. General Meade, who was commanding the troops approaching us at that time, had been sick, and he was some two miles to the rear of the troops that were attacking us or about to attack us.

General Horace Porter told me several years afterwards, at a meeting of the Army of the Potomac, that when Whittier brought back the letter to his commanding officer, whose name I do not recall, a staff officer was sent at once to General Meade, who was lying in his ambulance, indisposed. Porter told me — I may possibly make a little error, and I certainly do not want to make one to the discredit of General Porter — my recollection is that General Porter told me that he himself went back and pulled General Meade out of his ambulance and told him what was going to happen. General Meade immediately rode forward and joined the troops that were advancing to attack our rear guard.[5]

Whittier came back and told me that General Meade had come on the ground and that he had taken the liberty to suspend the attack until about 12 o'clock. I think this was after 10 o'clock. I told him I was glad to hear it; but he said General Grant was about four miles away — that he had gone round on our right — and that an officer had been sent to carry General Lee's letter to him. Just after Meade had given his order suspending operations, we heard guns in front and General Lee mounted his horse, rode forward rapidly, and got right up in front of Appomattox Court House in time to see General Fitz Lee bring in about two hundred prisoners; and that was the last fighting that was done in the war. Dearing was killed there, and I think Fitz Lee captured about two hundred prisoners and four pieces of artillery.

As soon as we arrived we stopped Fitz's activities and told him to be a good boy and not fight any more. Then we went down the slope of the hill on the other

---

[5] Lee caused Gordon to send a flag of truce simultaneously to Sheridan, who was blocking the Confederate front. Both Meade and Sheridan were at first suspicious that the request for a suspension of hostilities was a ruse to gain time; both, however, eventually agreed.

side of which stands Appomattox Court House. There was a bridge across a stream that ran at the foot of the hill, and we stopped on our side of the bridge, and, down near the foot of the hill, we made a little couch for General Lee under an apple tree. We put some rails down there, spread some blankets over them, and General Lee, who had been in the saddle all night long and who was very much fatigued, lay down and went to sleep. We stayed about him for an hour, perhaps, and then all saw an officer coming over the side of the hill from Appomattox Court House with a white flag — an officer with an orderly. I reported to General Lee that somebody was coming with a flag of truce, and he told me to go out and meet him. I went out and met Colonel Babcock, who was an officer on Grant's staff. Babcock told me that General Grant had received General Lee's letter which had been sent away around to him, and was coming on the road to Appomattox Court House. He said he was ordered to ask General Lee to appoint a place of meeting either in our own lines or in the Federal lines, whichever was preferable.

Colonel Babcock was then conducted to General Lee and delivered him the following letter : —

April 9, 1865

GENERAL R. E. LEE, Commanding C. S. A. —

Your note of this date is but this moment (11 : 59 A.M.) received. In consequence of my having passed from the Richmond and Lynchburg road to the Farmville and Lynchburg road, I am at this writing about four miles west of Walker's church, and will push forward to the front for the purpose of meeting you. Notice sent to me on this road where you wish the interview to take place will meet me.

U. S. GRANT, Lieut. General

General Lee got up and talked with Babcock a little while, and at last he called me and told me to get ready to go with him. I was in a very dilapidated state and I had to make some preparation before I could go. My friend Colonel Henry Young, of Charleston, who was Judge Advocate General of the Army, had a dress sword which he let me have. I had a very shabby sword that General Stuart had given me, one that he took from a Yankee, as we called them, on the field of battle. He gave it me and I have got it yet. I did n't care to wear that plain thing, so I borrowed Young's sword, which was very handsome. He also had a pair of gauntlets, a thing I did n't possess, and I put them on. He also lent me a clean shirt collar. I forget whether he gave me anything else or not. Then I mounted my horse and we started off — General Lee, Colonel Babcock, Colonel Babcock's orderly, one of our orderlies, and myself.

We struck up the hill towards Appomattox Court House. There was a man named McLean who used to live on the first battle field of Manassas, at a house about a mile from Manassas Junction. He did n't like the war, and having seen the first battle of Manassas, he thought he would get away where there would n't be any more fighting, so he moved down to Appomattox Court House. General Lee told me to go forward and find a house where he could meet General Grant, and of all people, whom should I meet but McLean. I rode up to him and said, "Can you show me a house where General Lee and General Grant can meet together?" He took me into a house that was all dilapidated and that had no furniture in it. I told

him it would n't do. Then he said, "Maybe my house
will do!" He lived in a very comfortable house, and
I told him I thought that would suit. I had taken the
orderly along with me, and I sent him back to bring
General Lee and Babcock, who were coming on behind.
I went into the house and sat down, and after a while
General Lee and Babcock came in. Colonel Babcock
told his orderly that he was to meet General Grant,
who was coming on the road, and turn him in when he
came along. So General Lee, Babcock and myself sat
down in McLean's parlour and talked in the most
friendly and affable way.

In about half an hour we heard horses, and the first
thing I knew General Grant walked into the room.
There were with him General Sheridan, General Ord,
Colonel Badeau, General Porter, Colonel Parker, and
quite a number of other officers whose names I do not
recall.

General Lee was standing at the end of the room
opposite the door when General Grant walked in.
General Grant had on a sack coat, a loose fatigue coat,
but he had no side arms. He looked as though he had
had a pretty hard time. He had been riding and his
clothes were somewhat dusty and a little soiled. He
walked up to General Lee and Lee recognized him at
once. He had known him in the Mexican war. General Grant greeted him in the most cordial manner, and
talked about the weather and other things in a very
friendly way. Then General Grant brought up his
officers and introduced them to General Lee.

I remember that General Lee asked for General
Lawrence Williams, of the Army of the Potomac.

That very morning General Williams had sent word
by somebody to General Lee that Custis Lee, who had
been captured at Sailor Creek and was reported killed,
was not hurt, and General Lee asked General Grant
where General Williams was, and if he could not send
for him to come and see him. General Grant sent
somebody out for General Williams, and when he came,
General Lee thanked him for having sent him word
about the safety of his son.

After a very free talk General Lee said to General
Grant: "General, I have come to meet you in accordance with my letter to you this morning, to treat
about the surrender of my army, and I think the best
way would be for you to put your terms in writing."
General Grant said: "Yes; I believe it will." So a
Colonel Parker, General Grant's Aide-de-Camp,
brought a little table over from a corner of the room,
and General Grant wrote the terms and conditions of
surrender on what we call field note paper, that is, a
paper that makes a copy at the same time as the note
is written. After he had written it, he took it over to
General Lee.

General Lee was sitting at the side of the room; he
rose and went to meet General Grant to take that paper
and read it over. When he came to the part in which
only public property was to be surrendered, and the
officers were to retain their side arms and personal baggage, General Lee said: "That will have a very happy
effect."

General Lee then said to General Grant: "General,
our cavalrymen furnish their own horses; they are not

THE SCENE IN McLEAN'S HOUSE AT APPOMATTOX

Government horses, some of them may be, but of course you will find them out — any property that is public property, you will ascertain that, but it is nearly all private property, and these men will want to plough ground and plant corn."

General Grant answered that as the terms were written, only the officers were permitted to take their private property, but almost immediately he added that he supposed that most of the men in the ranks were small farmers, and that the United States did not want their horses. He would give orders to allow every man who claimed to own a horse or mule to take the animal home.

General Lee having again said that this would have an excellent effect, once more looked over the letter, and being satisfied with it, told me to write a reply. General Grant told Colonel Parker to copy his letter, which was written in pencil, and put it in ink. Colonel Parker took the table and carried it back to a corner of the room, leaving General Grant and General Lee facing each other and talking together. There was no ink in McLean's inkstand, except some thick stuff that was very much like pitch, but I had a screw boxwood inkstand that I always carried with me in a little satchel that I had at my side, and I gave that to Colonel Parker, and he copied General Grant's letter with the aid of my inkstand and my pen.

There was another table right against the wall, and a sofa next to it. I was sitting on the arm of the sofa near the table, and General Sheridan was on the sofa next to me. While Colonel Parker was copying the letter, General Sheridan said to me, "This is very pretty country."

I said, "General, I have n't seen it by daylight. All my observations have been made by night and I have n't seen the country at all myself."

He laughed at my remark, and while we were talking I heard General Grant say this: "Sheridan, how many rations have you?" General Sheridan said: "How many do you want?" and General Grant said, "General Lee has about a thousand or fifteen hundred of our people prisoners, and they are faring the same as his men, but he tells me his have n't anything. Can you send them some rations?"

"Yes," he answered. They had gotten some of our rations, having captured a train.

General Grant said: "How many can you send?" and he replied "Twenty-five thousand rations."

General Grant asked if that would be enough, and General Lee replied "Plenty; plenty; an abundance;" and General Grant said to Sheridan "Order your commissary to send to the Confederate Commissary twenty-five thousand rations for our men and his men."

After a while Colonel Parker got through with his copy of General Grant's letter and I sat down to write a reply. I began it in the usual way: "I have the honor to acknowledge the receipt of your letter of such a date," and then went on to say the terms were satisfactory. I took the letter over to General Lee, and he read it and said: "Don't say, 'I have the honor to acknowledge the receipt of your letter of such a date'; he is here; just say, 'I accept these terms.'" Then I wrote: —

HEADQUARTERS OF THE ARMY OF NORTHERN VIRGINIA
April 9, 1865

I received your letter of this date containing the terms of the surrender of the Army of Northern Virginia proposed by you. As they are substantially the same as those expressed in your letter of the 8th instant, they are accepted. I will proceed to designate the proper officers to carry the stipulations into effect.

Then General Grant signed his letter, and I turned over my letter to General Lee and he signed it. Parker handed me General Grant's letter, and I handed him General Lee's reply, and the surrender was accomplished. There was no theatrical display about it. It was in itself perhaps the greatest tragedy that ever occurred in the history of the world, but it was the simplest, plainest, and most thoroughly devoid of any attempt at effect, that you can imagine.

The story of General Grant returning General Lee's sword to him is absurd, because General Grant proposed in his letter that the officers of the Confederate Army should retain their side-arms. Why, in the name of common sense, anybody should imagine that General Lee, after receiving a letter which said that he should retain his side-arms, yet should offer to surrender his sword to General Grant, is hard to understand. The only thing of the kind that occurred in the whole course of the transaction — which occupied perhaps an hour — was this: General Lee was in full uniform. He had on the handsomest uniform I ever saw him wear; and he had on a sword with a gold, a very handsome gold and leather, scabbard that had been presented to him by English ladies. General

Grant excused himself to General Lee towards the close of the conversation between them, for not having his side arms with him; he told him that when he got his letter he was about four miles from his wagon in which his arms and uniform were, and he said that he had thought that General Lee would rather receive him as he was, than be detained, while he sent back to get his sword and uniform. General Lee told him he was very much obliged to him and was very glad indeed that he had n't done it.[6]

After that a general conversation took place of a most agreeable character. I cannot describe it. I cannot give you any idea of the kindness, and generosity, and magnanimity of those men. When I think of it, it brings tears into my eyes.

After having this general conversation we took leave of General Grant, and went off to appoint commissioners to attend to the details of the surrender.

The next day General Grant sent a message to General Lee asking him to meet him. I did not accompany him on that occasion, but I think it was then he met General Grant under that famous apple tree, because I saw some Federal soldiers cutting down the tree the

[6] This little conversation is of peculiar interest because Lee first met Grant when he was a captain on General Scott's staff in the Mexican war, and Grant was a lieutenant of infantry. General Scott had issued an order that officers coming to headquarters were to do so in full dress. Grant had been making a reconnaissance and came to headquarters to report the result in his field dress, plentifully covered with the dust of Mexico, evidently thinking in 1847, as he did in 1865, that time was of more importance than appearance. Lee had to tell Grant to go back to his tent and return in full dress. One wonders whether, when apologizing to Lee a second time for his informal costume, Grant remembered what had happened eighteen years before.

By Courtesy of Harper and Brothers

LEE AND MARSHALL RIDING AWAY AFTER THE SURRENDER

next day. General Lee told me when he came back that General Grant asked him if he would go and meet Mr. Lincoln. He said he did not know where Mr. Lincoln was. He might be at Richmond, at City Point, at Fortress Monroe, or in Washington, he could not tell where — but he said, "I want you to meet him. Whatever you and he agree upon will be satisfactory to the reasonable people of the North and South." He said: "If you and Mr. Lincoln will agree upon terms, your influence in the South will make the Southern people accept what you accept, and Mr. Lincoln's influence in the North will make reasonable people of the North accept what he accepts, and all my influence will be added to Mr. Lincoln's."

General Lee was very much pleased and would have been delighted to do anything in the world that he could to bring about a pacification, but he said: "General Grant, you know that I am a soldier of the Confederate Army, and I cannot meet Mr. Lincoln. I do not know what Mr. Davis is going to do, and I cannot undertake to make any terms of that kind."

General Grant then said he would go himself at once, and while he understood the reasons of General Lee's position, he regretted that he could not go.

I think myself, and have always thought, that if General Lee and Mr. Lincoln would have met as General Grant proposed, we could have had immediate restoration of peace and brotherhood among the people of these States.

There remained a last duty to perform. On the night of April 9th after our return from McLean's house General Lee sat with several of us at a fire in front of

Hd Qrs Army Northern Virginia
10th April 1865

General Orders}
No 9 }

After four years of arduous services marked by unsurpassed courage and fortitude the Army of Northern Virginia has been compelled to yield to overwhelming numbers and resources.

I need not tell the brave survivors of so many hard fought battles, who have remained steadfast to the last, that I have consented to this result from no distrust of them, But feeling that valor and devotion could accomplish nothing that would compensate for the loss that must have attended the continuance of the contest, I determined to avoid the useless sacrifice of those whose past services have endeared them to their country

By the terms of the agreement Officers and men can return to their homes and remain until exchanged. You will take with you the satisfaction that proceeds from the consciousness of duty faithfully performed and I earnestly pray that a merciful God will extend to you his blessing & protection.

With an unceasing admiration of your constancy and devotion to your country and a *grateful remembrance of your kind and generous consideration for myself, I bid you all an affectionate farewell.*

R E Lee
Genl

Hd. Qrs. Army of N. Va.
April 10, 1865.—

General Orders
No. 9

Farewell to the troops.

"FAREWELL TO THE TROOPS"

Facsimile of Lee's last order, from a copy in the handwriting of Colonel Marshall, believed to be the original copy signed by Lee.

his tent, and after some conversation about the army and the events of the day in which his feelings towards his men were strongly expressed, he told me to prepare an order to the troops.

The next day it was raining and many persons were coming and going, so that I was unable to write without interruption until about 10 o'clock, when General Lee finding that the order had not been prepared, directed me to get into his ambulance, which stood near his tent, and placed an orderly to prevent anyone from approaching us. I made a draft in pencil and took it to General Lee who struck out a paragraph, which he said would tend to keep alive the feeling existing between the North and the South, and made one or two other changes. I then returned to the ambulance, recopied the order and gave it to a clerk in the office of the Adjutant General to write in ink.

After the first draft of the order had been made and signed by General Lee, other copies were made for transmission to the corps commanders and the staff of the army. All these copies were signed by the General and a good many persons sent other copies which they had made or procured and obtained his signature. In this way many of the orders had the General's name signed as if they were originals.

[The facsimile of the farewell order has been kindly supplied me by Mr. Charles A. Marshall. It was made from the copy found in his father's papers, which copy he believes to be the original one signed by Lee. Strictly, the original copy of an order is that signed by the issuing authority. There appears to be little doubt that Colonel Marshall's first draft which was amended by Lee has disappeared, but as this draft was not signed by Lee it cannot be considered as the original of the order.

The copy here reproduced is in Colonel Marshall's handwriting and is believed by his family to be his second pencil draft which was signed by Lee and then sent to the clerk to be copied. There is no doubt that Colonel Marshall thought that he had the original in his possession, but he appears also to have been under the impression that he had loaned the original and that it had not been returned to him. After Colonel Marshall's death the copy now in Mr. Charles Marshall's hands was found, and it was believed by the family that after all the original had been returned. This draft was retouched in ink in 1909, but Mr. Marshall does not remember if it was in ink or in pencil, for it was so badly faded as to make it difficult to read. If it was not in pencil it is not the original, and there is therefore some element of doubt. But the fact remains that Colonel Marshall frequently spoke in his lifetime of having had the original in his possession, and never referred to his possession of a second copy. It seems highly improbable that he should have retained for himself two copies of so precious a document, and equally improbable that he should not have mentioned the fact had he done so.

There is another claimant to the possession of the original in Mr. B. Bouldin. Mr. Bouldin's copy is in the handwriting of his wife's brother, William L. Ward, whom he believes to have been a member of Lee's headquarters staff, and the clerk to whom Colonel

Marshall gave his original draft to have it copied in ink and signed by General Lee. There is no record that Mr. Ward was attached to the headquarters staff, but in the circumstances of the time that is not conclusive. His name may have been overlooked. It is not, however, very probable that a clerk should have been permitted to retain the original of an important order signed by the Commander in Chief. There is, however, other evidence which seems to me more conclusive. There is a difference in the wording of Mr. Marshall's and Mr. Bouldin's copies. In the former the second sentence in the third paragraph runs: — "You will take with you the satisfaction that proceeds from the consciousness of duty faithfully performed." In the latter the corresponding sentence is: — "you will take with you the consciousness of duty faithfully performed." Now, having spent nearly two years in examining Colonel Marshall's papers and having read most of his drafts of Lee's dispatches, I have become familiar with his style, and I am convinced that what he wrote was the sentence as it is in the copy which his son possesses. Further, while it is not unnatural that a copyist should, in making his transcript, abbreviate what appeared to him redundant, it is not natural that he should add words which are not essential to the sense of the original. On these grounds it seems to me to be certain that Mr. Bouldin's is a later copy, and I am of opinion that the balance of evidence is in favour of Mr. Marshall's contention that he possesses the original copy of the famous order.]

INDEX

INDEX

ALLAN, COLONEL WILLIAM, his conversation with Lee, 248–252.

Anderson, General Richard H., 124, 134 and *n.*, 139, 140, 229, 232, 234.

Antietam. *See* Sharpsburg.

Appomattox, 253–280.

Armies, Confederate, volunteers called for, 11; reënlistment encouraged, 13; unwise reorganization, 14, 15, 16, 29, 30; lack of equipment, 15, 16, 17; difficulty of discipline, 17, 18; State Governors asked to enroll troops, 19, 20; inadequate numbers to meet Federal forces, 20, 21; new call planned by Lee, 30, 31, 32 and *n.*; its modification by Congress, 33 and *n.*, 34; practical working of the modified plan, 34, 35, 36, 37; serious mistakes by Commissary Dept., 44 and *n.*, 45, 46, 47; loss during the Seven Days, 117 and *n.*; lack of maps, 117 *n.*; campaign against Pope, 120–142; situation after second battle of Manassas, 144–148, 154, 155; in 1862–1863, 188; returning from Gettysburg, 243–248; Lee's farewell order to, 276–277, 278–280.

Armies, Federal, early enrolment in, 12 and *n.*

Armistead, General Lewis A., 114 *n.*, 240.

BABCOCK, COLONEL, at Appomattox, 268, 269.

Badeau, Colonel Adam, 269.

Banks, General Nathaniel P., in the Shenandoah Valley, 28, 53, 54; during the Seven Days, 120 *n.*

Beaver Dam Creek, battles around, 80–99.

Benjamin, Hon. Judah P., quoted on war legislation by the Confederacy, 14, 15 and *n.*, 16, 17, 18; on the Roanoke Island loss, 16, 17; handling of Lee's new plan for army, 32, 33.

Blesdoe, Dr. A. T., 165.

Boonsboro' Gap. *See* South Mountain.

Buell, General Don Carlos, in Tennessee, 29.

Buford, General John, 134 *n.*, 226 *n.*, 227 *n.*

Bull Run. *See* Manassas.

Burnside, General Ambrose E., 119, 120, 122, 123, 248, 249.

CEDAR RUN. *See* Slaughter's Mountain.

Chancellorsville, campaign of, 163–176.

Chartres, Duc de, 143.

Confederacy, the, its unpromising condition in spring of '62, 8 and *n.*, 9; peril of coast and river cities, 13; interstate jealousies, 17, 18; hampering effect of its theory of states' rights, 24, 25, 65; complicated problem of protecting civilians, 64, 65, 66, 67; population as compared with U. S. A., 68 and *n.*

Congress of Confederate States of America, offers President bill (vetoed) creating office of General-in-Chief, 3 and *n.*; Act providing staff for General on duty at seat of Government, 7 and *n.*, 8; first provisions for raising an army, 11, 12; further provision, 13; asks for information about foreign relations, 24 *n.*; changes Lee's plan for enlarging army, 33 and *n.*, 34, 35, 36, 37, 38 and *n.*

Conscription. *See* Armies.

Cornwallis, Lord, at Yorktown, 256, 257, 258 and *n.*

Cotton, European demand for, 10, 18, 19 and *n.*, 22, 25; proposals for secret purchase of, 26; later traffic, 27.

DAVIS, PRESIDENT JEFFERSON, vetoes bill creating office of General-in-Chief, 3 and *n.*; public criticism of his management, 4 and *n.*; his insist-

Davis (*continued*)
ence on his prerogatives, 5, 6; failure to see need of expert assistance, 7 *n.*; message of Feb. 1862 quoted, 15 and *n.*, 16; implied rebuke to, in Conscript Law of 1862, 38 *n.*; appoints Lee to command of the Confederate forces, 58 and *n.*, 59, 60; Lee's letters to, proposing Maryland campaign, 150, 151, 152, 153.
Donelson, Fort, 8.

EARLY, GENERAL JUBAL A., 115 *n.*, 138; in the invasion of Pennsylvania, 217; at Gettysburg, 227, 232, 233, 235, 236, 237, 238.
Earthworks and entrenchments, construction of, 78 and *n.*, 79, 80 and *n.*; retreat from behind, 105 *n.*
Evans, General Nathan G., 137, 138, 140.
Ewell, General Richard S., 52, 99 *n.*, 102, 104, 132 and *n.*, 133, 141; in Shenandoah Valley, 195; sent to advance into Pennsylvania, 196, 198, 199; Lee's letter regarding advance into Pennsylvania, 200, 201; Lee's letter about the order to Stuart, 203; advance into Pennsylvania, 216, 217, 218; at Gettysburg, 220, 227, 228, 229, 231, 232, 233, 234 *n.*, 236, 238, 239, 247, 248, 251, 252; surrenders at Sailor's Creek, 254 and *n.*
Exemption of Slaveholders, 40 and *n.*, 41, 42 and *n.*, 43.

FAIR OAKS, battle of. *See* Seven Pines.
Frayser's Farm, battle of, 108 and *n.*, 111 and *n.*
Fredericksburg, 187, 189 *n.*, 190, 191, 192, 193, 195 and *n.*
Frémont, General John C., 52, 120 *n.*
French, General William H., 121.

GAINES'S MILL, battles near, 96 *n.*, 97–103.
Garnet, General R. B., 240.
Gettysburg, battle of, 225–252.
Gordon, General John B., at Appomattox, 261, 262, 266 *n.*
Grant, General Ulysses S., 52; on the James River, 184, 185; at Appomattox, 253 *et seq.*; his desire for conference between Lee and President Lincoln, 275.
Griffith, General Richard, 86.

Groveton. *See* Manassas, second battle of.

HALLECK, GENERAL HENRY W., 120 *n.*, 122 *n.*, 127.
Hampton, General Wade, letter about the Seven Days action, 109, 110, 111, 112 and *n.*
Hampton Roads, naval engagement at, 49; Burnside at, 122.
Harper's Ferry, Federal garrison at, 149; Lee sends Jackson against it, 149, 150; Longstreet's criticism of movement, 156, 157; necessary to clear Shenandoah Valley, 157; its capture by Jackson, 158 and *n.*, 159; discussion about, 248, 249.
Henry, Fort, 8.
Heth, Major General Henry, at Gettysburg, 225, 226, 227, 239, 245, 246.
Hill, General Ambrose P., at Beaver Dam, 87, 88, 89, 91, 92, 93, 94, 95; at Gaines's Mill, 97, 99, 100, 101 and *n.*, 102; in movements about White Oak Swamp, 106, 107, 108 and *n.*, 114; in the campaign against Pope, 121 and *n.*, 133; at battle of Groveton (second Manassas), 137, 138, 141; at Fredericksburg, 195; moves over into Shenandoah Valley, 196, 198, 199; in invasion of Pennsylvania, 217, 218; at Gettysburg, 220, 225, 226, 227, 229, 230, 232, 234, 239, 247 *n.*
Hill, General Daniel H., in the Seven Days movement and action, 86 and *n.*, 88, 89, 91, 93, 95, 97, 101, 103; at White Oak Swamp and Malvern Hill, 106, 108 *n.*, 113, 114 and *n.*; moves to Richmond, 119; on the James River, 121, 124; at South Mountain, 159; at Sharpsburg, 160.
Holmes, Major General Theophilus H., 87, 107, 108.
Hood, General John B., 124, 135, 137, 138, 139, 140, 189 and *n.*; at Gettysburg, 228, 233, 234.
Hooker, General Joseph, 108 *n.*, 132 *n.*; at Chancellorsville, 163–170; his position at Fredericksburg, 191, 192, 193, 195 and *n.*; his movements to be watched by Stuart, 201, 202, 203, 208; advances North between Lee and Stuart, 214; his movements not reported to Lee, 216, 217; crosses Potomac, 219 *n.*

Hotchkiss, Major Jed, quoted, 166, 167.
Huger, General Benjamin, 17, 86, 105 and *n.*, 106, 107, 108 and *n.*, 114 and *n.*, 115.

IMBODEN, GENERAL JOHN D., 217, 243.
Intervention, foreign, Southern expectation of, 9, 10, 11, 22, 23, 24 and *n.*, 25.

JACKSON ("STONEWALL"), GENERAL THOMAS J., in Shenandoah Valley, 28, 52, 53, 54, 76; supported by Davis, 60; his delay in reaching Beaver Dam, 83, 84–101; pursues Federals after Gaines's Mill, 106, 107 and *n.*; delays at White Oak Swamp, 108 and *n.*, 109, 110, 111, 112 and *n.*, 113 and *n.*; moves to attack Pope, 124, 125, 128, 129 and *n.*; pursues him in retreat, 131, 132 and *n.*, 133 and *n.*, 134; at second Manassas, 136–142; moves against Harper's Ferry, 149, 150, 158 and *n.*, 159; question of responsibility for his movement at Chancellorsville, 163–170; Lee's message to him, 173.
Johnson, General Edward, 228, 232, 235, 238.
Johnston, General Albert Sidney, loses to Federal forces in the west, 8, 9, 20; distrust of his competency, 9; letter to Davis, 21 and *n.*; supported by Davis, 60.
Johnston, General Joseph Eccleston, his lack of men, 9, 21; position in March 1862, 28; movement to Peninsula, 43, 47, 48 and *n.*, 49; retreats from Yorktown, 50 and *n.*, 51; his inadequate force for protection of Richmond, 51; misunderstanding at Seven Pines, 56, 57 and *n.*, 58; movements near Richmond, 78 and *n.*; retreat before Sherman, 258.
Jones, General D. R., 86, 135, 136, 137, 140.
Jones, General William E., 240, 241.

KEARNY, GENERAL PHILIP, 108 *n.*, 142 and *n.*
Kemper, General James L., 137, 140.
Kentucky, Army of, 8, 9.

LEE, GENERAL FITZHUGH, 125, 126, 128 *n.*, 259, 266.

Lee, Light Horse Harry, quoted on Cornwallis, 257, 258.
Lee, General Robert E., appointed to general command of Confederate armies, 3, 5 and *n.*; this position merely advisory, 6 and *n.*, 7; is allowed a secretary and aides-de-camp and Col. Marshall comes into close relations with him, 7, 8 and *n.*; Lee's earlier responsibility for coast defenses, 17 and *n.*, 59; anxiety about inadequate troops, 30 and *n.*, plans a new draft bill, 30, 31, 32; made Commander-in-Chief, 58 and *n.*, 59, 61, 62; his unselfish devotion, 61, 62; his policy for the Confederacy, 63, 64, 65, 66, 67; essential unity of his plans, 67–76; new use of entrenchments criticised, 78 *n.*, 79, 80 and *n.*; the Seven Days battles, 77–118; concentration in Northern Virginia, 119, 120; begins campaign against Pope, 120, 122; sends troops to Gordonsville, 124; plans attack on Pope, 124, 125, 126; commands at second battle of Manassas, 126; miscarriage of movement on the Rapidan, 128 and *n.*, 129 and *n.*, 130 and *n.*; narrowly escapes capture, 134 and *n.*; in battle of Groveton (second Manassas), 137, 140, 142 and *n.*; his problem after second Manassas, 144–148; letter to Davis about proposed Maryland campaign, 150, 151, 152, 153; the "lost order" regarding Harper's Ferry, 158 and *n.*, 160 and *n.*, 161; letter to Mrs. Jackson, 163, 164; letter to Dr. Blesdoe, 165, 166; Marshall's anniversary tribute to Lee, 171–176; Lee's procedure in making up report on Gettysburg campaign, 178–181; letter to Ewell about advance into Pennsylvania, 200, 201; instructs Stuart as to cavalry movements, 201; his written order as to Stuart's advance into Maryland, 202, 203; writes Ewell about the order to Stuart, 203; sends the Stuart order through Longstreet, 204, 205; sends second order to Stuart, 207, 208 and *n.*, 209; lack of information about Hooker, 216, 217, 218, 220, 222; consequences of misunderstanding with Stuart, 223, 224 and *n.*; Lee at Gettysburg, 227, 228, 229, 230,

Lee (*continued*)
231, 232, 233, 234 and *n*., 238, 240; conversation with Allan about military campaigns, 248–252; receives Grant's first letter and replies, 254 and *n*., 255; might have avoided personal conference, 256, 257, 258; agrees to conference, 261; receives Grant's second letter, 263; meets Grant and accepts terms of surrender, 269–273; later interview under the apple tree, 274, 275; Lee's farewell order to the armies, 276–277.

Lee, Colonel S. D., 139, 140.

Lee, Colonel William H. F., 127.

Lincoln, President Abraham, calls for Federal volunteers, 12 and *n*.; his War Order No. 1, 23 *n*.; his policy and McClellan's, 55, 56; prospect of long-continued war, 73, 74; anxiety for Washington, 75, 76, 145; Grant's desire for him to confer with Lee after Appomattox, 275.

Long, Brigadier General Armistead L., 8; quoted on Lee's surrender, 254 *n*.

Longstreet, General James, at Seven Pines, 57 and *n*.; at Beaver Dam, 85 and *n*., 86, 91, 99, 101, 102; on the way to White Oak Swamp, 106, 107, 108 and *n*., 114; moves against Pope, 124, 125, 128, 129 and *n*., 133; at Thoroughfare Gap, 135, 136 and *n*.; at Groveton (second Manassas), 136–142; at South Mountain and Crampton's Gap, 159; at Sharpsburg, 160; at Suffolk, Va., 189 and *n*.; in the northward advance, 195, 196, 198; receives and forwards Lee's order to Stuart, 204, 205; his own letter to Stuart, 205, 206; in the invasion of Pennsylvania, 217, 218, 219 and *n*., 220; at Gettysburg, 228, 232, 233, 234 and *n*., 235, 237, 238, 239, 240; after Gettysburg, 245, 246, 248, 252; at Appomattox, 262.

Lost order of South Mountain, 158 and *n*.

MAGRUDER, GENERAL JOHN B., holding the Peninsula in spring of '62, 28, 29, 30; reënforced by J. E. Johnston, 47; in the Seven Days battles, 86, 105 *n*., 106, 107 and *n*., 108, 114, 115, 118 *n*.

Malvern Hill, action at, 113–118.

Manassas, first battle of, 7 *n*., 9, 11, 12 *n*., 15; second battle of, 130 and *n*., 134, 136–140.

Marshall, Colonel Charles, appointed an aide-de-camp of Lee, 8 and *n*.; begins to write a Life of Lee, 143; corresponds with the Comte de Paris, 144; explains Lee's plan for invasion of Maryland, 144–162; his Baltimore speech on Lee, 171–176; his account of the writing of Lee's report on the Gettysburg campaign, 178–181; explains necessity for Pennsylvania campaign, 190–194; his copy of Lee's farewell order, 276–277, 278–280.

Maryland campaign, Lee's, 143–162.

Mason, Hon. James M., quoted on probability of foreign intervention, 10, 11.

McCall, General George A., 108 *n*.

McClellan, General George B., 9; expected to advance on Richmond, 28; reaches Fortress Monroe, 30 and *n*.; advances to Yorktown, 50; his Peninsula forces, 51, 52; his policy of defense and offense, 55; movements in Northern Virginia, 56, 57 and *n*.; movements during the Seven Days, 78–118; during Pope's advance, 120, 121, 122 and *n*.; again at Malvern Hill, 123; sends reënforcements for Pope, 128 *n*., 129; his movements watched by Stuart, 148, 150; restored to Federal command after second Manassas, 149.

McDowell, General Irwin, 52, 120 *n*.

McIntosh, Major D. G., 225.

McLaws, General Lafayette, 86, 124, 228, 233, 234, 235.

Meade, General George G., 228, 229, 265, 266 and *n*.

NORTH, political parties in the, 22; delays and difficulties of military conscription, 38 *n*.

ORD, GENERAL EDWARD O. C., 269.

Orléans, Louis Philippe Albert d' (Comte de Paris), 143, 144, 153, 154.

PARIS, COMTE DE (Louis Philippe Albert d'Orléans), 143, 144, 153, 154.

Pegram, General John, 225.

Pender, General William D., 225, 226, 227, 232, 236, 237, 239.

Pendleton, Brigadier General William N., 121.
Perry, General E. A., 234.
Petersburg, 184, 185, 189.
Pettigrew, General James J., 225 and n., 232, 240, 245.
Pickett, General George E., 189 and n., 239, 240.
Pope, General John, advances from Washington, 120 and n., 121 and n., 122 and n.; at Cedar Mountain, 123; on the Rapidan, 124, 125, 126, 127; retires beyond the Rappahannock, 127, 128 and n., 130 and n., 133, 142 n.
Porter, General Fitz-John, 93 n., 96 n., 97 n., 100, 102 n., 104 n., 137 n., 138 n.
Porter, General Horace, 265, 266, 269.
Posey, General Carnot, 234.

REYNOLDS, GENERAL JOHN F., 227.
Richmond, the defense of, 55, 60, 61, 63, 65, 66, 69, 70, 71, 72, 73; its prospects after second battle of Manassas, 144, 145-148, 152; Lee's emphasis on its importance, 182, 183, 184, 185, 186.
Roanoke Island, 8 n., 16, 17.
Robinson, General B. H., 240, 241.
Rodes, General Robert E., 227, 232, 236, 237, 238.

SAILOR'S CREEK, 254 and n., 270.
Sedgwick, General John, 108 n., 195 n., 234 n.
Seven Days, battles of the, 77-118.
Seven Pines, battle of, 51 and n., 56, 57, 58.
Sharpsburg, 159, 160, 161, 162.
Shenandoah Valley, spring of 1862, 28 and n.; Jackson's campaign, 52, 53, 54, 76; first Harper's Ferry action, 149, 150, 158, 159; Ewell in, 195; Hill and Longstreet in, 198.
Sheridan, General Philip H., 52, 266 n., 269, 271, 272.
Sherman, General William T., 258.
Sigel, General Franz, 120 n.
Slaughter's Mountain, battle of, 123.
Slavery, as an issue, 39, 40, 41, 42 and n.; as an additional peril in war time, 64, 65.
Smith, General Gustavus W., 58.
South Mountain, 159, 161.
Starke, General William E., 138.

Stuart, General J. E. B., around Beaver Dam, 82, 88, 94 and n., 99 n., 104; expected to take part in attack on Pope, 125; delayed by non-arrival of Fitzhugh Lee, 125, 126, 127, 128 and n.; pursues Pope, 131, 132; at battle of Groveton (second Manassas), 137; raid around McClellan's army, 148 and n., 150; receives instruction from Lee as to movement of his cavalry, 201; Lee's letter to, regarding advance into Maryland, 202, 203; Longstreet's letter enclosing Lee's, 205, 206; a second order from Lee, 207, 208 and n., 209; Stuart's misunderstanding, 209 and n., 210; his own report of his movements, 210-216; consequences of the mistake, 222-224 and n., 229, 230, 231; his own movement to Gettysburg, 241, 242; returning from Gettysburg, 244, 247.
Suffolk, 189 n.

TALCOTT, MAJOR T. M. R., appointed an aide-de-camp of Lee, 8; quoted, 168, 169.
Taliaferro, General William B., 133.
Taylor, Brigadier General Richard, 132.
Taylor, Major W. H., 8.
Thoroughfare Gap, 135, 136 n.
Trimble, General Isaac R., 239, 240.

VENABLE, LIEUTENANT COLONEL CHARLES S., 8.
Virginia, Northern, strategic importance of, 70-76; officially designated Army of, 119 and n.
Volunteers. See Armies, Confederate and Armies, Federal.

WASHINGTON, movements or threats against, 54, 55, 71, 75, 76, 123, 131 n.; its situation after second battle of Manassas, 144-148, 155; the Maryland campaign, 185; and after the Wilderness, 185.
White Oak Swamp, action around, 107-112.
Whiting, General W. H. C., 111, 112, 113.
Wilcox, General Cadmus M., 135, 136, 137, 138, 140, 234, 235, 239.
Williams, General Lawrence, 269, 270.
Wise, General Henry A., 16, 17.
Wright, General A. R., 234, 235.